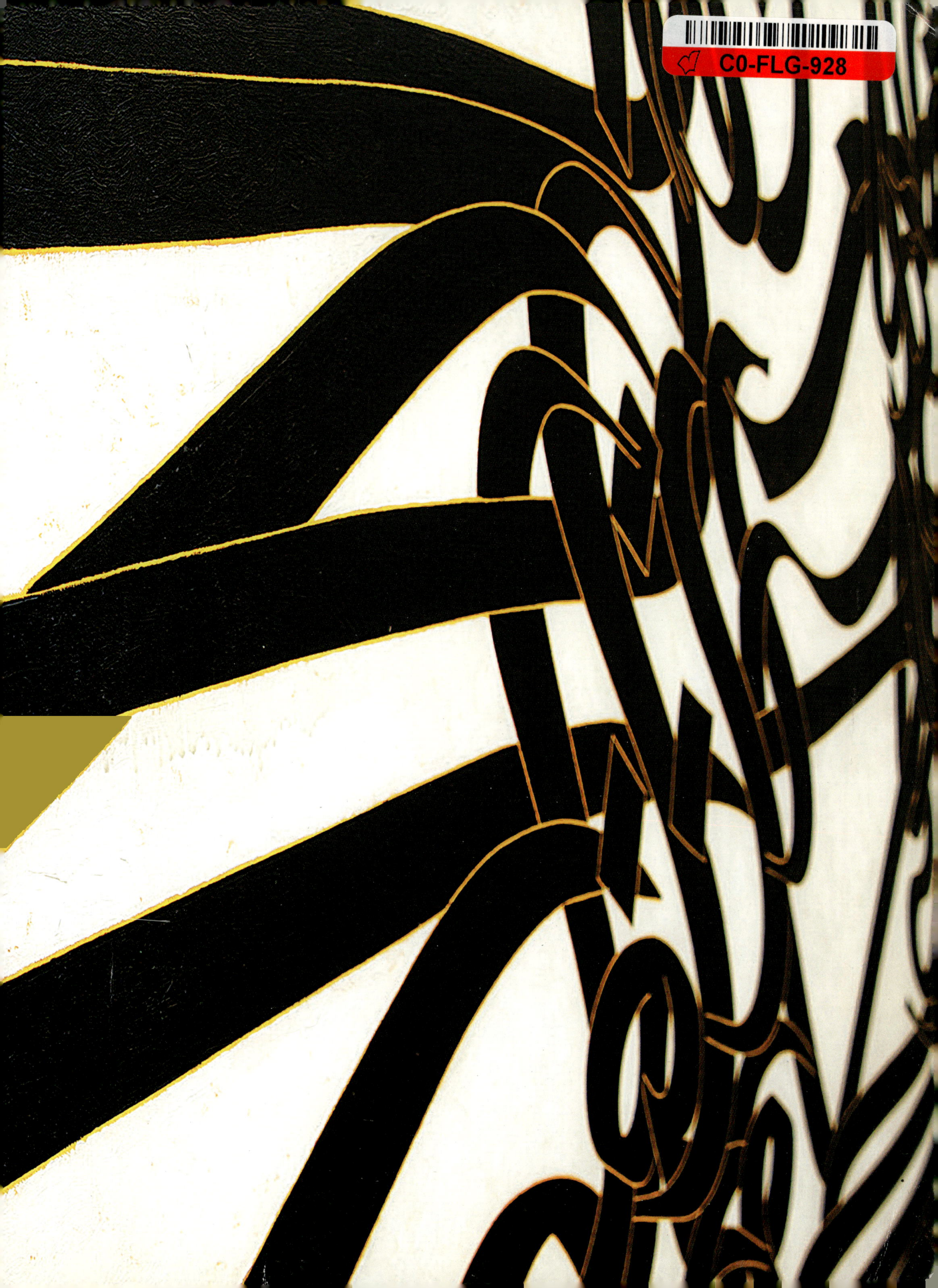

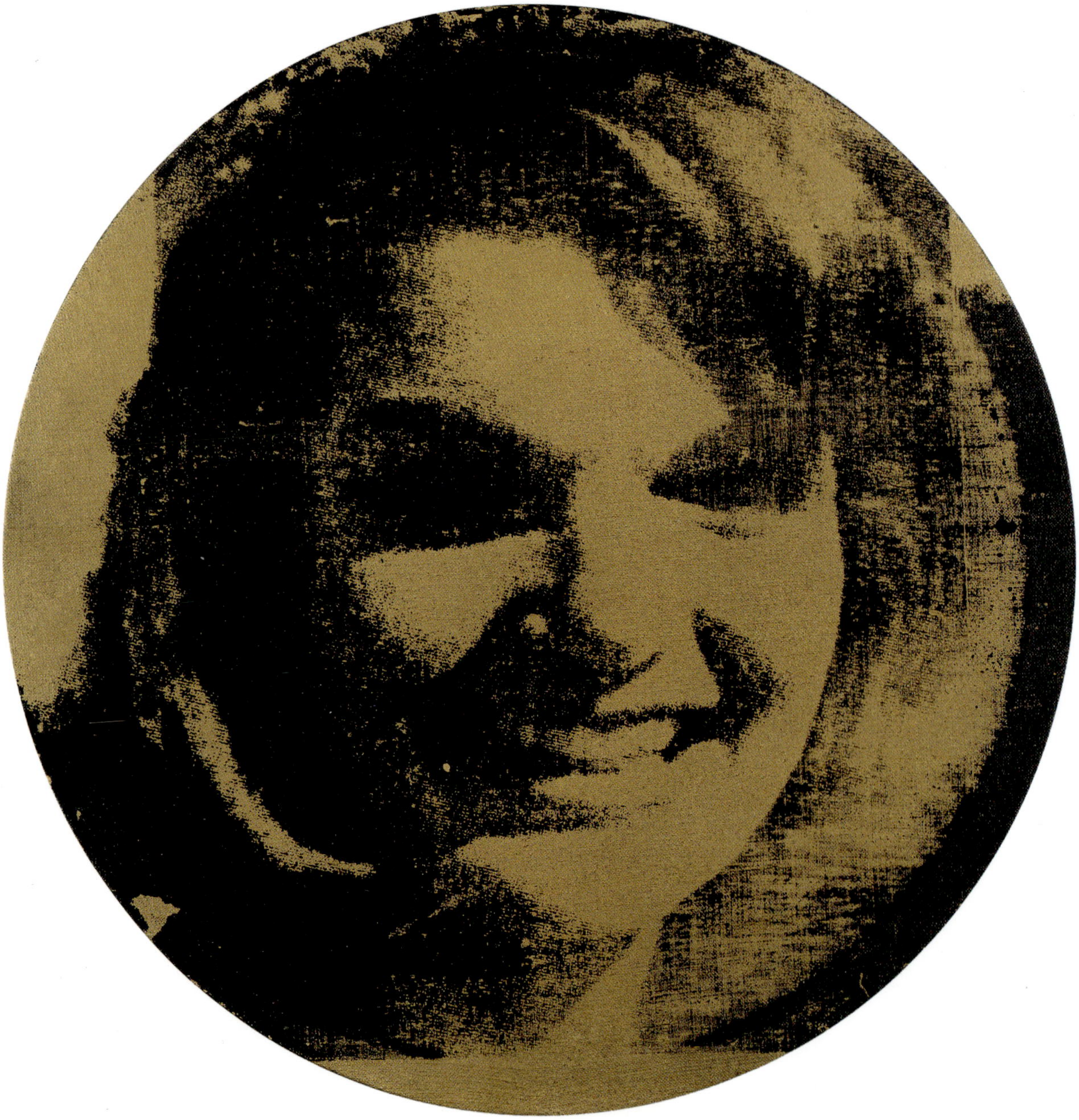

Contemporary Art

AUCTION IN DOHA WEDNESDAY 18 MARCH 2009 | 20.00

EXHIBITION

Saturday 14 March
13.00 – 15.00 | By Appointment Only
15.00 – 22.00 | Public View

Sunday 15 March
9.00 – 11.00 | Ladies Only
11.00 – 15.00 | By Appointment Only
20.00 – 22.00 | Public View

Monday 16 March
9.00 – 11.00 | Ladies Only
11.00 – 15.00 | By Appointment Only
15.00 – 17.30 | Public View

Tuesday 17 March
9.00 – 11.00 | Ladies Only
11.00 – 15.00 | By Appointment Only
15.00 – 22.00 | Public View

For an appointment please call +974 (0)452 8333
(+974 (0)409 7155 | 14–20 March only)
or email qatar@sothebys.com

PAYMENT AND COLLECTION

Wednesday 18 March | until 22.00
Thursday 19 March | 10.00 – 22.00
Friday 20 March | 10.00 – 20.00

THE RITZ CARLTON, DOHA
WEST BAY LAGOON, P.O. BOX 23400, DOHA – STATE OF QATAR

GULF REGION ENQUIRIES

For a full listing of our offices and salerooms worldwide with detailed information on all of Sotheby's services, visit sothebys.com

Roberta Louckx
roberta.louckx@sothebys.com
+1 646 244 6666

Pittman Shay
pittman.shay@sothebys.com
+1 646 515 8100

John Stevenson
john.stevenson@sothebys.com
+44 (0)777 552 1704

Doha
Nigel Harrison
nigel.harrison@sothebys.com
+974 (0)452 8333

Egypt
Ali Can Ertug
alican.ertug@sothebys.com
+1 646 732 3727

Kingdom of Saudi Arabia
Maria Al Zahrani
+971 509 901034

Kuwait
Ali Can Ertug
alican.ertug@sothebys.com
+1 646 732 3727

Bahrain
John Stevenson
john.stevenson@sothebys.com
+44 (0)777 552 1704

United Arab Emirates
Roxane Zand
roxane.zand@sothebys.com
+44 20 7293 6200
Ameera Samy
+971 501 325007

Turkey
Oya Delahaye
oya.delahaye@sothebys.com
+90 212 335 6442

OTHER AUCTIONS IN DOHA

A comprehensive calendar of international auctions, in addition to all sale results, can be viewed at sothebys.com

A Collection of Orientalist Art
18 March 2009
Doha

Important Watches
19 March 2009
Doha

Arts of the Islamic World
19 March 2009
Doha

The Pearl Carpet of Baroda
19 March 2009
Doha

Important Notice Please note that all lots are sold subject to our Conditions of Business for Buyers and Authenticity Guarantee, which are set forth at the back of this catalogue and Conditions of Business for Sellers, which are available from Sotheby's offices on request.

For all lots marked with a ○, △, □, ⩡, ⋑ or ✪ please refer to the Guide for Prospective Buyers.

SPECIALISTS AND AUCTION ENQUIRIES

For further information on lots in this auction please contact any of the specialists listed below.

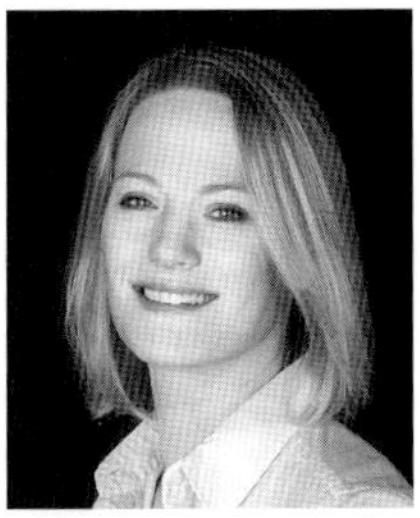

Cheyenne Westphal
Chairman, Contemporary Art, Europe
+44 (0)20 7293 5391
cheyenne.westphal@sothebys.com

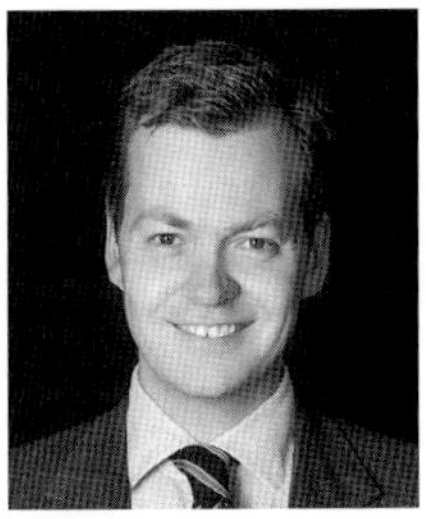

Oliver Barker
Senior International Specialist
+44 (0)20 7293 5494
oliver.barker@sothebys.com

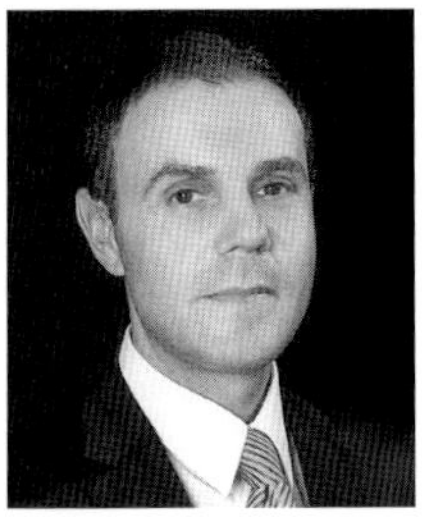

Saul Ingram
Managing Director
+44 (0)20 7293 5764
saul.ingram@sothebys.com

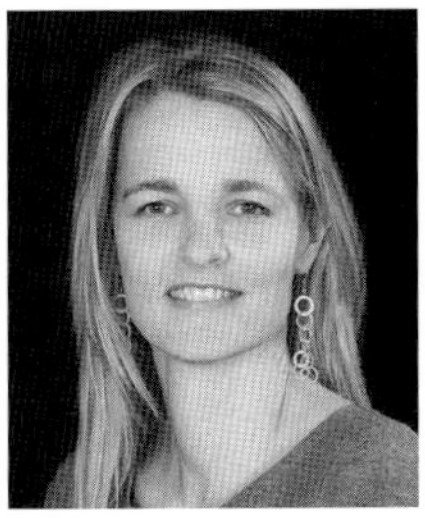

Miety Heiden
Senior Vice President
+1 212 894 1050
miety.heiden@sothebys.com

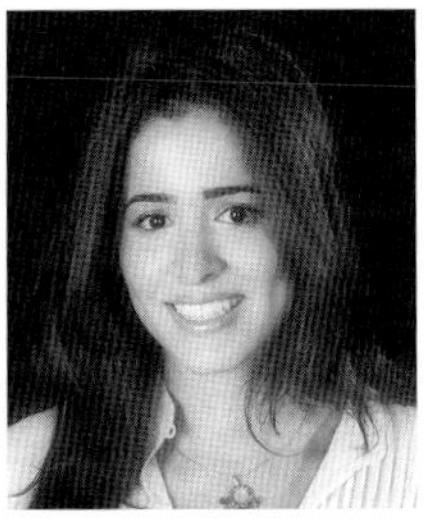

Lina Lazaar
Specialist
+44 (0)20 7293 5826
lina.lazaar@sothebys.com

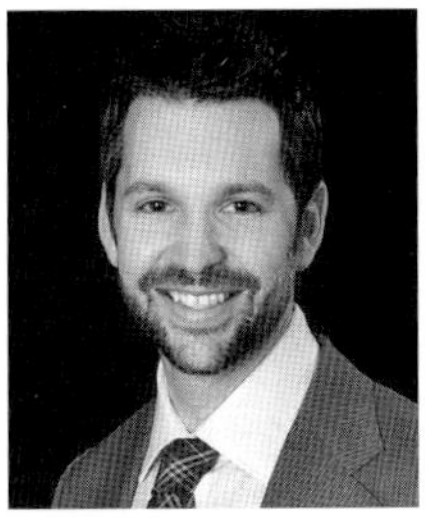

Scott Nussbaum
Specialist
+1 212 894 1319
scott.nussbaum@sothebys.com

Sale Number
D09001

Sotheby's Qatar
+974 (0)452 8333
FAX +974 (0)452 8334

From 14–20 March only
Sotheby's c/o The Ritz Carlton, Doha
+974 (0)409 7100
FAX +974 (0)409 7101

Absentee Bids
+974 (0)452 8333
FAX +974 (0)452 8334
FROM 14–20 MARCH ONLY
+974 (0)409 7120
FAX +974 (0)409 7102

Telephone Bidding
+974 (0)452 8333
FAX +974 (0)452 8334
FROM 14–20 MARCH ONLY
+974 (0)409 7120
FAX +974 (0)409 7102
Telephone bid requests should be received 24 hours prior to the sale.

Payment
BUYERS
Andrew McGarry
andrew.mcgarry@sothebys.com
+44 (0)20 7293 5270
FAX +44 (0)20 7293 5926
SELLERS
Catherine Mac
catherine.mac@sothebys.com
+44 (0)20 7293 5025
FAX +44 (0)20 7293 5951
FROM 14–20 MARCH ONLY
+974 (0)409 7130
FAX +974 (0)409 7103

Condition Reports & Image Requests
Joanne Carter
joanne.carter@sothebys.com
+44 (0)20 7293 6276
FAX +44 (0)20 7293 5921

Sale Administrator
Lee-Ann Cameron
leeann.cameron@sothebys.com
+44 (0)20 7293 5398
FAX +44 (0)20 7293 5980

Business Director
Emma Paleschi
emma.paleschi@sothebys.com
+44 (0)20 7293 6246
FAX +44 (0)20 7293 6903

Private Client Group
LONDON
Sarah Bourghardt
sarah.bourghardt@sothebys.com
+44 (0)20 7293 6420
NEW YORK
Susan Barrett
susan.barrett@sothebys.com
+1 212 606 7087
FROM 14–20 MARCH ONLY
+974 (0)409 7150
FAX +974 (0)409 7101

Shipping
EXPORTS
Martin de Meyer
martin.demeyer@sothebys.com
+31 20 550 2249
FAX +31 20 550 2349
IMPORTS
Sue Swan
sue.swan@sothebys.com
+44 (0)20 7293 5353
FAX +44 (0)20 7293 5952
FROM 14–20 MARCH ONLY
+974 (0)409 7140
FAX +974 (0)409 7103

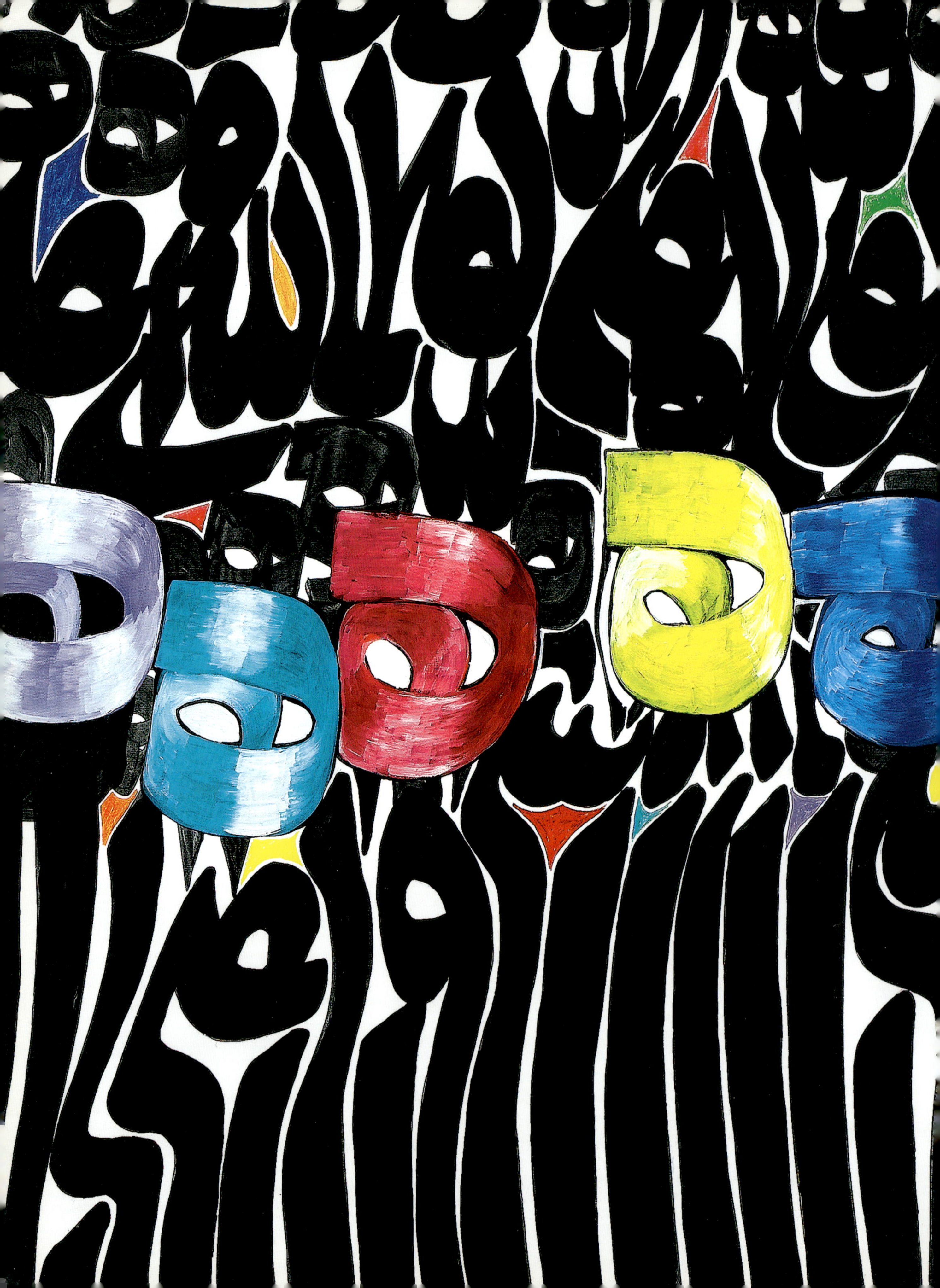

CONTENTS

FRONT COVER LOT 116 Farhad Moshiri *Diamond Head*
ENDPAPER LOT 104 Mohammad Eshai *Afarinesh (Creation)*
FRONTISPIECE LOT 117 Andy Warhol *Round Jackie*
OPPOSITE LOT 123 Hossein Zenderoudi *Ganje Paindjom*
PAGE 9 LOT 112 Anish Kapoor *Untitled*
BACK COVER LOT 119 Gerhard Richter *Heu*
BACK ENDPAPER LOT 114 Damien Hirst *Ulysses*

كلمة ترحيب

بقلم لينا لازار وسكوت نوسباوم

An Introduction

BY LINA LAZAAR AND SCOTT NUSSBAUM

يسرنا ويشرفنا أن نضع بين أيديكم هذه التشكيلة الإستثنائية من الأعمال الفنية العالمية، ويشرفنا أكثر أن يأتي طرحها خلال مزاد هو باكورة مزادات الفنون المعاصرة التي نقيمها في الدوحة. إن هذا المزاد هو ثمرة الجهود الهائلة التي بذلها «قسم الفنون المعاصرة» لدى «ساذبيز»، الذي طاف أرجاء المعمورة ليجمع قطعاً نادرة تقدم لهواة جمع المقتنيات النفيسة ولمديري المتاحف والصالات الفنية فرصاً غير مسبوقة لاقتناء لوحات ومخطوطات ومنحوتات على أرفع المستويات.

بين معروضات المزاد، تبرز بشكل خاص اللوحة النادرة جداً التي أبدعها آندي وارهول باللون الذهبي وبشكل مستدير عام ١٩٦٤ تحت عنوان «جاكي»، ولوحة متلألئة ذات مقاسات ضخمة أنجزها على القماش الفنان غيرهارد ريختر ضمن سلسلته الشهيرة المسماة «رسومات تجريدية». إلى جانب ذلك، يتضمن المزاد لوحة مذهلة على القماش للفنان فرهاد مشيري، الذي يعتبر في طليعة كوكبة جديدة من المواهب التي انطلقت من قلب الشرق الأوسط لتستقطب الأضواء على الساحات العالمية للفن المعاصر. وعلى صعيد المنحوتات، يأتيكم مزادنا بعدد من الروائع المعاصرة في فنون النحت المخصصة للعرض الخارجي، ومنها رائعة روبرت إنديانا التي أسماها «الحب»، وتحفة برنار ڤينيه المسماة «خطوط غير محددة». وتجدون في المزاد أيضاً لوحات فاخرة للفنان داميان هيرست من تشكيلته التي استوحاها من الفراشات، ومنحوتات جدارية مفعمة بالسحر والغموض للفنان آنيش كاپور، إلى جانب أعمال فذة لأسماء لامعة من رواد عالم الفن، ومن بينهم شفيق عبود، پول غيراغوسيان، بالإضافة إلى نبيل نحاس.

وإذ نحظى بشرف استضافة العاصمة القطرية لأول مزاداتنا فيها، يشرفنا أن يتضمن هذا المزاد أعمالاً لكوكبة متميزة من المبدعين القطريين، مثل يوسف أحمد، علي حسن، فرج دهمان، وسلمان المالك. من خلال الأعمال الإستثنائية لهذه الكوكبة المبدعة، نستشفّ معاً مدى الحيوية التي يتمتع بها المشهد الثقافيّ في قطر.

ختاماً، فإنه من دواعي سرورنا أن يتضمن المزاد أعمالاً لأسماء من شتى المشارب والثقافات، بدءاً من جوزيف آلبرس إلى حسين زندرودي، ليكون بذلك نموذجاً للحوار بين الحضارات، فيسلط الضوء على فنانين ينتمون إلى خلفيات متباينة في ثقافتها وتاريخها وفنونها. تفضلوا بمطالعة هذه الصفحات، لتكتشفوا المزيد مما يجعلنا نفتخر بتنظيم هذه التظاهرة الفنية الفريدة، والمزيد مما يقدم فرصاً تاريخية لهواة جمع المقتنيات النفيسة.

We are extremely pleased and honored to offer an exceptional selection of international works of Art in our inaugural sale of Contemporary Art in Doha. An effort of Sotheby's Contemporary Art department worldwide, this sale presents a superlative opportunity for collectors and curators to acquire paintings, works on paper and sculpture of the highest quality.

Highlighting the sale are an extremely rare and magnificent gold Jackie tondo painting by Andy Warhol from 1964 and a shimmering large-scale canvas by Gerhard Richter from his celebrated Abstraktes Bild series. Additionally, a dazzling canvas by Farhad Moshiri, a leader of the flourishing community of young Contemporary Middle Eastern artists, is included. Works such as Robert Indiana's iconic LOVE and Bernar Venet's lyrical Indeterminate Lines are magnificent examples of contemporary outdoor sculpture. Damien Hirst's exquisite butterfly paintings and Anish Kapoor's enigmatic wall sculpture are truly breathtaking. And notable works by artistic luminaries such as Chafik Abboud, Paul Guiragossian and Nabil Nahas feature prominently in this extraordinary sale.

Furthermore, we are particularly privileged to offer a distinguished group of works by leading artists of Qatar including Youssef Ahmed, Ali Hassan, Faraj Dahman and Salman al-Malik. These outstanding artworks illuminate the vitality of Qatar's vibrant culture.

From Josef Albers to Hossein Zenderoudi, this wonderful selection of works encourages a cross-cultural dialogue between artists of diverse backgrounds and histories. We are honored to participate in this groundbreaking event and thrilled for the opportunity to present the works on the following pages for your collecting enjoyment.

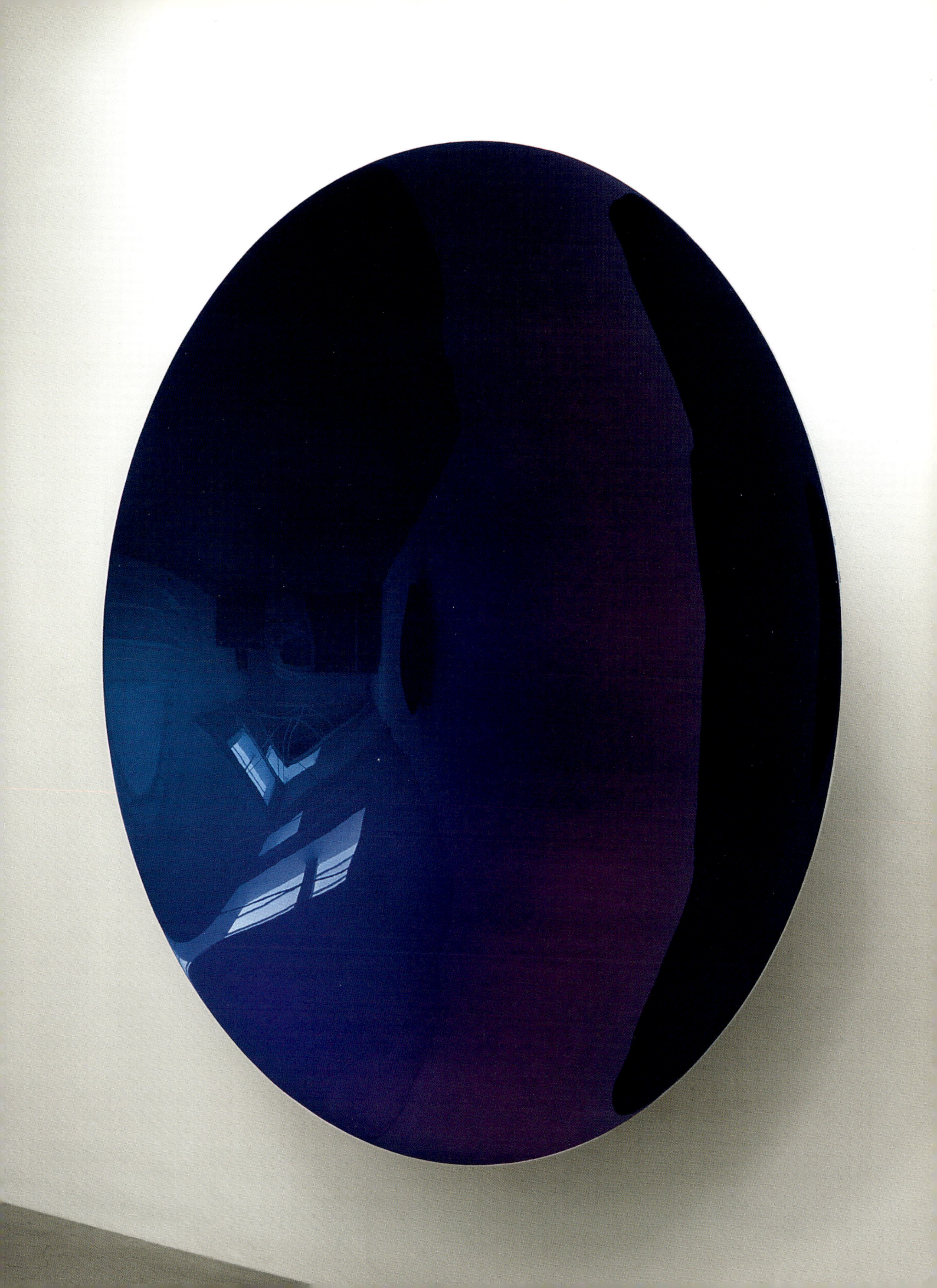

101

Yousef Ahmad

b. 1955

UNTITLED

signed and dated *08*
oil on canvas
120 BY 120CM.; 47¼ BY 47¼IN.

25,000-35,000 US$
91,000-128,000 QAR

PROVENANCE
Artspace Gallery, Dubai
Acquired directly from the above by the present owner

Immediately after graduating with a Masters degree in Fine Arts from California University in 1982, Yousef Ahmad held an exhibition in Washington D.C. that would mark an important turning point in his career. His artistic training had begun almost a quarter of a century before, when - although just a toddler - he would take the coals with which his mother used to light the cooking fire and scribble short phrases on the walls of his home in Qatar. A precocious child with an artistic spirit, he pursued this innate passion for graphic design. At early as primary school, he discovered the potential versatility of colours, which he explored throughout secondary school and at the university in Cairo. Yet throughout this journey, Ahmad held those first calligraphic exercises on the walls of his house very close to himself, which - after nearly twenty years of artistic training - he developed into his mature work which he describes as the result of "using and subjugating the Arabic calligraphy and letters in order to find new artistic solutions." (Y. Ahmad, YousefAhmad.com).

Untitled embodies the artist's original artistic treatment of traditional Arabic calligraphy. The forms projected onto the canvas do not merely present an aesthetically pleasing design, but invite the discerning viewer to question the origins of these forms that make up the Arabic alphabet. Indeed, these curving shapes and the carefully adorned surface on which they are exhibited appear to be a snapshot of ever-changing figures that the artist has been able to capture. Palestinian artist Kamal Boullata praises Ahmad's technique, highlighting the ability with which he 'brings spontaneity to painting, introducing in the kingdom of geometry some Arabic calligraphy' (M. King, *Art Contemporain Arabe*, Paris 1988, p. 68).

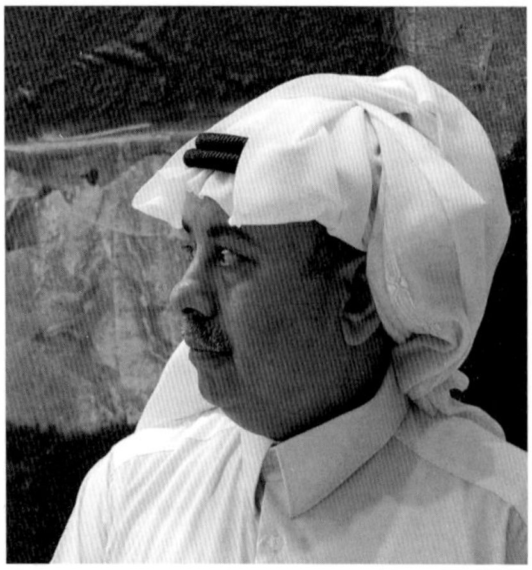

YOUSEF AHMAD, 2008, COURTESY OF THE ARTIST

Ahmad's talent does not only lie in his original treatment of Arabic calligraphy. Throughout his career, he has experimented with a large variety of colour schemes that have an equally strong impact on the dynamism and narrative of his work. His earlier paintings, which are decorated in various shades of brown and black, could be said to recall the "ephemerality of signs drawn onto the sand as they disappear with the sweeping desert winds." (Brahim Alaoui, Nicole de Pontcharra and Nabil Naoum, *Perspective on Contemporary Arab Art*, Paris 2002, pp. 114-5). Ahmad's careful treatment of blue, turquoise and yellow tones in *Untitled* is a beautiful attempt to evoke the colourful beaches of his native Qatar.

In *Untitled*, Yousef Ahmad masterfully combines colour and shape, engaging his audience in a vibrant composition of motion. The pseudo-calligraphy, surrounded by a meticulously detailed frame, proves the artist's comprehensive understanding of surface. Nevertheless - beneath these chromatic layers and twirling brushstrokes - an inquisitive viewer can find the same inspiration that led young Ahmad to trace his first carbon drawings: an instinctive curiosity for creation and innovation.

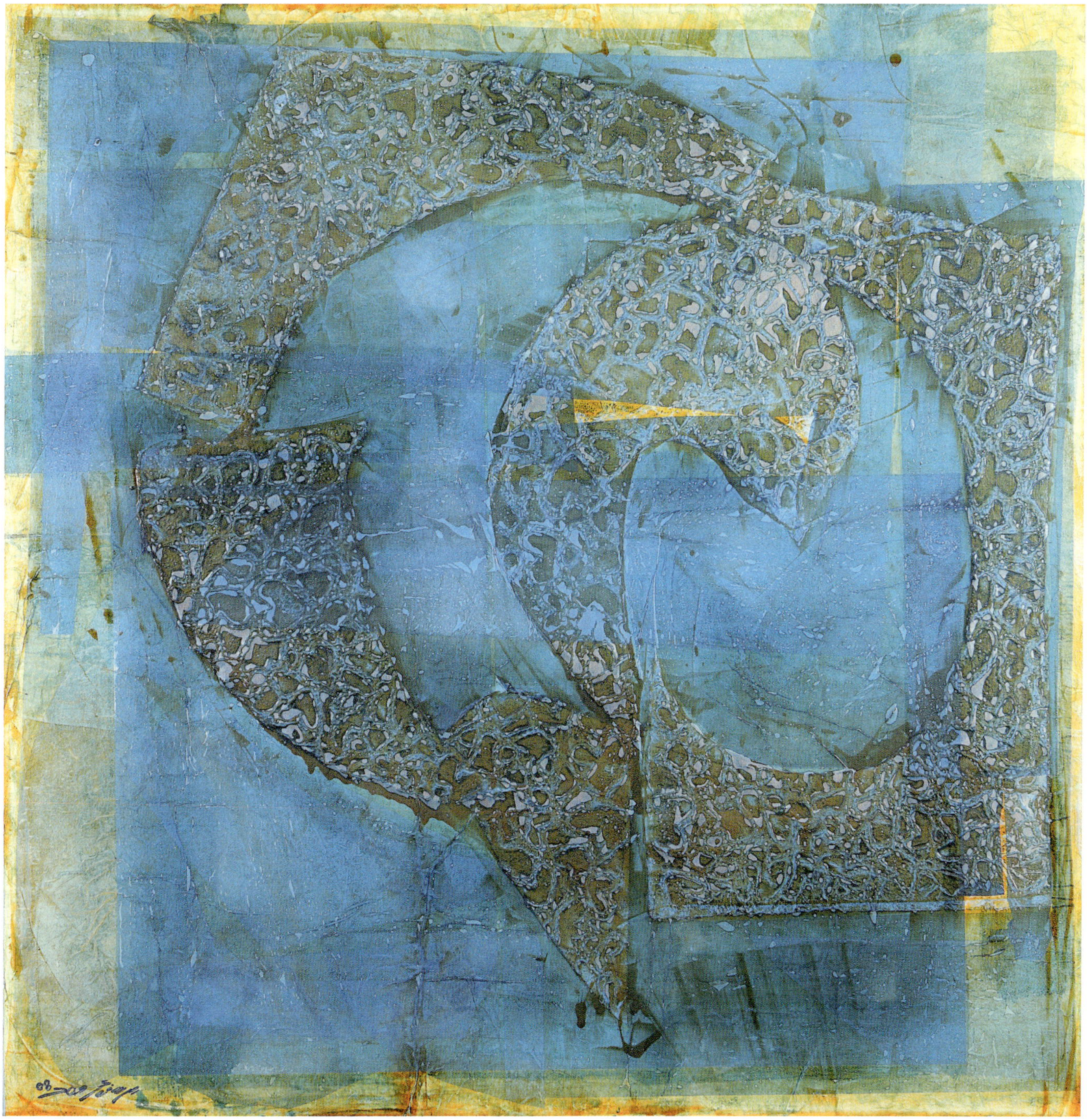

102

Kader Attia

b. 1970

BLACK CUBE 4

signed on a label affixed to the reverse
acylic on canvas
203.2 BY 203.2CM.; 80 BY 80IN.

Executed in 2005.

20,000-30,000 US$
73,000-110,000 QAR

PROVENANCE
Andréhn-Schiptjenko, Stockholm
Acquired directly from the above by the present owner

"This space in between [...] it is the experience of what may be perceptible tomorrow, when it will become an empiricism, and when the world will have changed its balance or maybe its thought. Then, maybe, a thing and its contrary will not be as important as what binds them."

The artist cited in: Kader Attia, *Black and White- Signs of Times*, Navarra 2008, n. p

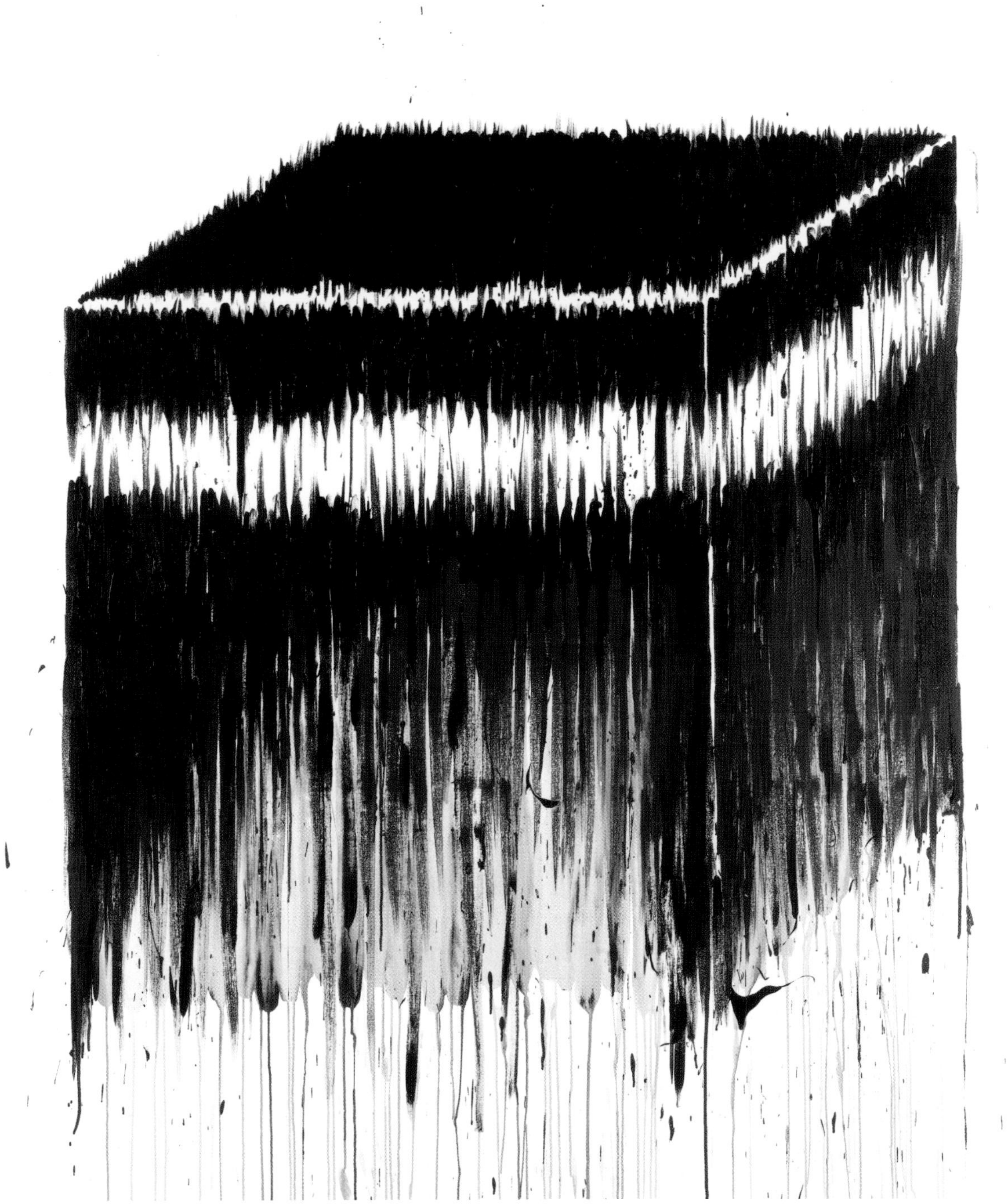

103

Mona Hatoum

b. 1952

∞

signed, signed with initials, dated *91* twice and numbered *4/8* on the underside of the table

bronze

60.1 BY 34.1 BY 34.1CM.; 23⅝ BY 13⅜ BY 13⅜IN.

35,000-45,000 US$

128,000-164,000 QAR

PROVENANCE

Private Collection, Europe

LITERATURE

Exhibition Catalogue, Santiago de Compostela, Centro de Arte de Salamanca; Centro Galego de Arte Contemporánea, *Mona Hatoum*, 2000, p. 97, illustration of another example

In the course of her international career, Mona Hatoum has produced a body of work exploring a variety of media, including performance, sculpture, video, installation and photography. The subjects are addressed through the use of familiar, everyday domestic objects which are powerfully transposed into a foreign, uncanny realm.

At first, the present work appears to be a conventional coffee table on which have been placed children's bronze figurines in a figure of 8. It soon becomes clear that a deeper iconography of war is explored as toy soldiers with guns pointing forward are aligned in a chain pursuing one another in a perpetual cycle forming the Infinity symbol. A deadly reminder of the vicious and never-ending cycle of war, where soldiers march relentlessly in pursuit of the unseen enemy, oo negotiates the controversial belief that some wars are a necessary evil in order to secure long-lasting peace and universal freedom.

Born to a Palestinian family in Beirut, Hatoum's experience is one of double exile: first, that of her Palestinian family in Lebanon, and subsequently, her own move to England due to Lebanon's civil war in the 70's. And, although the artist often avoids being too didactic and autobiographical, her work has inevitably been shaped by her personal story and perceptions. ∞ is therefore a poignant metaphor for the state of living in a nation fraught with constant war and conflict.

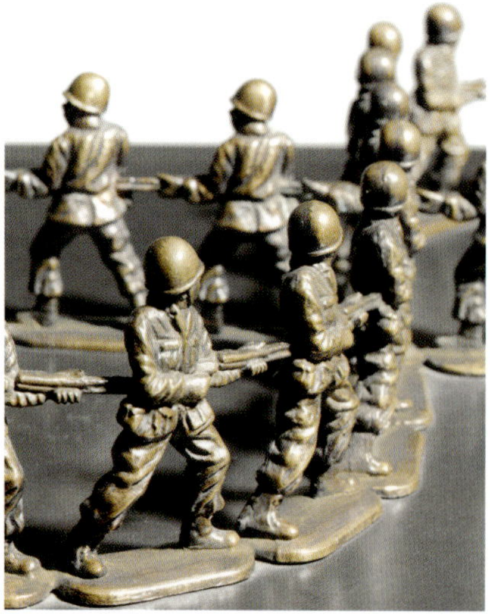

DETAIL OF PRESENT WORK

In Hatoum's work, everyday objects become unusable and often transformed into threatening sculptures, displaying a vision of the world as a dangerous place caught up in constant conflict and unrest. Their meaning is subverted and no longer belongs to the safe context of their everyday function, suspending the viewer between perceived normality and impending danger. ∞ does not provide a specific meaning but instead forces the viewer to wonder about the nature of power relationships, about who is oppressing or manipulating whom.

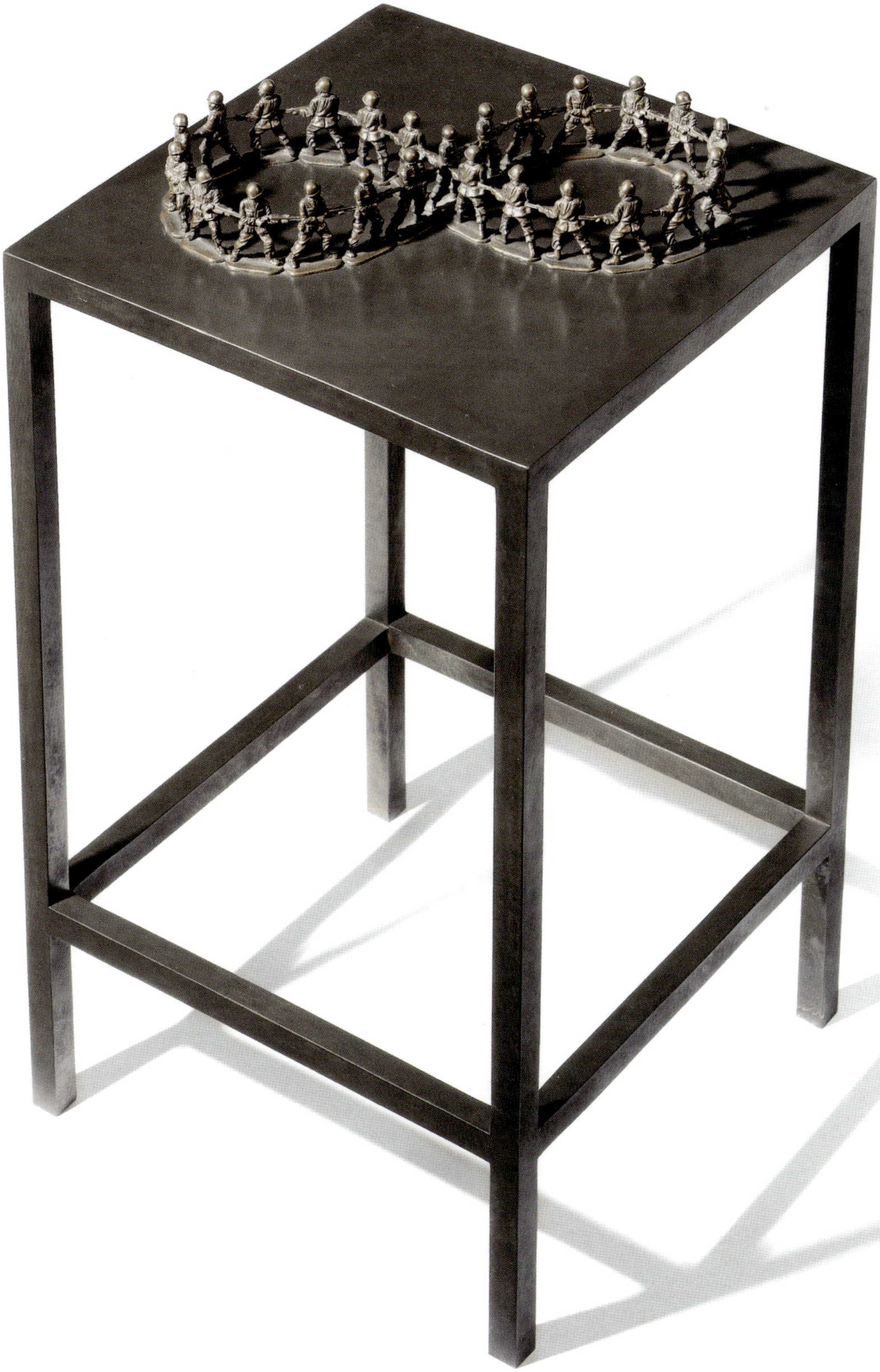

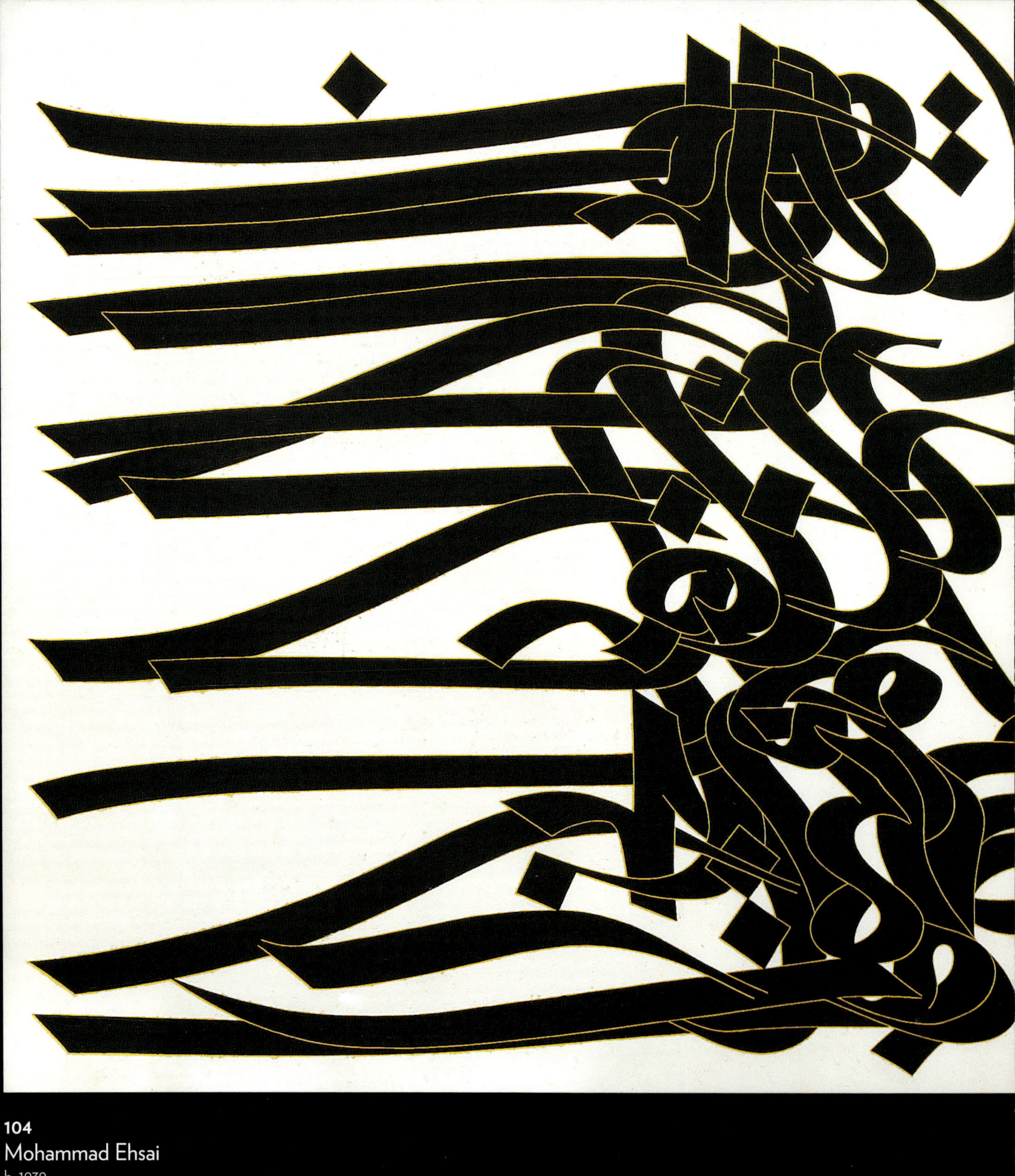

104

Mohammad Ehsai

b. 1939

AFARINESH (CREATION)

signed and dated *2008*

oil on canvas

204 BY 394CM.; 80⅜ BY 155⅛IN.

300,000-400,000 US$ 1,100,000-1,460,000 QAR

PROVENANCE

Acquired directly from the artist by the present owner

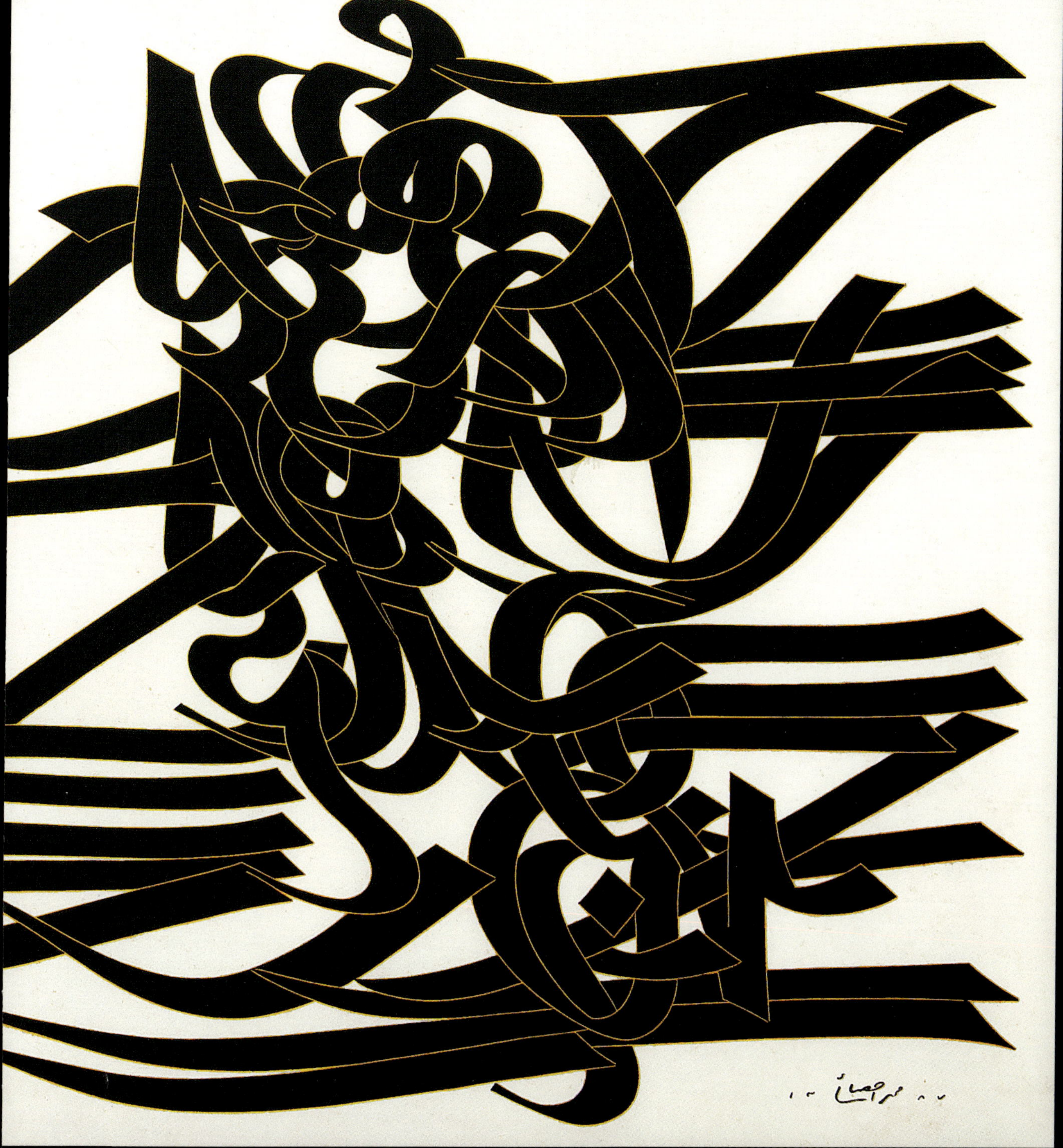

﴿ وَلَقَدْ خَلَقْنَا الْإِنسَانَ وَنَعْلَمُ مَا تُوَسْوِسُ بِهِ
نَفْسُهُ وَنَحْنُ أَقْرَبُ إِلَيْهِ مِنْ حَبْلِ الْوَرِيدِ ﴾

"And indeed Allah has created man, and knows whatever thoughts his inner self develops,
and is closer to him than the very vein in his neck"

Extract from Quran's Chapter 50: Surat Qaf ,16

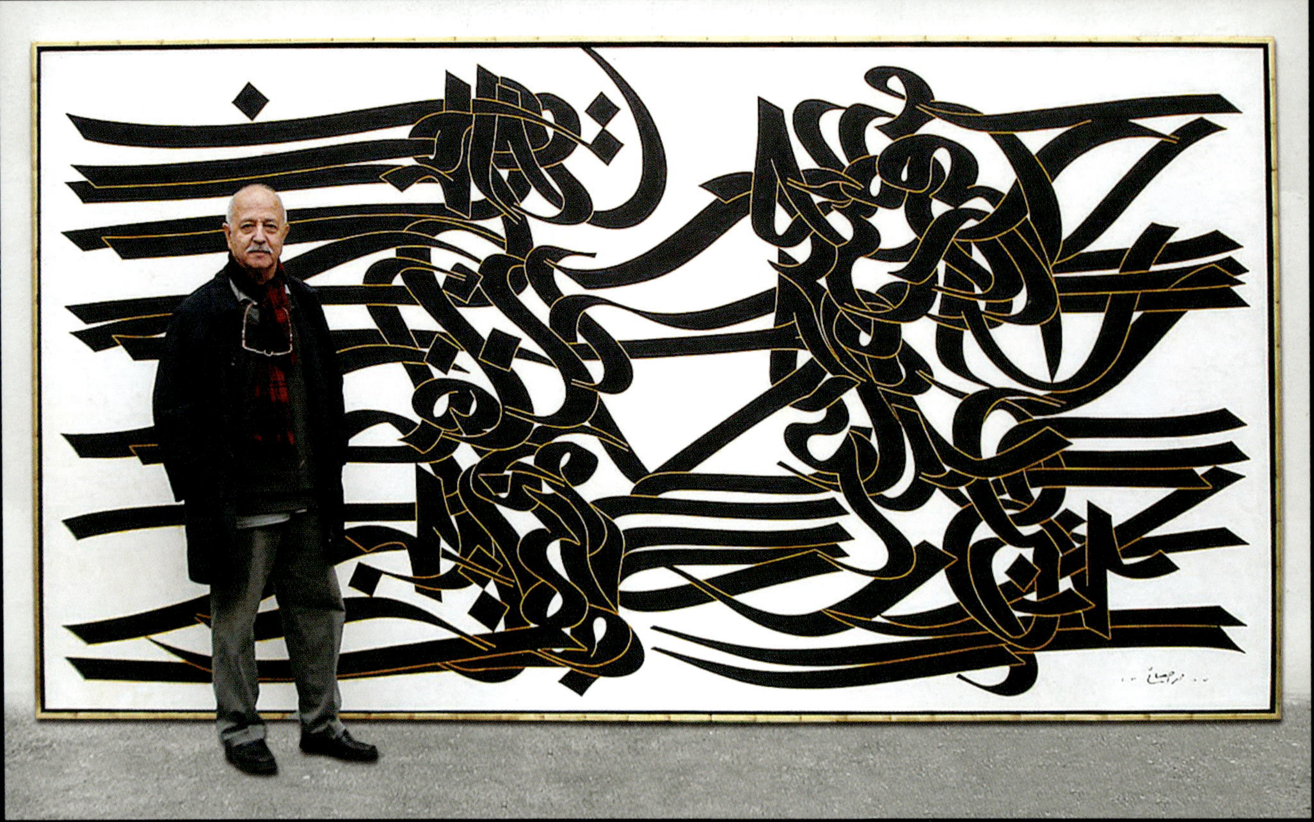

THE ARTIST IN FRONT OF THE PRESENT WORK

Mohammad Ehsai is undoubtedly one of the most gifted Iranian calligraphers of the past century. An erudite academician as well as a master of his craft, Ehsai synthesized the technical expertise of his formal training within a strictly contemporary visual schema, and counts as one of the rare few who can combine the vision of the artist with the craft of the calligrapher, producing works whose technical excellence is unrivalled, and whose conceptual makeup is both reflective and profound.

A master and lifelong disciple of traditional Persian calligraphy, in *Creation* Ehsai demonstrates a consummate technical skill in an unprecedented scale, but also a diversity and innovation of style that affirms a true willingness to break from the classical formalism of the calligraphic orthodoxy.

Known for his tightly composed intricate calligraphy, the present work breaks from the rigid structure of the past with a deft fluidity of execution, asserting a high level of spatial awareness and fluency of form. Letterforms are given new life, freed from the classical monotone. *Creation* is itself reviving with an extraordinary bright outline, fanning elegantly outwards in streaming, stem-like strokes from an intertwined nucleus.

In the present work, Ehsai explores the repetition of divine and benedictory phrases, and descriptive terms denoting the chief attributes of God, sourcing his inspiration from the Surat Al Qaf of the Quran, in which God exclaims the closeness to man's to be more perceptible than his own "jugular vein", whilst dismissed as a literal physical description, the verse serves as a spiritual testament to mans closeness with God, and concurs with the Sufi's central mystical belief that an element of God lives within the soul of every man, and that unity with the divine represents the pinnacle of spiritual consciousness, one that can be experienced through physical practices of religious adoration, such as meditation, poetry, song, or calligraphy.

By drawing on these divine sources, Ehsai acknowledges his place within a tradition spanning over one thousand years, pioneered by artists whose aim was to capture in words the attributes of heavenly perfection. His recognition of this legacy is enacted with a fluency, simplicity, and poise, all of which supersede the obscurity of hitherto calligraphic production. Dominant, graceful and profound, *Creation* is a magnificent testament to the continuation of a historical practice contextualised in a modern era.

Ultimately, his oeuvre not only pays tribute to century long traditions, but at the same time makes the more profound artistic statement that sanctity and perfection can be related through visual beauty, and that the graceful aesthetic of the letter-form reveals qualities and attributes that shed light on aspects of the divine which are otherwise unfathomable.

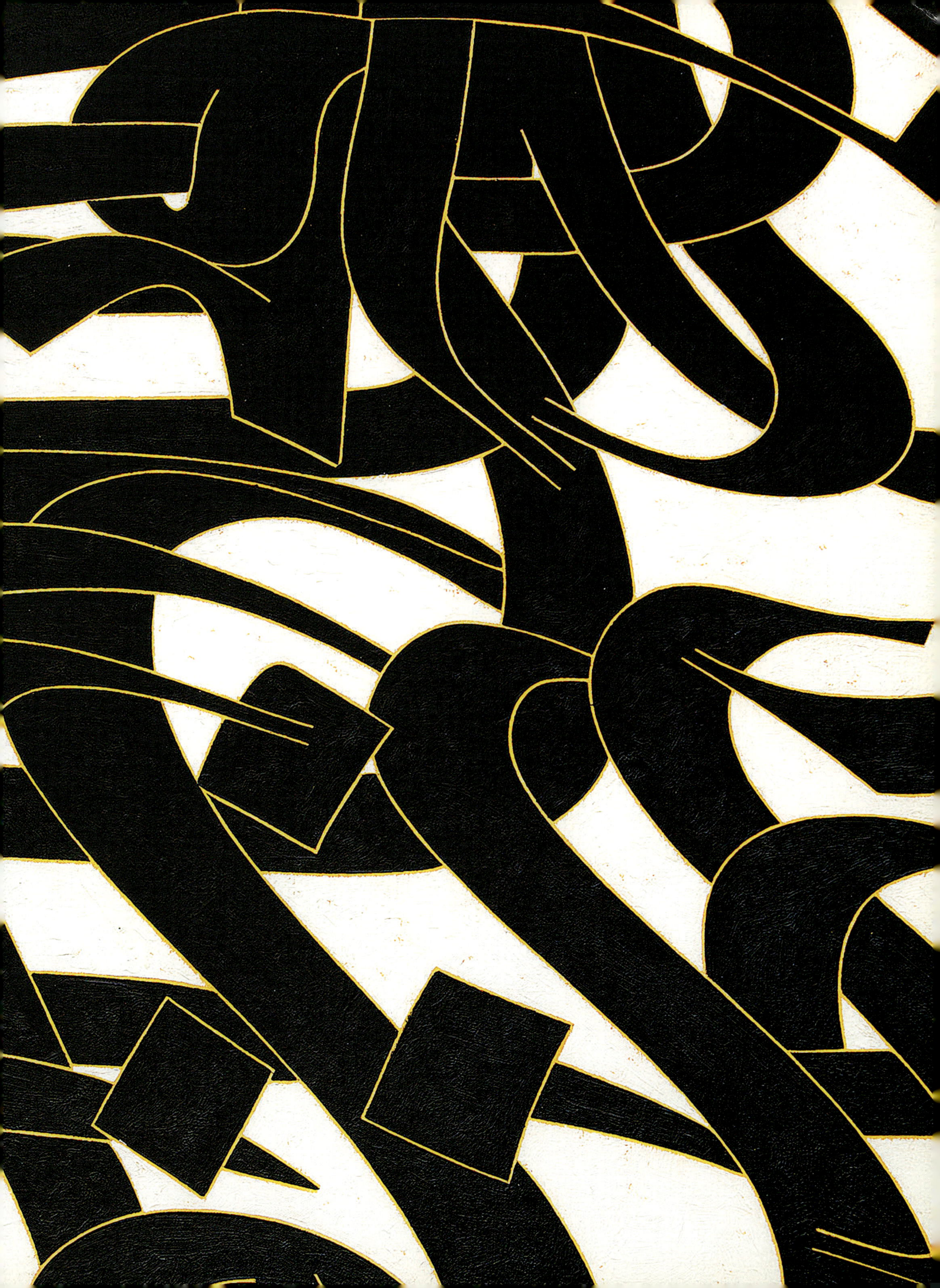

105

Ali Hassan

b. 1956

HORSE IN THE DESERT

signed and dated *08*; signed and dated *08* on the reverse
acrylic on canvas
150 BY 200CM.; 59 BY 78¾IN.

20,000-25,000 US$
73,000-91,000 QAR

PROVENANCE
The Artist

"At the beginning I used all the 28 Arabic letters, but after being with letters for a while I thought to present the place and the flexibility of it through a single letter which is the letter *Nun*, because I have an inner fascination with it. Furthermore to reveal the value of it from different aspects and to prove that a human can use one letter all his life because of its strength and the position of the Arabic letters."

Ali Hassan cited in: Exhibition Catalogue, Bonn, Kunstmuseum, *Languages of the Desert*, 2005, p. 144

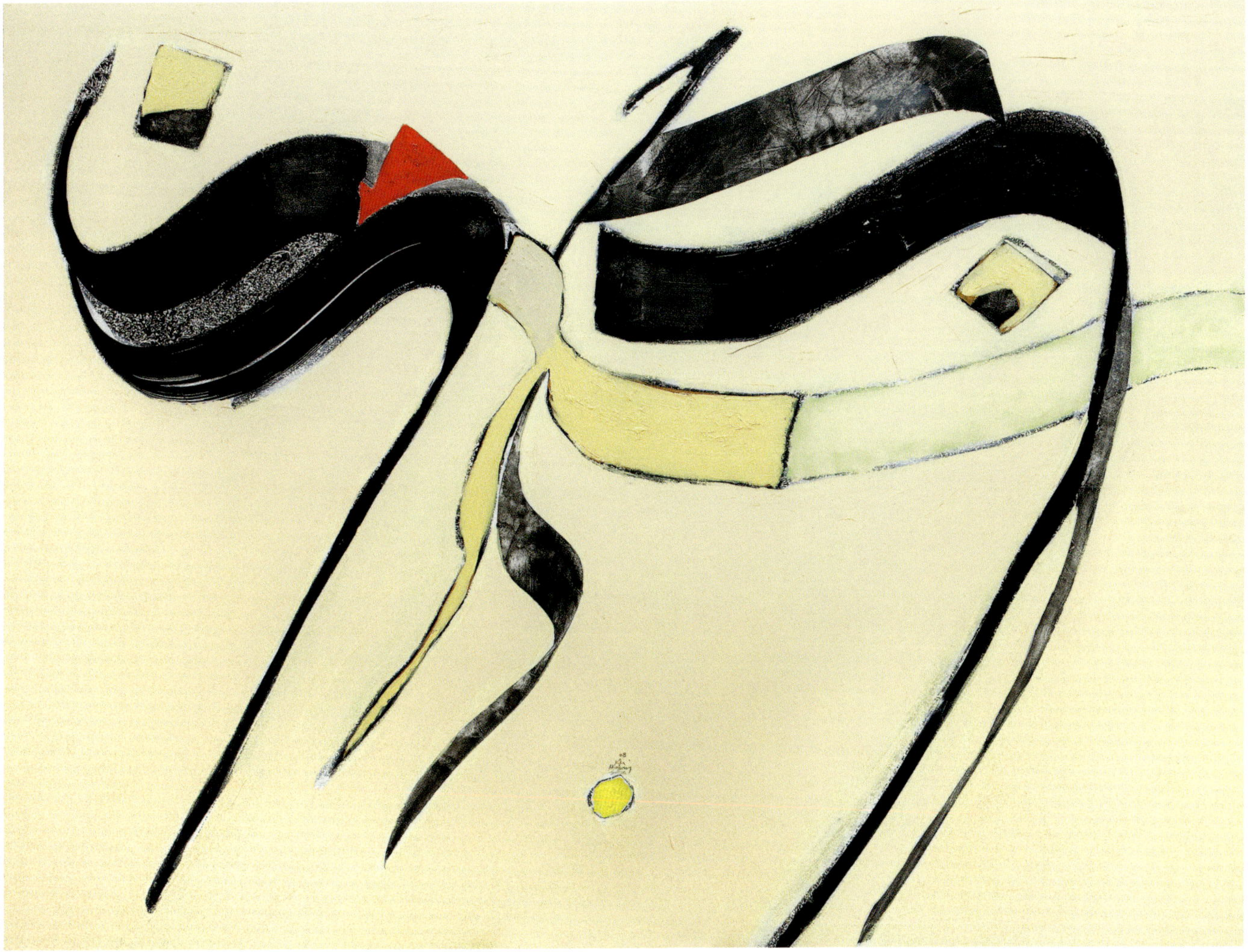

106

Ayman Baalbaki

b. 1975

ABEL

signed, titled and dated in Arabic *08*
acrylic, gold leaf and neon on wood
235 BY 150CM.; 92½ BY 59IN.

20,000-30,000 US$
73,000-110,000 QAR

PROVENANCE
Private Collection, Lebanon

Like many Lebanese citizens, Ayman Baalbaki's life has often been disrupted by displacement. Born in the southern village of Odeisse in 1975, civil war compelled his family to move to the downtown Beirut section of Wadi Abu Jamil. Shortly thereafter, gentrification of this neighbourhood triggered development of luxury villas and high-end apartment buildings pricing his family out and forcing them to relocate to the southern suburb of Haret Hreik. In 2006, once again, Baalbaki's life was fractured by the destruction of his family's home and his own studio during the most recent conflict. This frequent dislocation, borne from clashes between adversaries within and from afar, the rich and the poor, the old and the new is translated and transformed in his art with brilliant dexterity, skilfully articulating a duality between modern art theory and contemporary society.

Though his radical paintings and installations would seem to mark a break from historical and modern formal concerns, Ayman's art is deeply rooted in tradition. His mixed media work pays tribute to contemporary artists such as Robert Rauschenberg, Keith Sonnier and Jasper Johns while the dazzling use of gold leaf is reminiscent of medieval manuscripts and religious iconography. As the artist notes, "In Arabic and Islamic culture, we use a lot of gold [...] It's tradition. The colour exists in dancers' costumes, on Christian icons and in Islamic texts." (The artist cited in: Kaelen Wilson-Goldie, *The Art of War*, The National, www.thenational.ae, cited 05/02/2009)

However, unlike his artistic predecessors, Baalbaki's art is concerned less with philosophies of art and more in philosophies

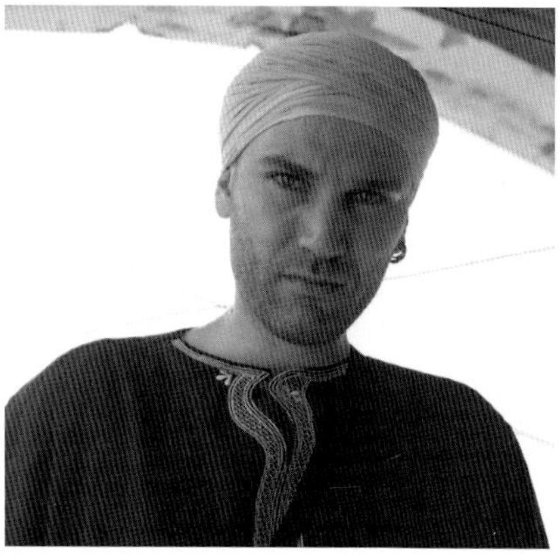

AYMAN BAALBAKI, COURTESY OF THE ARTIST

of life; specifically contemporary Lebanese life. In *Abel*, 2008, a strong portrait of a man hovers above the name "Abel", elevating the figure to the status of stardom and compelling the viewer to question the reasons for such notoriety. However, while the name evokes the biblical fratricidal victim of Cain, the portrait depicts an anonymous male who could stand in for anyone in Lebanese society. This juxtaposition of contemporary Lebanese culture with a reference to the past lends his work an impact and immediacy that demands attention and introspection. As Kaelen Wilson-Goldie observes, "The artist's underlying themes also dig into the dark corners of Lebanon's collective psyche. Baalbaki's works reference civil war, the economic inequities of the post-war reconstruction era and the devastation wrought by the conflict with Israel in the summer of 2006 [...] They call attention to the vibrant visual culture of Lebanon's lower classes [...] they also grapple with the consequences of the so-called war on terror on one hand, the rising tide of militant Islam on the other." (*Ibid.*) Thus, while the medium of his work is familiar, the message is quite new.

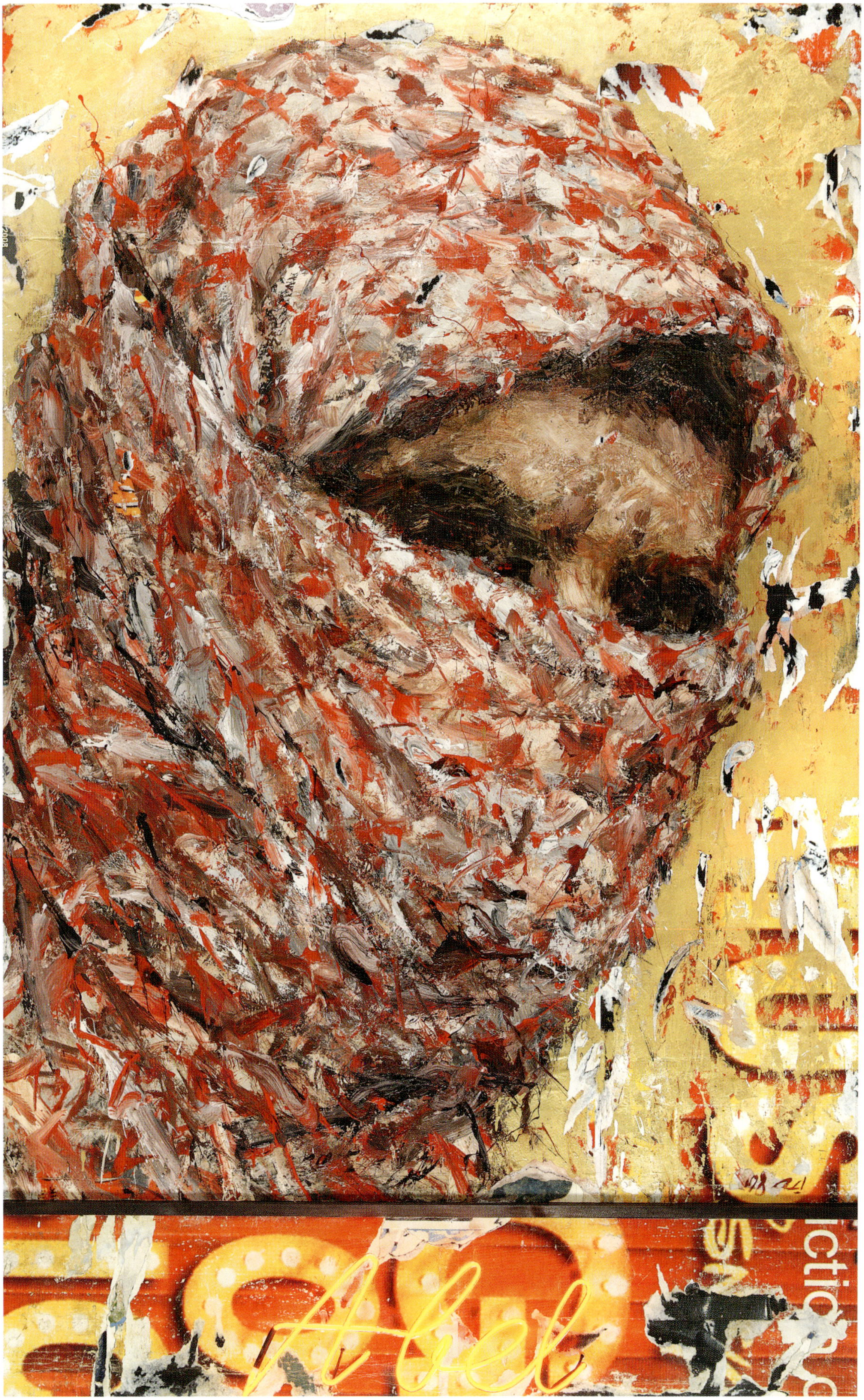
Abel

107

Nabil Nahas

b. 1949

CEDAR

signed on the reverse
acrylic and gold pigment on canvas
244 BY 153CM.; 96 BY 60¼IN.

Executed in 2005.

90,000-120,000 US$
328,000-437,000 QAR

PROVENANCE
Private Collection, Lebanon

"The cedars became a vehicle to express the grandeur and tragedy of Lebanon over the last few thousand years. Like a [Diego] Rivera painting of a girl holding calla lilies embodies the soul of Mexican culture, I hope my cedars... accomplish the same for the Middle East."

Nabil Nahas (Yasmine Mohseni, "Nature and Beyond: Nabil Nahas", *Canvas Magazine*, volume 4, issue no. 5, pg. 147)

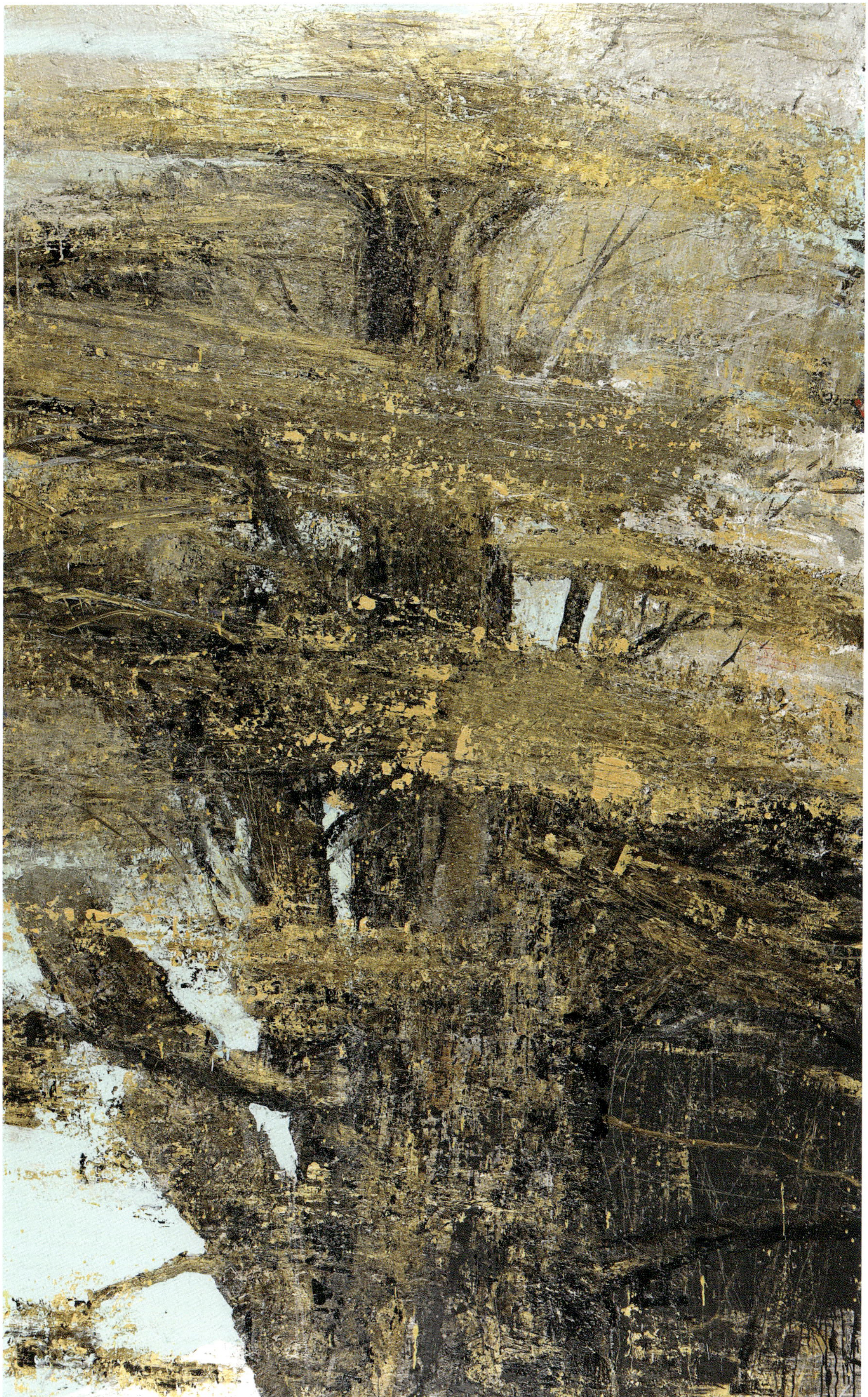

108

Yousef Ahmad

b. 1955

LETTER COMPOSITION

signed and dated *1977*
oil on canvas
60 BY 50.5CM.; 23⅝ BY 19⅞IN.

35,000-45,000 US$
128,000-164,000 QAR

PROVENANCE
Collection of the Artist

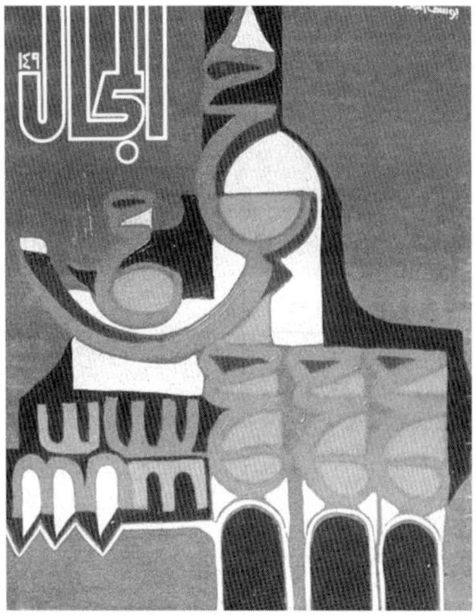

COVER OF EXHIBITION CATALOGUE, QATAR, 1980

"Historically in Islamic art, calligraphy has played an important role and I have utilized the Arabic alphabet throughout my career. I always start with a given unity that I abstract until it fades into the surface of the work, often using different raw materials to integrate the alphabet and produce a harmonious ensemble."

Yousef Ahmad in conversation with Sotheby's Preview, January 2008

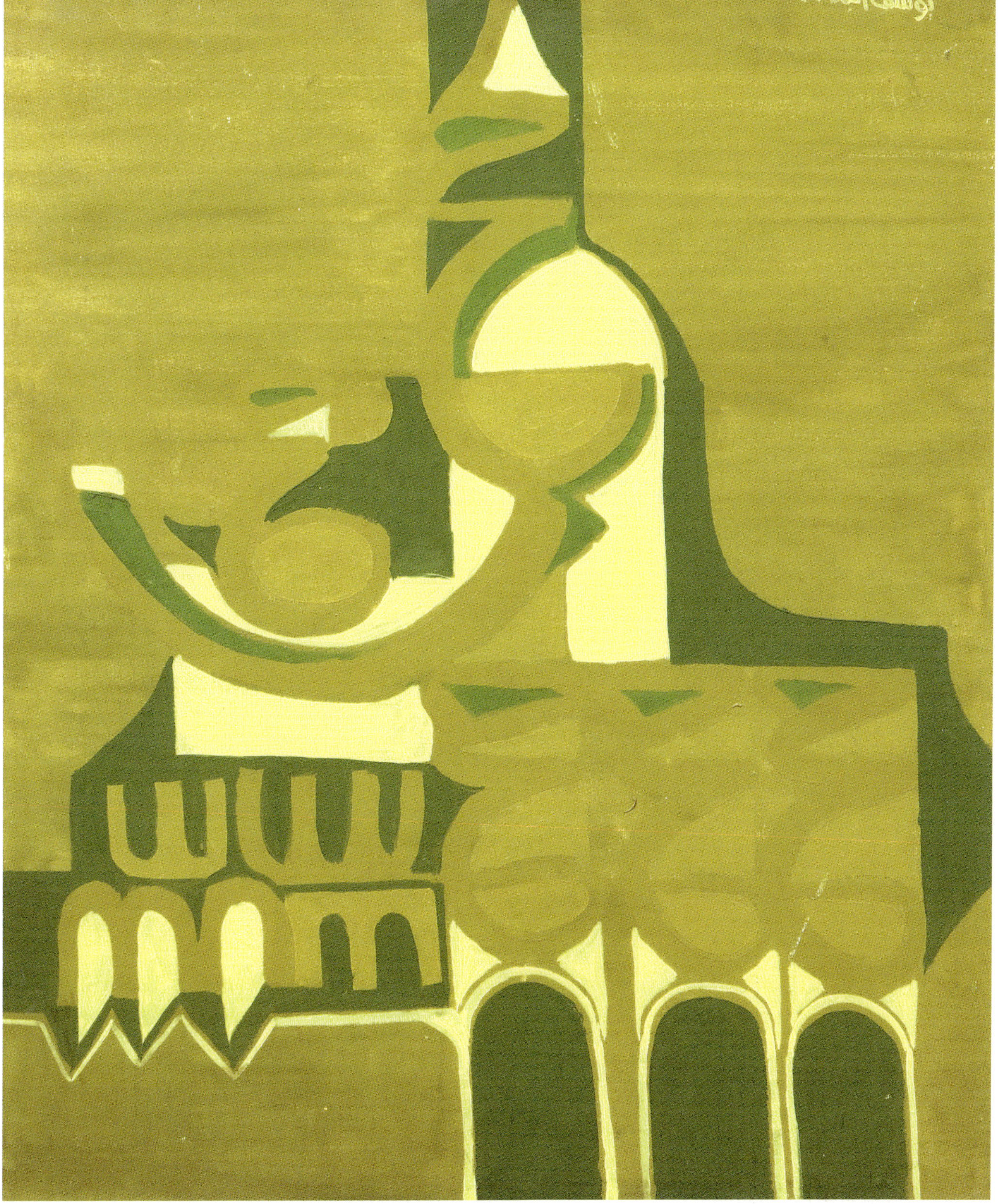
يوسف احمد ٧٧

109

Koorosh Shishegaran

b. 1945

UNTITLED

signed and dated in Farsi *86* (A.P./A.D. 2007); signed and dated in Farsi *1386* (A.P./A.D. 2007) on a label affixed to the reverse
oil on canvas
149.8 BY 149.8CM.; 59 BY 59IN.

50,000-70,000 US$
182,000-255,000 QAR

PROVENANCE
Private Collection, Tehran (acquired directly from the artist)
Private Collection, New York
Acquired directly from the above by the present owner

EXHIBITED
Tehran, Saba Art and Cultural Institute, *Tehran Contemporary Biennial*, 2008

Koorosh Shishegaran is one of the few artists of his generation to embrace a truly contemporary visual schema whilst maintaining a strong link with the key spiritual elements that characterise Iran's artistic landscape. Having developed a distinct, free-flowing style inspired by an abstraction of calligraphic letterforms, Shishegaran's early works consisted of pseudo-figurative depictions weaved by curvilinear strokes. Yet as his artistic style evolved, his works were thrust further into abstraction, demonstrating technical and conceptual refinement in the absence of figurative clarity.

Untitled is a superlative example of Shishegaran at his most visually mature. Gone is the semblance of bodily form, gone is the suggestion of figurative representation, and it is at this height of abstraction where Shishegaran's agenda is brought to sublime fruition. Latent in the composition the viewer is caught in the terse conflict between what appear to be arbitrary, stray brushstrokes and what are in actual fact meticulously executed forms; a visual characteristic that points to the profound contrast between apparent chaos in the worldly realm and an underlying divine order.

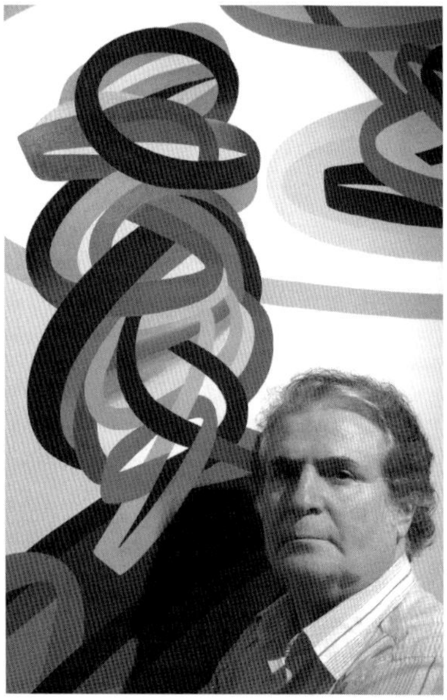

KOOROSH SHISHEGARAN IN HIS STUDIO, 2007, COURTESY OF THE ARTIST

Shishegaran's present composition is played out on a commanding scale. In it, he makes heavy use of bright, vivid hues of yellows in combination with bold, towering intertwined linear forms. The artist then contrasts some clearly defined linear depictions with opaque, indistinct and blurred sections that dominate the centre of the canvas. This is representative not only of a clear progression in Shishegaran's mode of expression, but perhaps points towards deeper conflicts between appearance and essence, challenging our senses to distinguish between mere perceptions and actual forms.

In style, execution, scale and schema, the present work is demonstrative of Shishegaran at his most artistically astute. A painter willing to at once break free from the traditional formalism of his artistic milieu, whilst retaining the spiritual essence that breathes life-force into his compositions, Shishegaran's works are emblematic of an artistic impulse that is liberal in execution whilst remaining profound in conception.

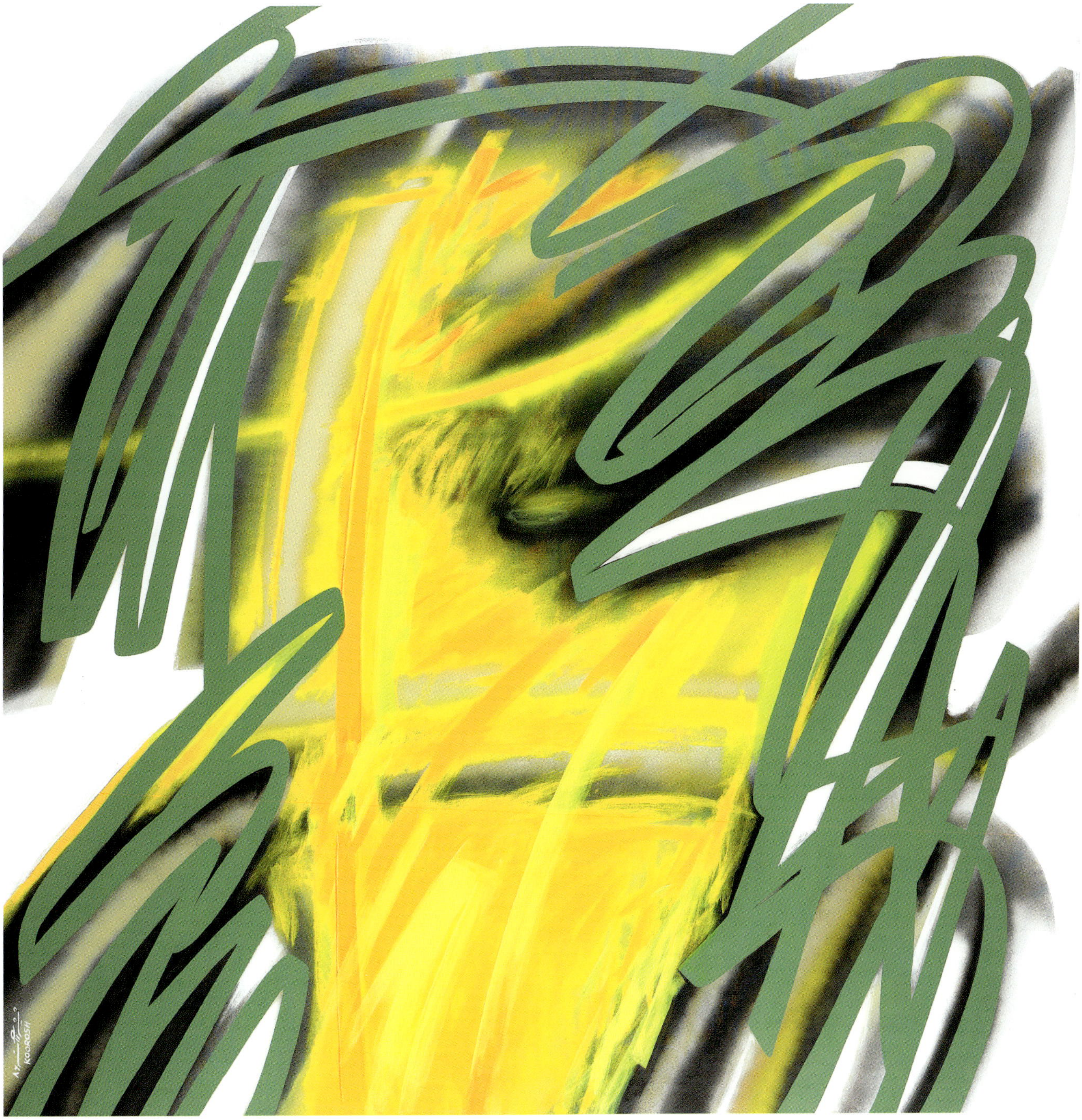
KOOROSH

110

Farhad Moshiri

b. 1963

14S8

signed, titled and dated *2004* on the reverse
oil and acrylic on canvas
152.3 BY 152.3CM.; 60 BY 60IN.

70,000-100,000 US$
255,000-364,000 QAR

PROVENANCE
Acquired directly from the artist by the present owner in 2004

"The fragile network of crackled lines conveys the sense of time's ravages on an ancient material. It evokes mosque tiles (an impression strengthened by the gridded creases) or old weathered shop signs [...] Here he brings the past and the present together in an uneasy union, as if commenting obliquely on the tensions between tradition and modernity in post-revolutionary Iran."

John Ravenal cited in: [http://www.blackbird.vcu.edu/v5n2/gallery/ravenal_j/intro.htm]

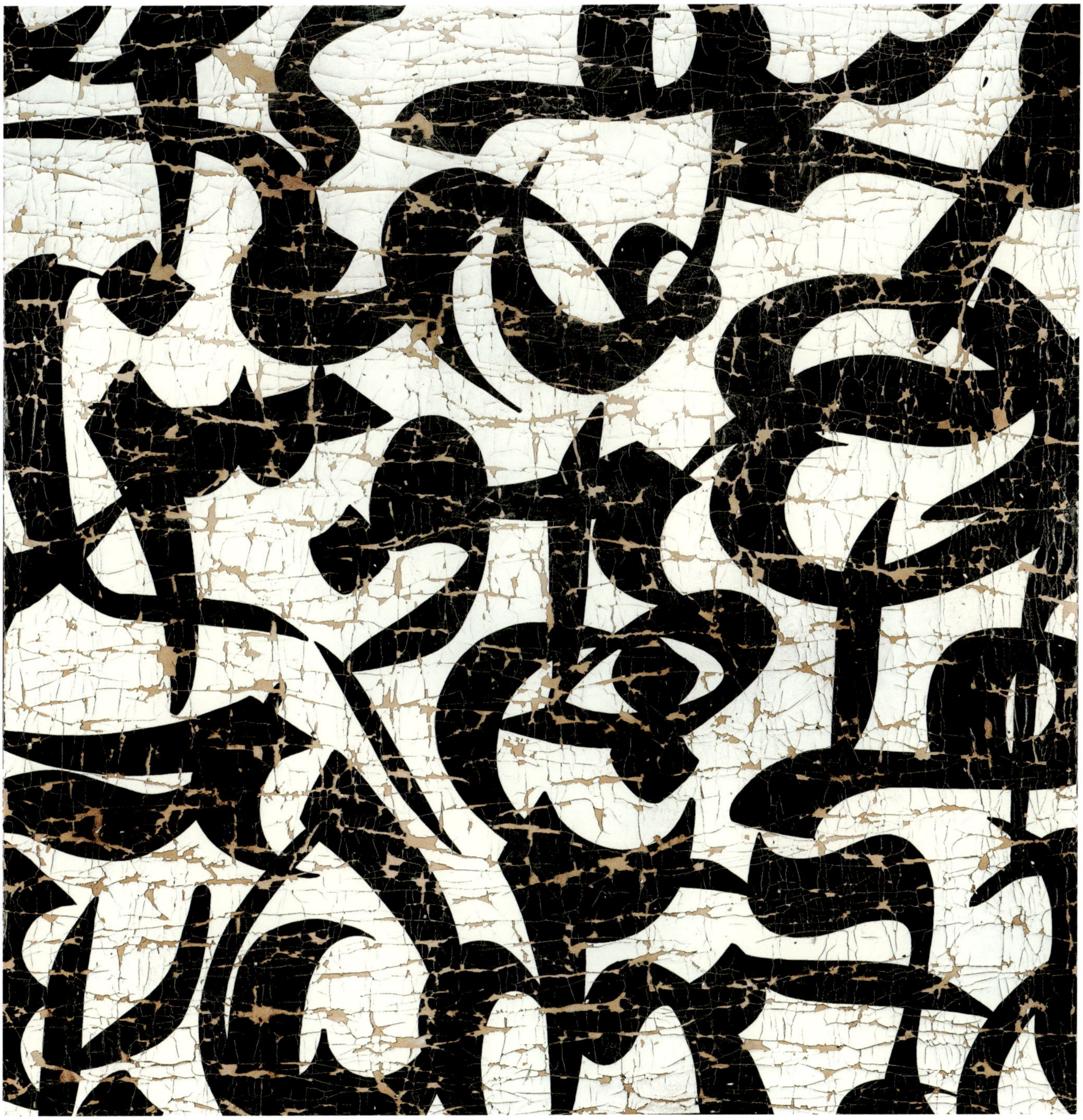

111

Damien Hirst

b. 1965

PAPILIO ULYSSES

signed, titled and dated *2008* on the reverse
butterflies and household gloss on canvas
213.4 BY 213.4CM.; 84 BY 84IN.
INCLUDING FRAME: 276.5 BY 276.5 BY 13.5CM.; $108\frac{5}{8}$ BY $108\frac{5}{8}$ BY $5\frac{3}{8}$IN.

650,000-850,000 US$
2,370,000-3,100,000 QAR

PROVENANCE
The Artist

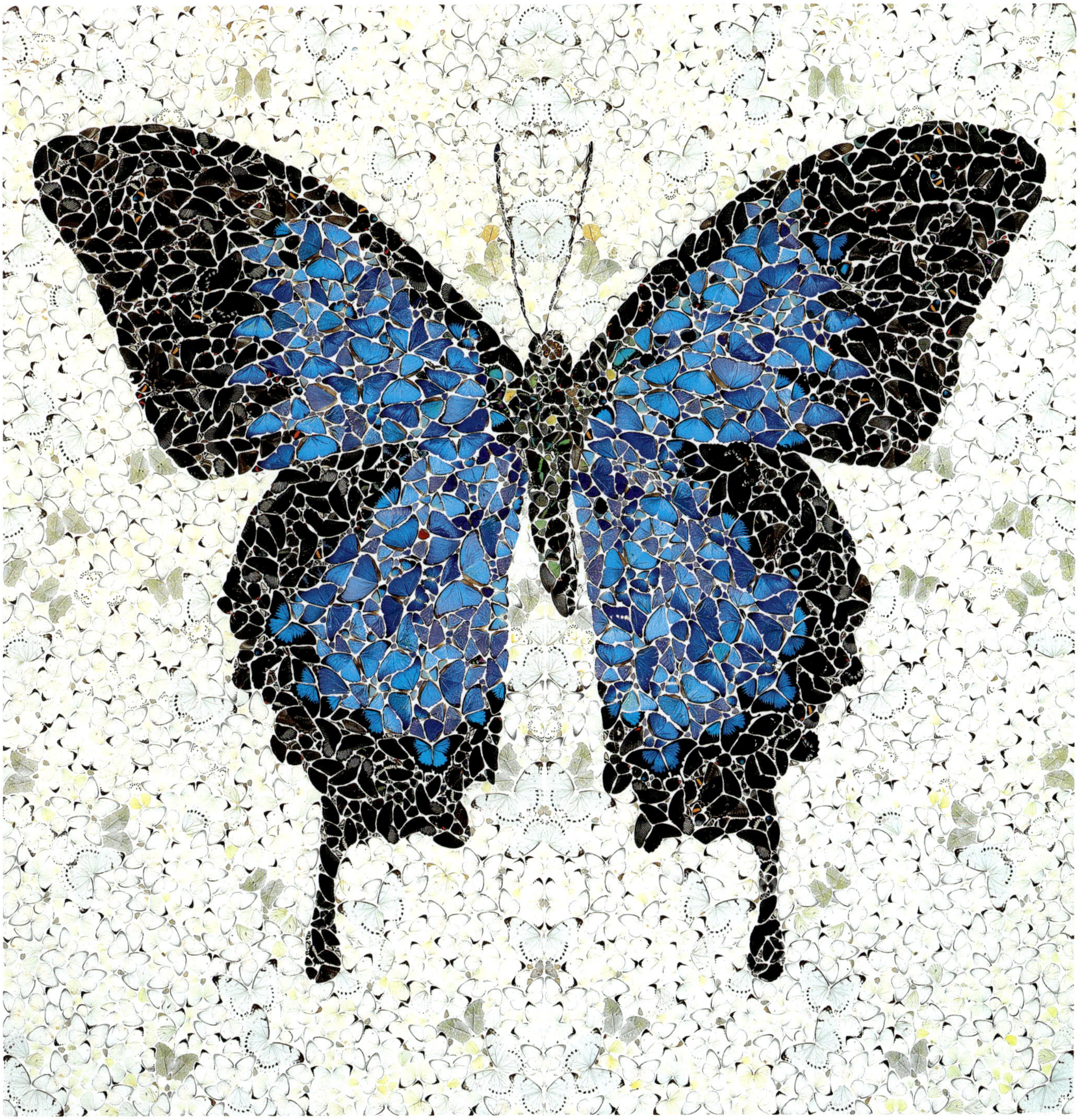

Majestic Butterfly Paintings by Damien Hirst

LOTS 111, 114 AND 137

From the final series of Hirst's butterfly wing pieces and executed before the seminal Beautiful Inside My Head Forever sale, *Papilio Ulysses* is a uniquely powerful work, both in scale and execution. With its literal and iconographic description of this spectacular butterfly from Australia, the painting is a seven-foot monument to Hirst's cycle of life philosophy. Literally the sum of its parts, the vast image of the Papilio Ulysses is itself composed of thousands of butterfly wings, whose motionless forms have been united to breathe life into a vital contemporary work.

In the present work, Hirst chooses to represent a particular species of butterfly, the *Papilio Ulysses*. In doing so, he consciously references one of Greek mythology's most ubiquitous figures; a particularly potent combination of subject and substance, given the prevalence of the mosaic in the iconography of ancient Greek and Roman life. Yet Hirst's painting does far more than merely acknowledge a tradition of Western Art. By selecting such iridescent natural materials, and amplifying their aesthetic impact through the judicious use of pure white gloss, the artist emboldens nature's rich tapestry. With *Papilio Ulysses*, we are simultaneously faced with the spectacles of both death and artistic creation: the monumental form of the butterfly before us grants immortality to those that perished in its creation.

The monochrome butterfly canvases were first exhibited in his *In and Out of Love* exhibition of 1991 at the Woodstock Gallery in London. This was one of the artist's most important installations, a tropical environment complete with live butterflies and monochrome canvases. Focusing upon their tragically short lives and alluding to the pointlessness and inherent fragility of human existence, Hirst fastened pupae ready to hatch on white monochrome canvases in the upstairs gallery space, with flowers and sugar-water on shelves attached to the bottom of paintings to sustain the butterflies once they had emerged. As the real butterflies flew around the gallery space upstairs, it seemed as if the butterflies below had alighted upon the different coloured monochrome canvases lining the walls before dying and falling to the floor. Their lifespan from birth to death was spent on and around the canvases, linking them to Hirst's work both physically and conceptually. As Hirst recalls, the effect was, "More real than de Kooning, where colour leaps off the canvas and flies around the room" (the artist in: Damien Hirst, *I want to spend the rest of my life everywhere, with Everyone, One to one, Always, Forever*, London 1997, p. 120).

In the butterfly paintings, as is the case with Hirst's finest work, the underlying concept is often complex, but the vehicle he uses to carry these ideas is characterised by an overriding freshness and vitality. The butterfly for Hirst holds considerable iconographic power and meaning. As he explained, "You need to find universal triggers, everyone's frightened of glass, everyone's frightened of sharks, everyone loves butterflies" (Ibid., p. 132). Butterfly paintings can be read as a development from abstract monochrome painting, long seen as the essence of purity in art and the location for art as a form of minimised ritual. In Hirst's butterfly gloss and grid paintings, the monochrome is adapted, becoming a commentary on contemporary existence. By attaching butterflies to paintings, the purity of the flat surface is transformed into a beautiful object.

The appearance of *Papilio Ulysses* changes when viewed from different distances and perspectives. From afar, the individual wings resemble jewel-like tesserae in a mosaic, brimming with azurite, pearl and ebony hues, each intense colour subservient to the chromatic design of the overarching composition. The blue butterflies, with iridescent wings as rich in hue as lapis-lazuli, reflect the light to such a degree that the surface scintillates and shimmers, so that the butterfly image reflects and refracts colour as if it were alive. Up close, the individual specimens become discernible. A panoply of different species – some large some small, some brightly coloured, others chosen for their calming opalescence – seem fragile and painfully mortal, enshrined in household gloss. For Hirst, this moment of realisation contains the oxymoronic beauty of horror, and horror of beauty. In a complex echo of the cyclical nature of life on earth, the caterpillar dies in its chrysalis, and is reborn as a butterfly. This delicate creature dies, but in doing so gives birth to a beautiful object, the work of art. As ever in Hirst's work, beauty is laced with death. From the empty shells of dead butterflies Hirst has created an object of extraordinary, almost totemic, power which eloquently encapsulates the precepts underpinning his art.

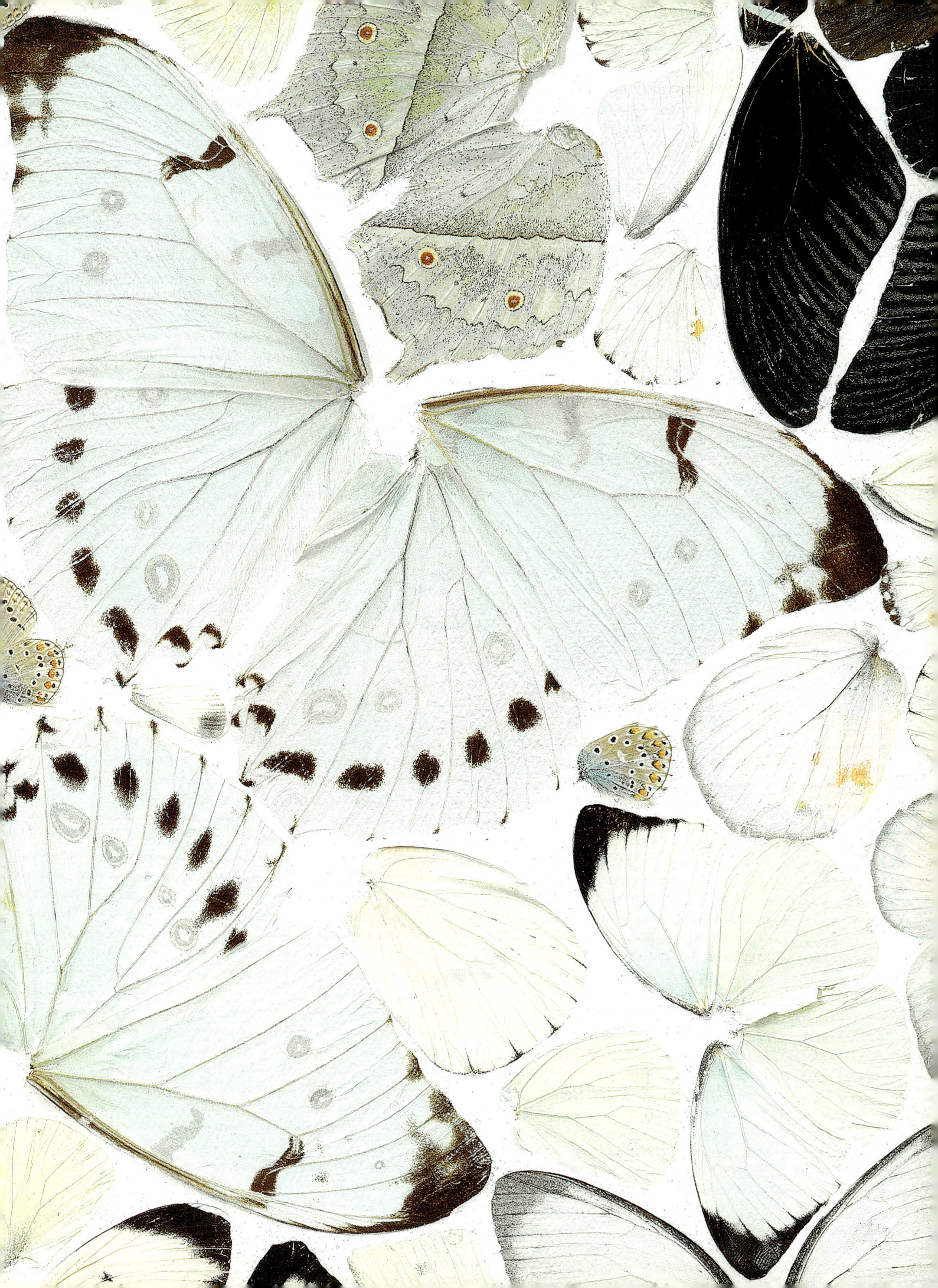

112

Anish Kapoor

b. 1954

UNTITLED

stainless steel and paint

230 BY 230 BY 70CM.; 90½ BY 90½ BY 27½IN.

Executed in 2003.

900,000-1,400,000 US$

3,280,000-5,100,000 QAR

PROVENANCE

Lisson Gallery, London

Acquired directly from the above by the present owner in 2003

The perfect concave sphere of Anish Kapoor's *Untitled*, 2003 emanates a profound colouristic effect whose warmth instantly enshrouds the viewer into its welcoming, yet slightly disconcerting, infinite space. Luscious reflected hues of tanzanite blue, han purple and deep turquoise seem to dance across its shimmering metallic surface, changing with every angle and colliding with each other to create a mesmerising 'skin' which at once reflects the outside world whilst also drawing the viewer into the depths of its seemingly interminable void.

Sublimely fashioned from stainless steel, painted and polished to reflective brilliance, Kapoor here makes sensitive light of the heavy industrial material as its harmonious balance is suspended as if weightless on the wall. This sunken, metallic abyss of light evinces one of the key conflicts in art that permeates all of Kapoor's work: that of the issue of balance between the visible and the spiritual; between the concrete material of a work and its idea; between the form and the void.

At a height of 270cm., the work is taller than the average person and there is instantly a human relationship that develops from an encounter with it. Much as Yves Klein made his first investigations into the Void in the late 1950s, Kapoor's best work always employs human dimensions as the origin from which to discover a material space which is beyond our senses. Eternally divided between its inner and outer realms, Kapoor's *Untitled* fuses the world of the viewer with that of its object self. Kapoor here has developed Klein's early investigations and expanded them into a more sophisticated sculptural presence. Its concave form activates the transformative properties of the polished steel, capturing the eternally changing natural world within its fixed, artificial grasp. The very act of looking, places the viewer as the link uniting the two - a dialectic function usually performed in Kapoor's work by the hollow or void itself. Compared to the impenetrable darkness of his earlier void works of the late 1980s and early 90s, *Untitled's* forever reflecting luminosity is affirmed by its environment and audience. Immaculate in surface and form and existing as if self-created, elements of light, space and colour all fuse into a new quality that witnesses the transcendence of the material and the spiritual.

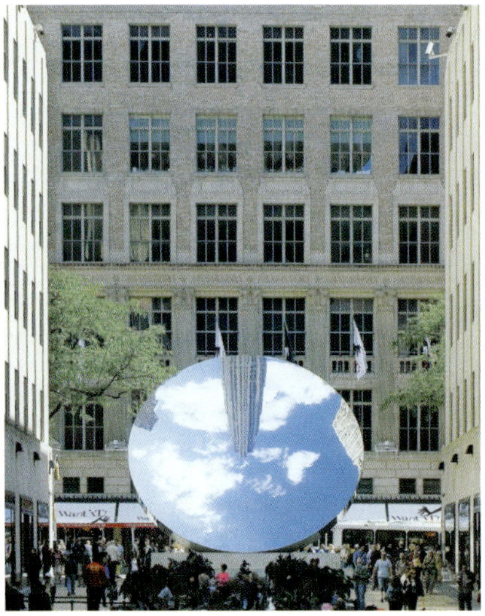

ANISH KAPOOR, *UNTITLED*, 2006, PRESENTED BY TUMI AT ROCKEFELLER CENTER, ORGANIZED BY PUBLIC ART FUND, HOSTED BY TISHMAN SPEYER. COURTESY PUBLIC ART FUND. PHOTO: SEONG KWON PHOTOGRAPHY

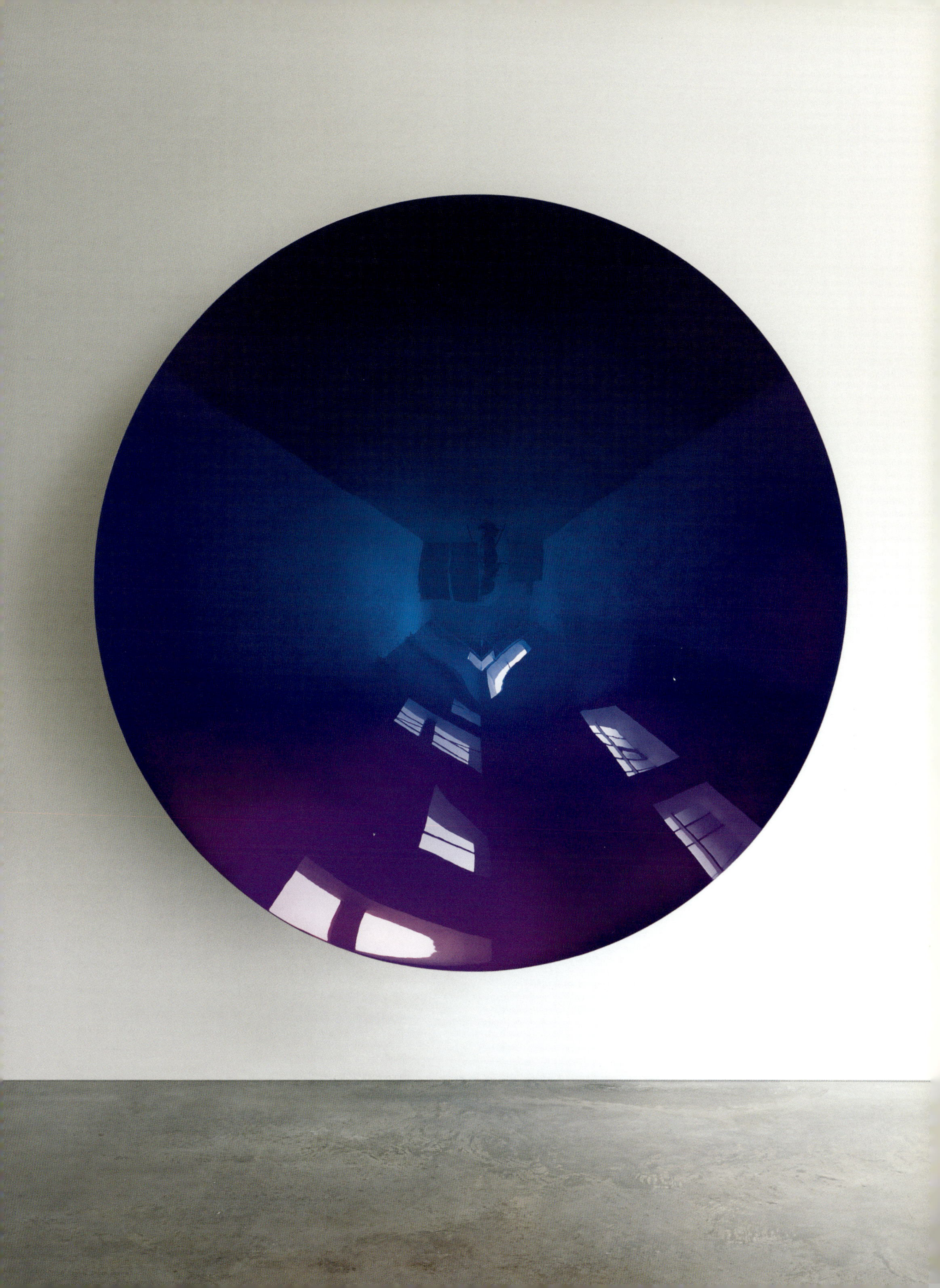

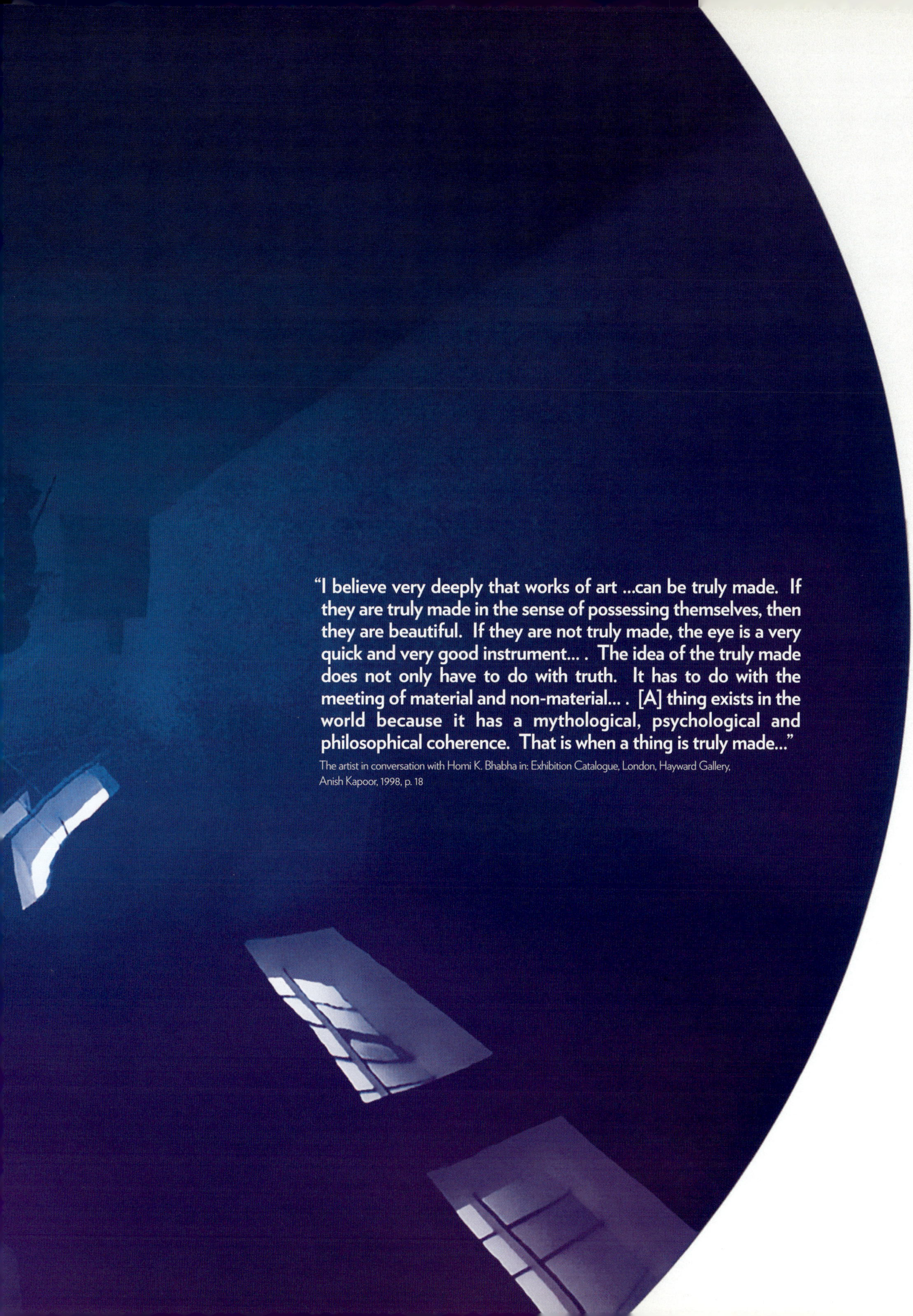

"I believe very deeply that works of art ...can be truly made. If they are truly made in the sense of possessing themselves, then they are beautiful. If they are not truly made, the eye is a very quick and very good instrument... . The idea of the truly made does not only have to do with truth. It has to do with the meeting of material and non-material... . [A] thing exists in the world because it has a mythological, psychological and philosophical coherence. That is when a thing is truly made..."

The artist in conversation with Homi K. Bhabha in: Exhibition Catalogue, London, Hayward Gallery, Anish Kapoor, 1998, p. 18

113

Olafur Eliasson

b. 1967

NATIONAL CAREER LAMP

acrylic, stainless steel, aluminium, optical lighting film and light bulbs

120 BY 120 BY 55CM.; 47¼BY 47¼BY 21¾IN.

Executed in 2007, this work is number 5 from an edition of 10.

60,000-80,000 US$

219,000-292,000 QAR

PROVENANCE

Christian Larsen, Stockholm

Acquired directly from the above by the present owner

Widely heralded for his ability to create multisensory experiences, Olafur Eliasson nimbly merges art, science, and natural phenomena in an effort to emphasize the role of the viewer and blur the boundaries between perception, representation, art and life. His diverse oeuvre including sculpture, photography and large-scale installations all seek to challenge the passive nature of traditional art-viewing and engage the observer as an active participant. Relying on sensorial stimulation such as aroma, temperature and light, his works stimulate a dialogue between the art work and the onlooker so that the piece itself becomes a manifestation of the way the viewer perceives it.

Eliasson's *National Career Lamp* takes the form of a pulsating eye with electric red, orange and yellow swirls radiating from its retina. Capturing your gaze as well as your reflection, it allows you to *see yourself see*. Like many of his works, *National Career Lamp* is rooted in Eliasson's fascination with human perception and sensory cognition – how time, space, color, light and sensation occur as phenomena for us. Specifically the twisted louvers that form the lampshades of the lamp are clad with a foil of microscopic prisms that reflect both the viewer and their surrounding space. But this foil further functions to break light waves into colors illustrating how color materializes when light is reflected off of our retinae. In other words, the lamp serves to demonstrate the mechanics of perception or more simply put, *how* we see.

At the Tate Modern In *The Weather Project* (2003), one of the artist's most renowned installations, Eliasson strived to bring about a similar perceptual awareness though a dramatic optical illusion. He allowed gallery-goers to bask, meditate and picnic in the light of a huge sun. This "sun' consisted of hundreds of mono-frequency lamps placed in a semi-circle under a mirrored ceiling which doubled the perception of the light effect and reflected the audience's image in the work. Most importantly though, the installation's mirrors, lamps and electrical cables lay exposed on the reverse side of the artificial sun so that visitors were invited behind the Oz's proverbial green curtain. Access to the actual construction of the work allowed for a concrete, visual understanding of perception.

As illustrated, Eliasson's oeuvre necessitates participation. His pieces, especially his large-scale installations are dictated by the viewers' physical relation and orientation to the piece. "How can I set up a practice of having people interact with a work in a way that doesn't formalize the process into telling them how to experience it? How can the piece constantly change with every new visitor? How can the piece be one thing one day and the next day something else?" (Olafur Eliasson from Daniel Birnbaum in conversation with Olafur Eliasson, in *Olafur Eliasson*, Phaidon Press, New York, 2002, p. 35). Eliasson's sentiment is epitomized in his most recent installation, *New York City Waterfalls* on Manhattan's East River. The work's essence is determined by whether it is viewed from the FDR Drive (the highway), the Brooklyn Bridge, a barge on the river or a plane overhead.

Like his predecessor Marcel Duchamp, Olafur Eliasson is an artist who seeks to question the role of art in contemporary society and the meaning of the art-object. Are we looking at lamps and urinals or great artistic masterpieces? According to Eliasson, that is for us to decide. "My work is you, the onlooker," he says. His creations are simply tools he uses to teach, shape and challenge us.

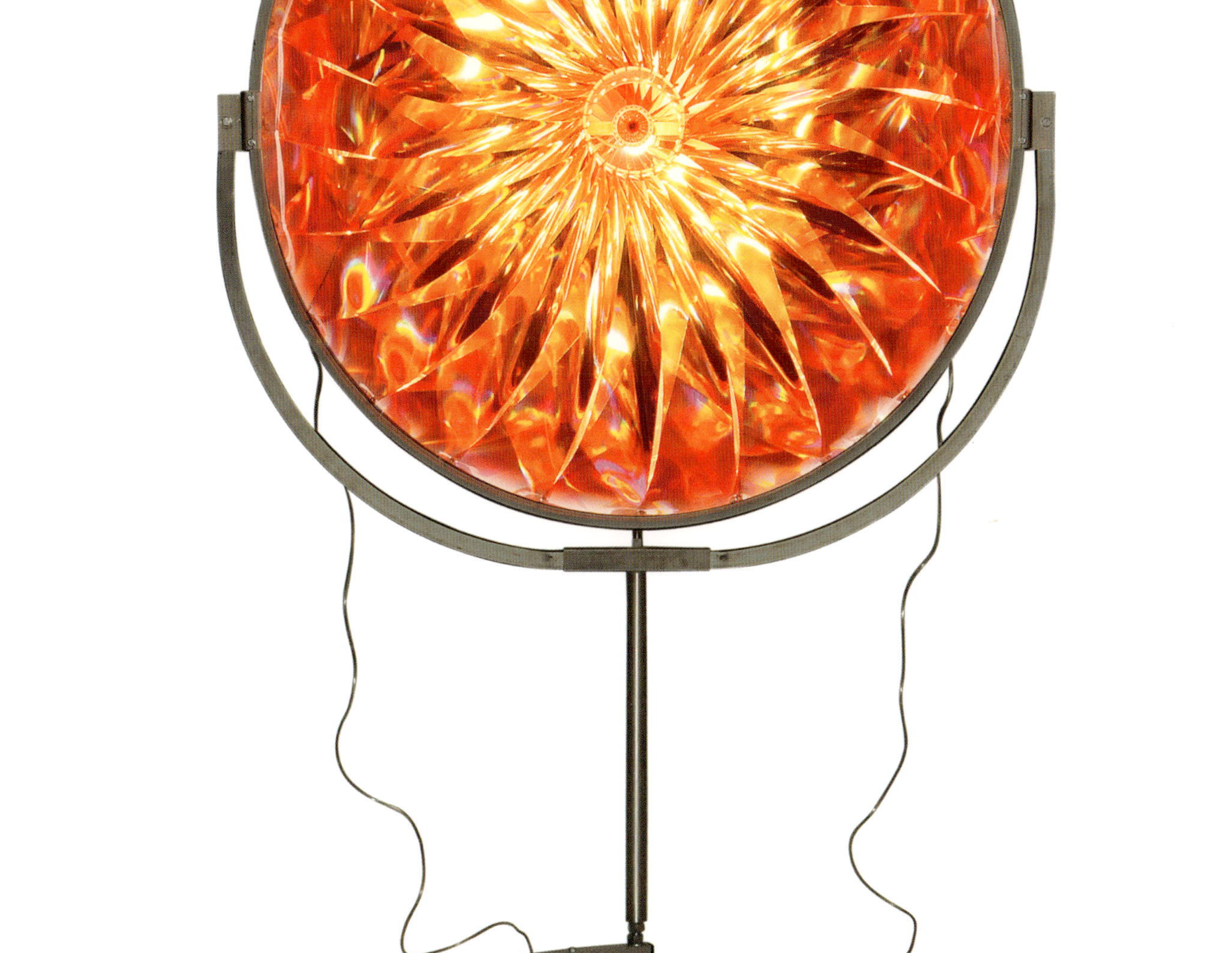

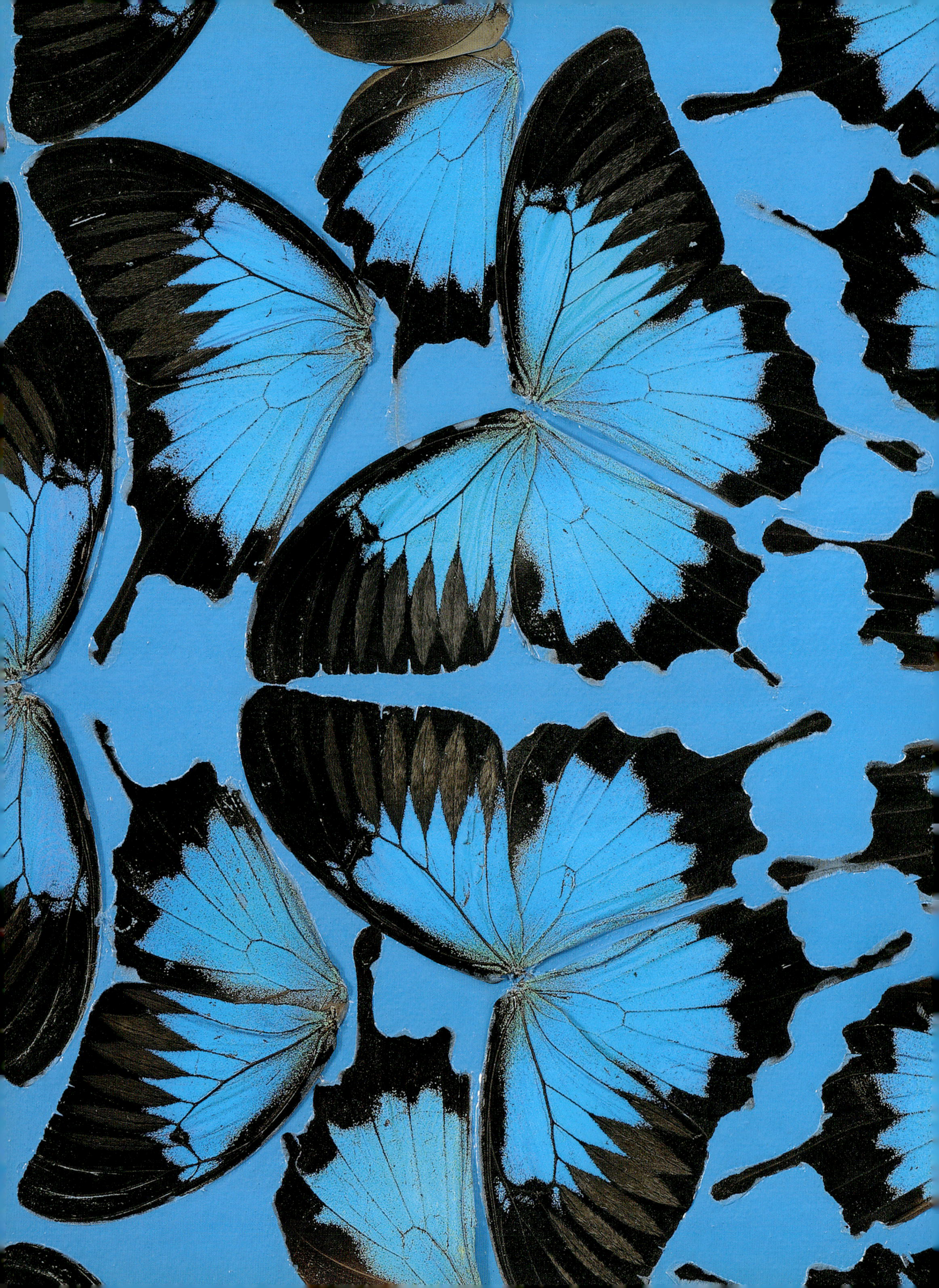

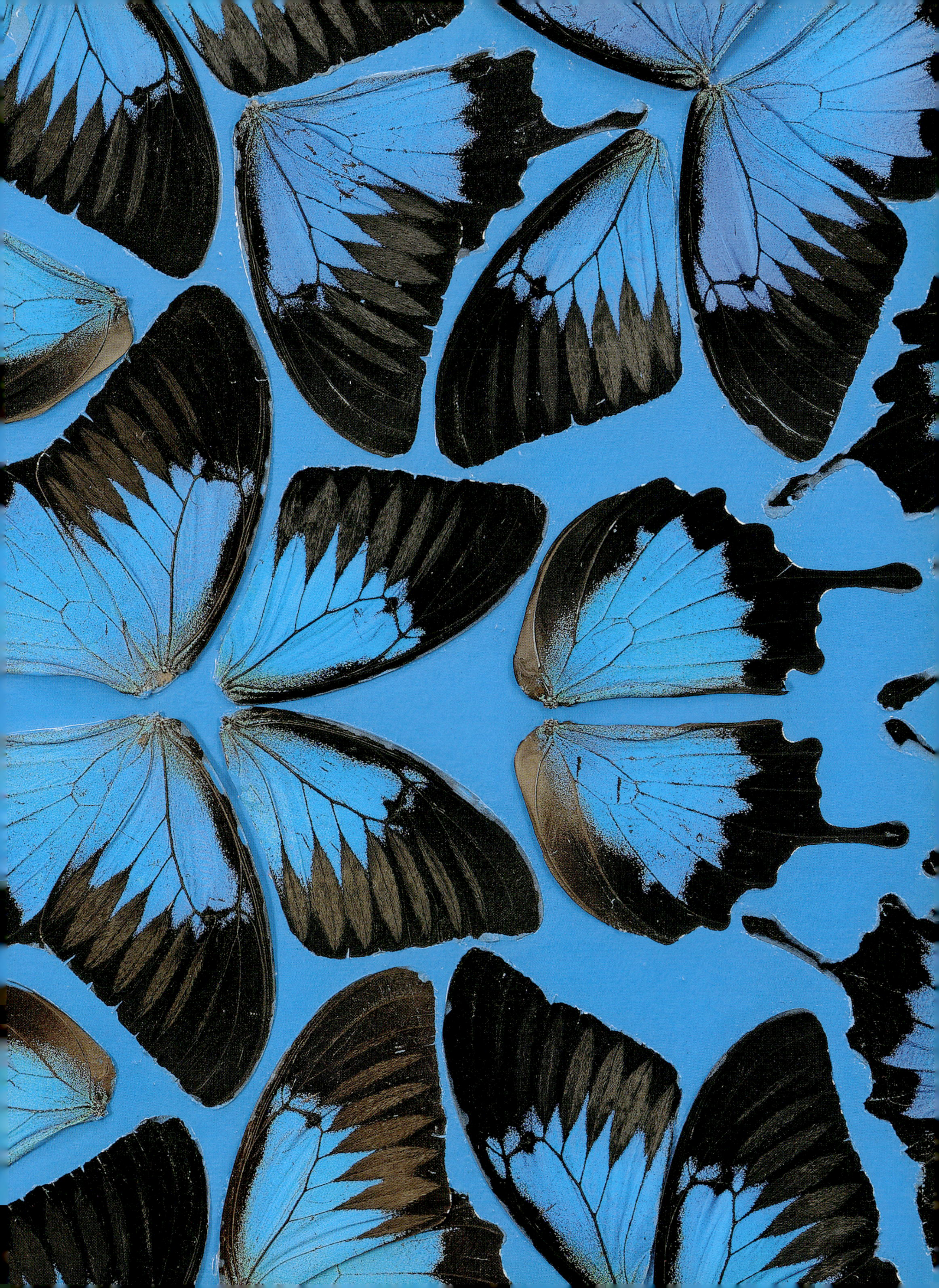

114

Damien Hirst

b. 1965

ULYSSES

signed, titled and dated *2008* on the reverse
butterflies and household gloss on canvas
DIAMETER: 213.36CM.; 84IN.
DIAMETER INCLUDING FRAME: 268.5 BY 13.5CM.; 105½ BY 5⅜IN.

800,000-1,200,000 US$
2,920,000-4,370,000 QAR

PROVENANCE
The Artist

"I was born in mid-backtrack... I have a butterfly mind. I hate being pinned down."

Damien Hirst cited in: Exhibition Catalogue., Mexico City, Galeria Hilario Galguera, *The Death of God. Towards a Better Understanding of a Life Without God Aboard the Ship of Fools*, 2006, p. 14

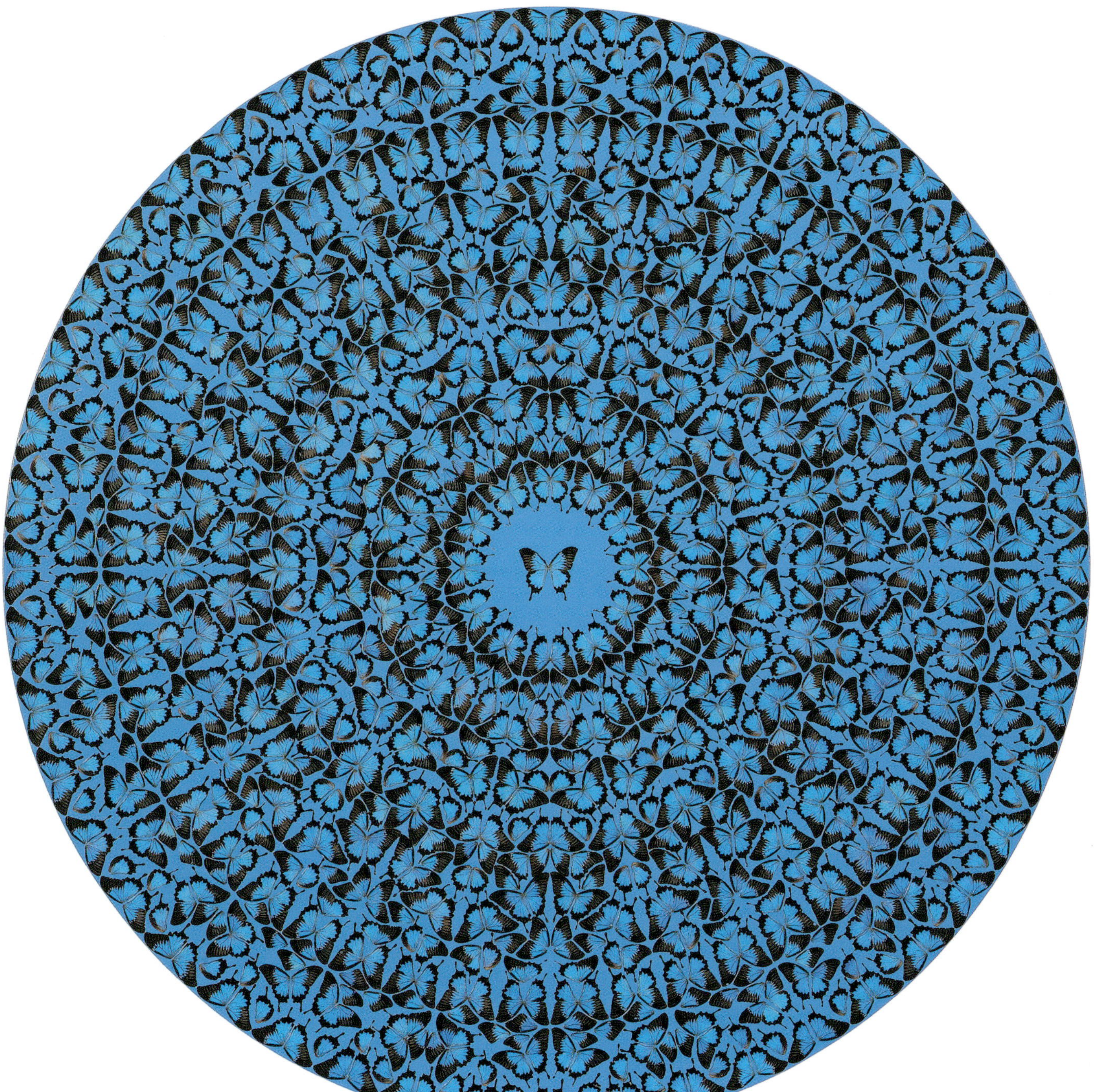

115

Andy Warhol

1928-1987

UNTITLED (LEG AND SHOE)

pen, watercolour and lithograph on paper
66 BY 50.8CM.; 26 BY 20IN.

Executed *circa* 1956.

20,000-30,000 US$
73,000-110,000 QAR

PROVENANCE
Robert Galster (a gift from the artist)
Nicholas J. Sands, New York

EXHIBITED
Taipei, Fine Arts Museum, *Andy Warhol: A Private Collection 1928-1987,* 1994, p. 34, illustrated
Lausanne, Fondation de l'Hermitage, *Andy Warhol: Collection Jose Mugrabi, 1995,* p. 34, no. 7, illustrated
Helsinki, Kunsthalle, *Andy Warhol: Samlingen Jose Mugrabi*, 1997, p. 47, illustrated
Warsaw, National Museum; Crakow, National Museum, *Andy Warhol, Works from a Private Collection*, 1998, p. 49, illustrated
Kochi, The Museum of Art; Tokyo, Bunkamura Museum of Art; Umeda-Osaka, Daimaru Museum; Hiroshima, City Museum of Contemporary Art; Kawamura, Memorial Museum of Art; Nagoya, City Art Museum; Niigata, City Art Museum, *Andy Warhol*, 2000-2001, p. 56, no. 20, illustrated

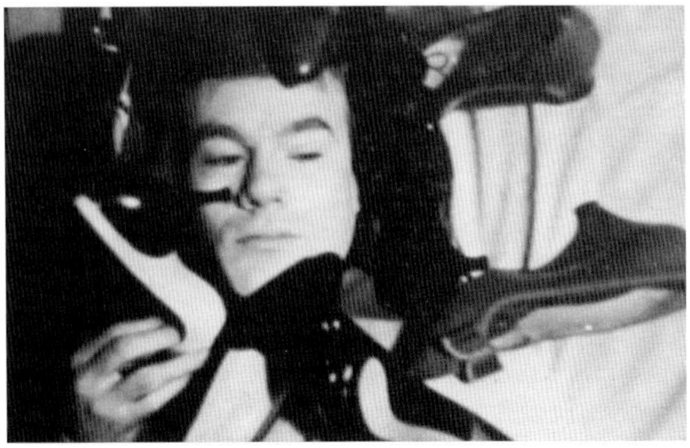

ANDY WARHOL, NEW YORK, 1950S. PHOTOGRAPH: EDWARD WALLOWITCH

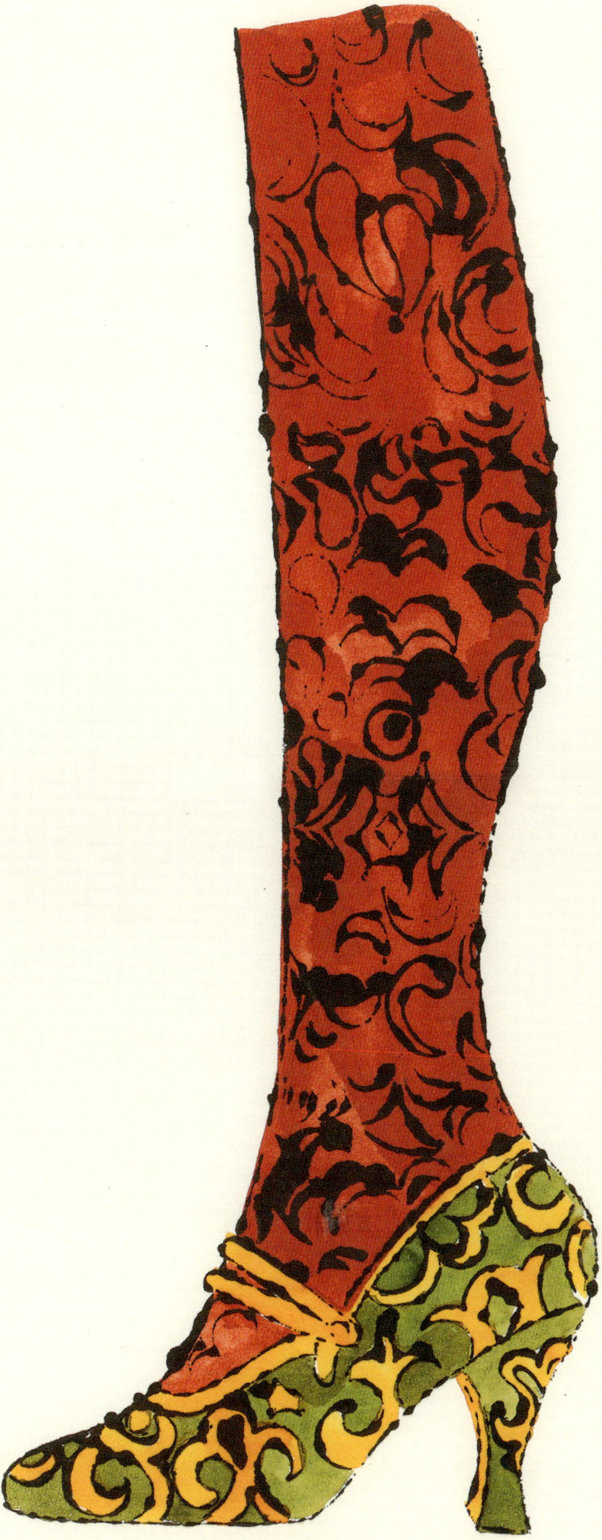

116

Farhad Moshiri

b. 1963

DIAMOND HEAD

signed, titled and dated *2007* on the overlap
oil, acrylic, glue and Swarovski crystals on canvas mounted on board
200 BY 170CM.; 78¾ BY 66⅞IN.

250,000-350,000 US$
910,000-1,280,000 QAR

PROVENANCE
Private Collection, Dubai (acquired directly from the artist)
Acquired directly from the above by the present owner

Residing in the very top tier of Farhad Moshiri's illustrious output, *Diamond Head* is an iconic work by the foremost artist currently working in Iran. It is both immediately recognisable as part of Moshiri's widely lauded and critically acclaimed canon, yet also exactly embodies the conceptual diversity and perpetual desire for technical innovation that characterises his best work. Harnessing the tension between conflicting symbols of tradition and contemporaneity, *Diamond Head* epitomises the artist's manipulating of convention and confronting issues of perception in a world dominated by homogenising mass-media and popular culture. For Moshiri, this conceptual dynamism is the ideal metaphor for deeper cultural anomalies which arise when western culture is 'translated' for consumption in the Middle East. Enlisting kitsch imagery in the name of visual satire, Moshiri continues the important post-Modern subversive enquiry of Jeff Koons, inventively re-presenting the values of competing socio-cultural priorities and contrasting conflicting expectations.

Diamond Head broadcasts Moshiri's untiring appetite for methodological development: re-inventing the possibilities of the painted canvas to re-classify the two dimensional picture plane and challenge the viewer's assumptions about the ornamented surface. Close inspection of the foundation canvas weave reveals that it was first painted black, before a thick layer of brittle, gold-covered gesso-like material was applied on top. Typically Moshiri builds up his painted surfaces in multiple layers, folding and crushing the canvas once each paint film has dried to create a deliberate matrix of craquelure across the composition, before finally sealing the surface with a transparent resin. This creates a grid of lines throughout that recalls the tiled interiors of Mosques or creased pages of ancient texts. With *Diamond Head* the artist has manipulated the canvas and with pressure cracked the entire surface in an irregular broken network of underlying black veins.

The extant gold fragments that have remained and been consolidated on the substrate have delicately curved edges that lift up to become subtly concave reflective tesserae, glittering a transcendent golden shimmer as the viewing light and perspective changes. The dense and sophisticated texture of the gold and black background is thus highly sculptural and extremely tactile. This provides the backdrop for the luscious brushstrokes of thick white paint, which describe the wings and body of the bird, in turn framed by a broad outline of solid gold. Crowning both this extraordinary surface diversity and the figure of the bird itself is a simply awe-inspiring crescendo: over a thousand brilliant Swarovski crystals, stitched into the canvas to demarcate this mystical bird's head. This sparkling bejewelled crown transforms this bird into a creature of truly indefinable transcendence: a literally extra-ordinary radiant being.

The ornithological form of this bird is determinedly ambiguous. Its outline principally evokes a bird of prey, the hooked beak implicates that perfected through millennia of evolution to tear meat rather than peck vegetation. As such it is reminiscent of a falcon

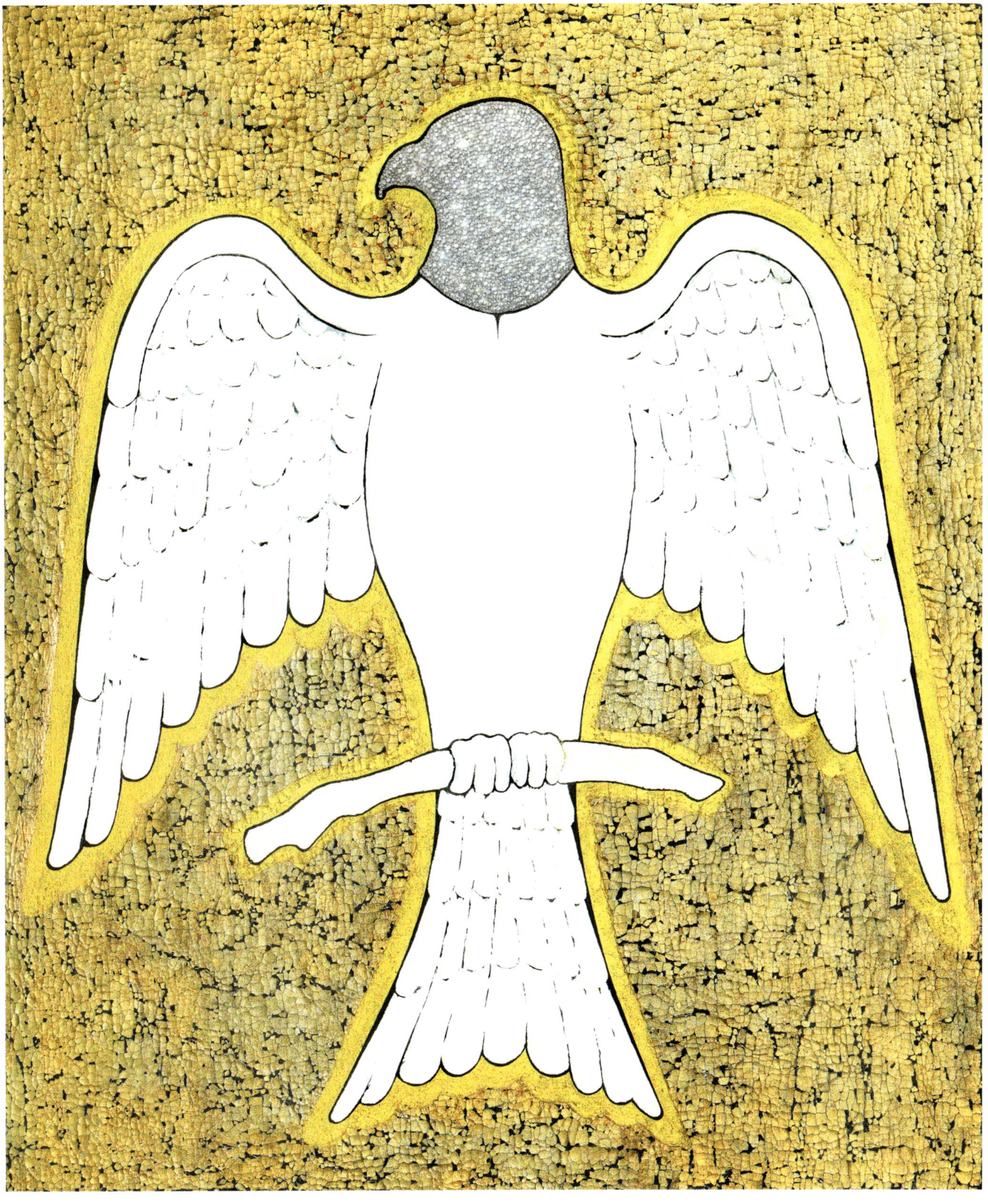

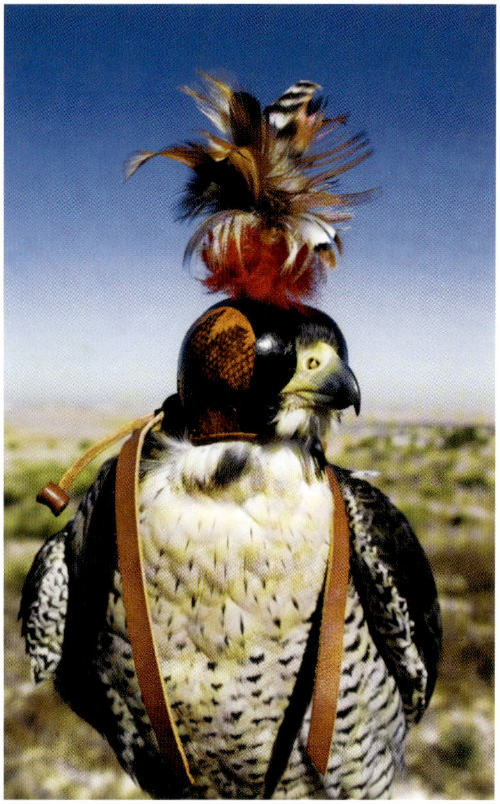

SKY HUNTERS: THE PASSION OF FALCONRY. COURTESY TRANSGLOBE PUBLISHING LTD, LONDON. IMAGE © ROBERT M. PALMER.

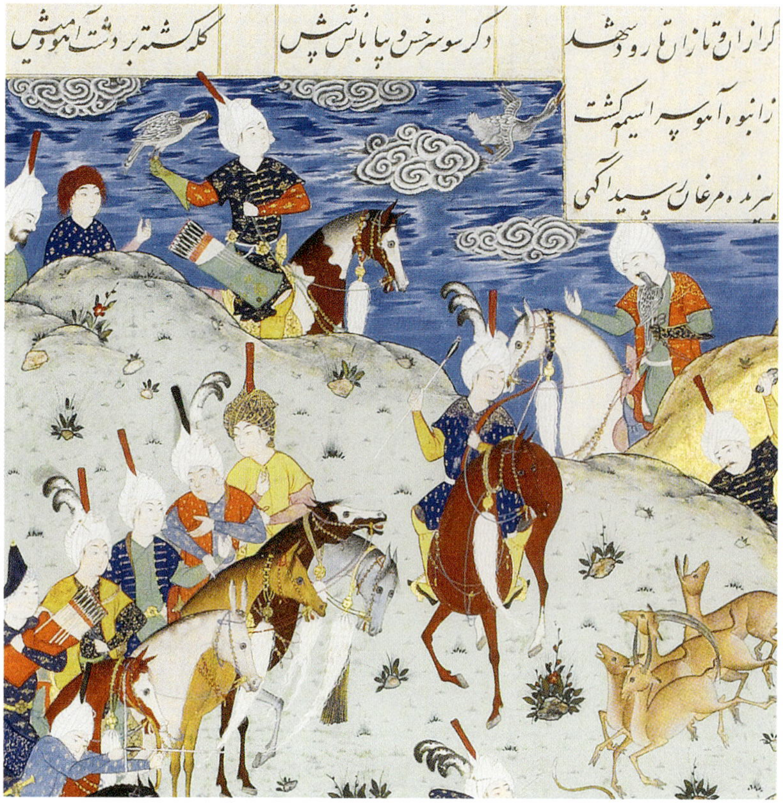

ATTRIBUTED TO MIR SAYYID ALI, *RUSTAM AND THE SEVEN WARRIORS HUNTING SCENE* FROM 'HOUGHTON' SHAHNAMEH KHALILI COLLECTION, LONDON

or an eagle, both of which carry heavy symbolic and historical connotations. Of course falcons give their name to the ancient sport of falconry, which has a very substantial and important history throughout the entire Middle Eastern region. A form of hunting once depended on as a survival necessity, it is loaded with cultural and social significance as various ceremonies and traditions have been associated with it through the ages. By contrast, the eagle is more usually connected to the wilds of nature and, perceived as untameable, it is usually depicted soaring unrestricted around the highest mountain tops. Furthermore, if we momentarily disregard the shining bright head and its carnivorous beak, the bright white colour, plump breast and rounded wings make the body of this bird also reminiscent of a dove, the ancient, multivalent and omnipresent symbol of peace, and the object it carries in its feet could perhaps be the dove's ubiquitous olive branch. The dove possesses a vast catalogue of semiotic referents, having been loaded throughout history with symbolic association. In Ancient Greek mythology, Aphrodite, the goddess of love, rode a chariot that was drawn by doves; the Aztec goddess Xochiquetzal descended in the form of a dove to give humankind the gift of speech; the Hindu deity Kamadeva was often depicted riding a dove; and in north American indigenous cultures the spirits of the dead took the form of a dove immediately on departing the body.

Moshiri's subject thus holds dense layers of sophisticated meaning and implication, which is intrinsically tied into the artist's working method. Despite standing fundamentally as a contemporary artwork, the ostensible fragility of the painting's surface and its weathered appearance convey a sense of the ravages of time on some ancient material and comment on the deterioration of both Moshiri's metaphorical subjects and the literal physicality of the painting itself. The allegorical erosion of the background hints at the waning appreciation of traditions and ancient art forms and even of Persian culture itself in the face of unifying globalisation.

However, as announced by the work's title, the core conceptual project of this painting resides in Moshiri's incorporation of sublime crystals for the bird's head. With this highly inventive use of media the artist makes explicit reference to the commoditising of socio-cultural traditions. The precious 'diamond head' acts both as ornament to beautify the head and as currency to denote the value of the bird symbol. However, as the artist has himself stated, this commodification is not contrived to criticise or isolate, but is rather representative of a global and inevitable trend: "To blur the boundaries between merchandizing and art making has become an essential part of my work...Let's be real. As object makers, we're all packaging our ideas. I just laugh when people criticize me for commodifying exoticism!" (the artist interviewed by Sotheby's, June 2008)

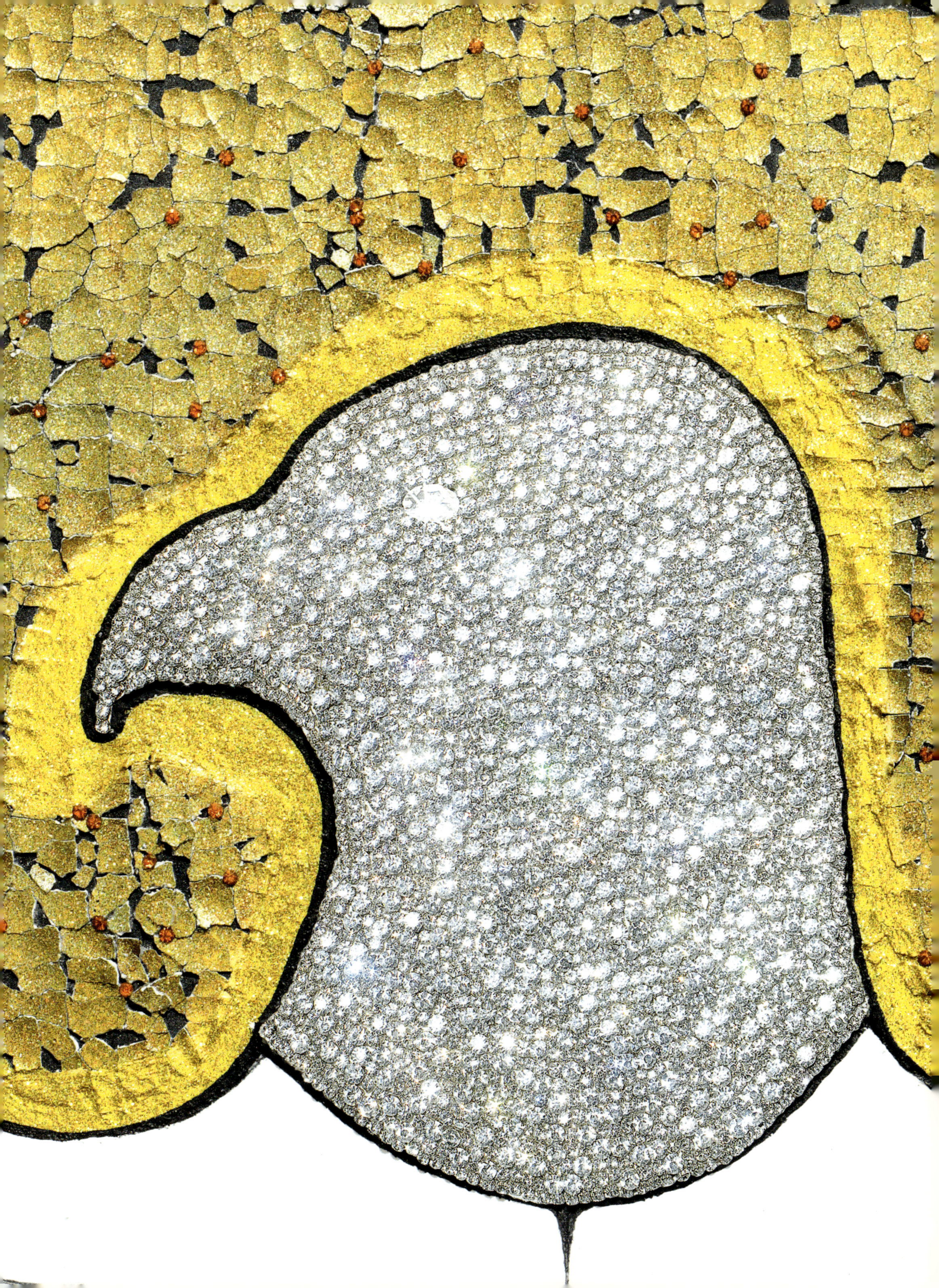

ROUND JACKIE BY ANDY WARHOL

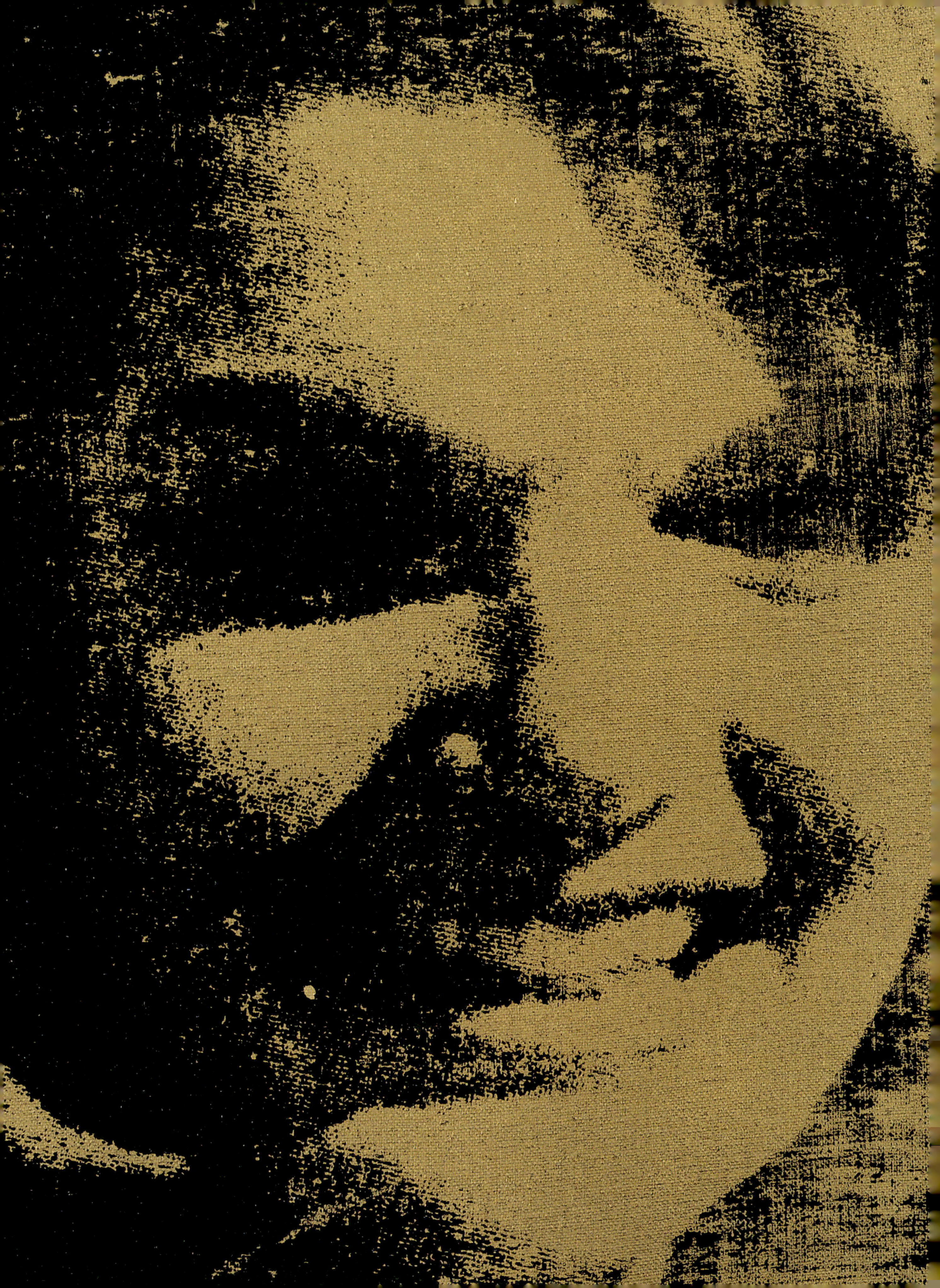

PROPERTY FROM THE COLLECTION OF JANE HOLZER, NEW YORK

117

Andy Warhol

1928-1987

ROUND JACKIE

stamped with the artist's signature and authenticated
by Vincent Fremont on the overlap
gold paint and silkscreen ink on canvas
DIAMETER: 44.8CM.; 17⅝IN.

Executed in 1964.

2,500,000-3,500,000 US$
9,100,000-12,740,000 QAR

PROVENANCE
Leo Castelli Gallery, New York (LC 791)
Jon J. Leibowitz, New York
Private Collection, New York
Sale: Sotheby's, New York, *Contemporary Art*, 9 May 1990, Lot 339
Private Collection, London
Sale: Sotheby's, New York, *Contemporary Art*, 17 November 1992, Lot 46
Acquired directly from the above by the present owner

EXHIBITED
Boston, Institute of Contemporary Art, *Andy Warhol*, 1966, no. 937, illustrated in colour
New York, C&M Arts, *Women of Warhol: Marilyn, Liz and Jackie*, 2000
Minneapolis, Walker Art Center; Chicago, Museum of Contemporary Art; Toronto, Art Gallery of Ontario, *Andy Warhol/Supernova: Stars, Deaths and Disasters, 1962-1964*, 2006 (only exhibited in Chicago)

LITERATURE
Rainer Crone, *Andy Warhol*, New York 1970, p. 292, no. 125
Rainer Crone, *Andy Warhol*, New York 1976, p. 292, no. 125
George Frei and Neil Printz, Eds., *The Andy Warhol Catalogue Raisonne: Paintings and Sculptures, Volume 2A: 1964-1969*, New York 2004, p. 108, no. 939, illustrated in colour

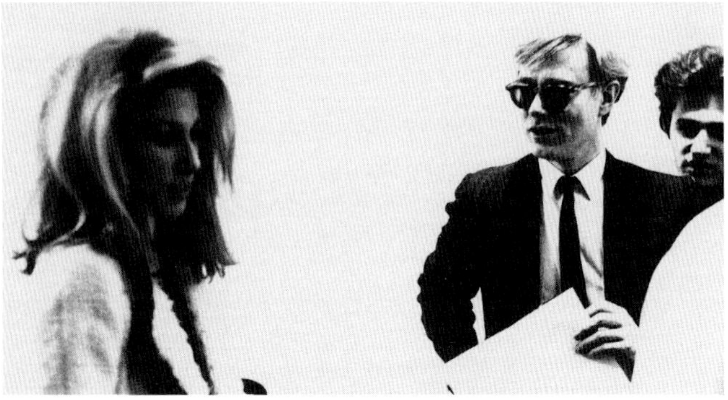

JANE HOLZER, ANDY WARHOL AND GERARD MALANGA AT STABLE GALLERY, 1964,
PHOTOGRAPH BY BILLY NAME. © BILLY NAME, 2009

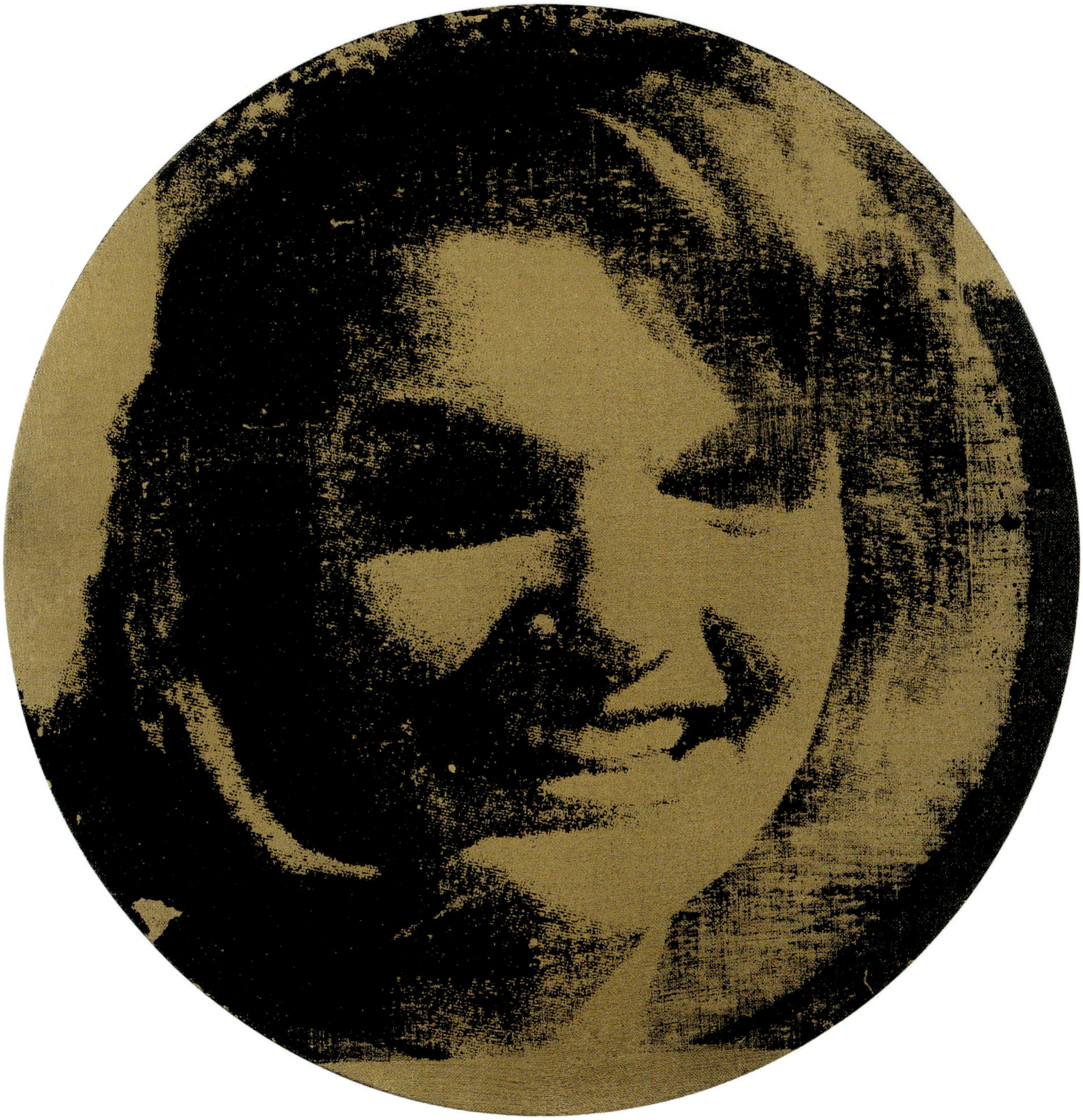

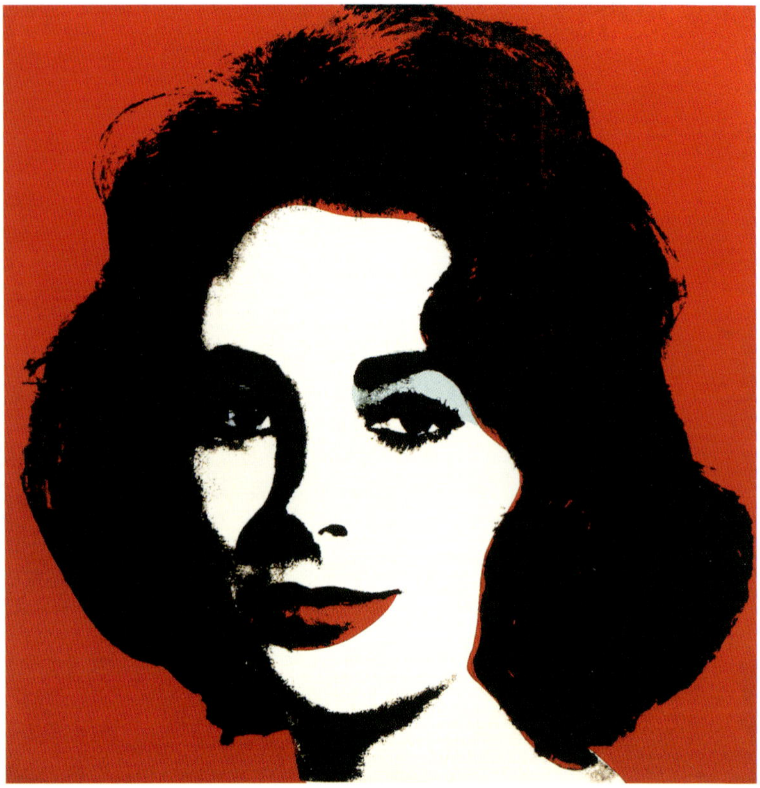

ANDY WARHOL, *LIZ*, 1963. PRIVATE COLLECTION. © THE ANDY WARHOL FOUNDATION FOR THE VISUAL ARTS / ARTISTS RIGHTS SOCIETY (ARS), NEW YORK / DACS, LONDON 2009.

ANDY WARHOL, *GOLD MARILYN MONROE*, 1962. THE MUSEUM OF MODERN ART, NEW YORK. GIFT OF PHILIPS JOHNSON. © THE ANDY WARHOL FOUNDATION FOR THE VISUAL ARTS / ARTISTS RIGHTS SOCIETY (ARS), NEW YORK / DACS, LONDON 2009.

Executed in 1964, *Round Jackie* is an exceptionally rare and immensely important paragon of Pop Art from the very heart of Andy Warhol's most celebrated period. One of just eight *Jackie* canvases that the artist made in this distinguished round gold format, which were themselves very possibly the first in the entire illustrious *Jackie* series, this is truly a Pop masterpiece and absolutely central to this golden age of Contemporary Art. Epitomising the moment when Warhol's work advanced from the cosmopolitan avant-garde to become a global phenomenon, *Round Jackie* is central to his revolutionising of iconography, which has so fundamentally shaped the development of visual culture ever since. With the most brilliant artistic and conceptual economy, this work encapsulates the allure of unlimited celebrity, critiques the manipulative power and replicating effects of mass-media, and is a groundbreaking response to one of the most tragic moments of twentieth-century American history.

The rarity, provenance and quality of *Round Jackie* makes it truly worthy of the most exceptional museum collection. Indeed, two of the other round gold *Jackies* now reside in The Art Museum of Princeton University, having been exhibited with the present work at the Institute of Contemporary Art in Boston in 1966. However, whereas the gold colour of the two Princeton paintings was sprayed onto the canvas, this *Round Jackie* was lavished with more attention by being hand-painted gold. The extraordinary metallic and reflective qualities of gold held particular importance for Warhol, and outstanding highlights of the *Jackie* series depend upon the predominance of the colour such as *The Week That Was I*, and *Jackie Frieze*, which is almost entirely gold. In fact Warhol's use of gold was exceptionally rare: outside the *Jackie* works, two round *Marilyns* of 1962, two *Ethel Sculls* of 1963 and the dramatically iconic *Gold Marilyn Monroe* of 1962 in the Museum of Modern Art in New York are exceptional instances of gold canvases in Warhol's entire 1960s output. Furthermore, the eminent provenance, which includes the Leo Castelli Gallery and one of Warhol's first superstars Jane Holzer, is impeccable. The round format is also virtually unique, being used elsewhere only in the two *Marilyn* works. Here the circular canvas outline serenely frames and echoes the rounded curves of Jackie's beautiful visage as well as evoking other uses of the format from the Renaissance *tondo* to profile portraits stamped on coins and medallions. Indeed, evoking the head of an empress or monarch on a golden coin, *Round Jackie* perfectly symbolises the currency of celebrity and as an icon deserving reverential adoration, Warhol's subject becomes the consummate deity of Pop Art.

The editors of Warhol's 2004 catalogue raisonné cite an early photo of the artist's legendary factory to suggest that *Round Jackie* was one of the inaugural paintings he made of Jacqueline Kennedy after the tragedy of her

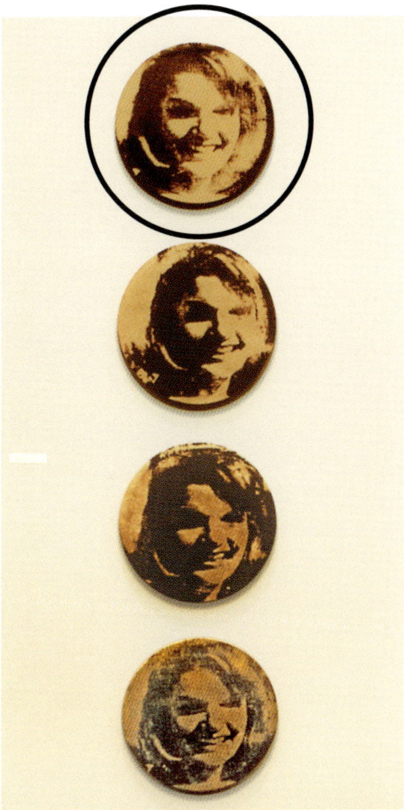

ANDY WARHOL, *FOUR ROUND JACKIE TONDOS* EXHIBITED AT THE INSTITUTE OF CONTEMPORARY ART, BOSTON, 1966. © THE ANDY WARHOL FOUNDATION FOR THE VISUAL ARTS / ARTISTS RIGHTS SOCIETY (ARS), NEW YORK / DACS, LONDON 2009.

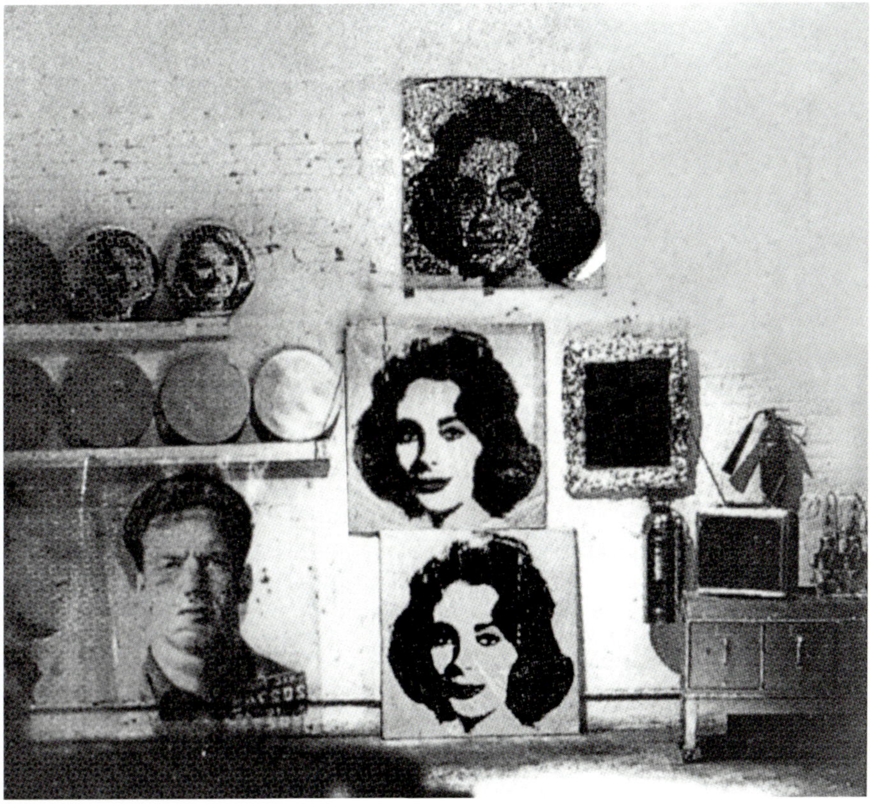

THE FACTORY, EARLY 1964. PHOTOGRAPH BY BILLY NAME. © BILLY NAME 2009

husband's assassination. As such this painting would directly presage the golden canvases included in celebrated masterpieces of the *Jackie* corpus now residing in The Metropolitan Museum of Art, New York, the Philadelphia Museum of Art, and The Gallery of Modern Art, Iwaki. Furthermore it would predate all the celebrated *Jackie* works on blue and white canvases, examples of which are celebrated in prestigious institutions from the Walker Art Center, Minneapolis, to the Museum Ludwig in Cologne and the Staatliche Museem zu Berlin, Nationalgalerie.

From the moment her husband was voted President of the United States in November 1960, Jackie Kennedy had been an inspirational heroine to millions in the optimistic climate of a newly rejuvenated post-war America. Physically epitomising youth, beauty and style, she became the ideal of a wife, mother and First Lady. In *Round Jackie* the illumination of her smile eerily portends the historic tragedy that has become synonymous with the letters J.F.K. Sourced in a photo taken at Dallas Love Field airport on the morning of 22nd November 1963, *Round Jackie* immortalises the final moments before an open-top limousine journey and a sniper's bullet devastated the emotional landscape of a nation. "Then, for the first time, there were many who experienced the banality of illustrious death, time being measured by the flash: a gasping instant" (Remo Guidieri, "JFK", in: Exhibition Catalogue, Houston, The Menil Collection, *Andy Warhol: Death and Disasters*, 1988-89, p. 29).

Kennedy's assassination was followed two days later by his burial in Arlington National Cemetery near Washington, D.C. While the route of the cortege was lined by 800,000 mourners, broadcasting agencies and news editors assembled their valedictory testimonials to a hero. As an entire population sank into the shared psychosis of bereavement, the media's carefully choreographed narration precipitated one of the most prodigious critiques of mass communication ever conceived. This traumatizing national experience, one of the earliest to be mediated by the media, is arguably also the first to be implanted in the public's consciousness by means of ubiquitous photographic images. In this climate Warhol was immediately intrigued by "the way television and radio were programming everybody to feel so sad" (Andy Warhol and Pat Hackett, *POPism: The Warhol '60s*, 1980).

The tension between public and private personae is at the root of much of Andy Warhol's art. He had earlier portrayed Jackie Kennedy in 1962 in the frontal, movie-star format used in his similar paintings of Marilyn Monroe and Elizabeth Taylor. Although these three celebrities each possessed private turmoil and personal tragedy, it was the glittering surface persona that the public wanted and that the media celebrated. Warhol grasped intuitively that a public image shown

"The woman whose feelings were reproduced in all the media to such an extent that no better historical document on the exhibitionism of American emotional values is conceivable"

Rainer Crone, *Andy Warhol*, New York 1970, p. 29

pervasively through the mass media was a merely artificial construct. For Jackie Kennedy, the enormity of her tragedy in 1963 personified a wider sense of national loss, and her inner trauma became her public persona. Advancing themes initiated in his highly acclaimed *Death and Disaster* series, Warhol here narrates the catastrophe through the mirror of Jackie's face, relating the horror by depicting its closest witness. For the viewer, there is an overwhelming sense of dramatic irony in knowing the subsequent outcome of the day's events: Jackie's radiant smile soon to be transformed by mourning desolation into the widow's shadow holding a fading memory of the iconic husband. Indeed, by appropriating potent imagery and re-presenting narrative through implication and absence *Round Jackie* should be considered as a poignant history painting of the Twentieth Century.

Warhol scoured the popular press for portraits of Jackie Kennedy, eventually selecting eight and cropping each to about three and-a-half by three inches. Warhol ordered a large screen for the eight photos together in which each image was enlarged to twenty by sixteen inches, so that the entire mechanical was eighty inches high. To make individual canvases the other seven images were covered before the ink was pushed through the silkscreen onto the canvas. In *Round Jackie* it is possible to make out the adjacent screen image from the original mechanical towards the right edge, at about the two o'clock position on the rim of the circle where the black suddenly turns gold next to a straight vertical line.

Round Jackie enshrines on canvas one of the defining moments of modern American history, in an image which is deeply personal, revealing the private side of a very public event. The smiling idol of lost halcyon tranquility, literally a vestige of Camelot, Jackie Kennedy will always re-tell an epic tragedy. Frei and Printz have assessed how Warhol "brought her into close-up, making her the dramatic focus and emotional barometer of the Kennedy assassination, shifting the historical narrative into a series of affective moments or portraits that register the subject over time" (Georg Frei and Neil Printz, Eds., *The Andy Catalogue Raisonné, Vol. 2A, Paintings and Sculptures 1964-1969*, London and New York 2004, p. 103). Without historical perspective and working immediately after the event, Warhol identified the media's capacity to fix this association between icon and story exceptionally early. In keeping with his very best work, celebrity, tragedy and the spectre of death inhabit every pore of this magnificent painting. The profuse repetition of Jackie's silk-screened portraits mirrors the shattering of moments when time stands still. Replicating a lost moment in the stark reality of tonal duality, suffused in a circular pool of transcendent reflective gold, this perfect *Round Jackie* is the iconic paean to an individual's struggle with disaster.

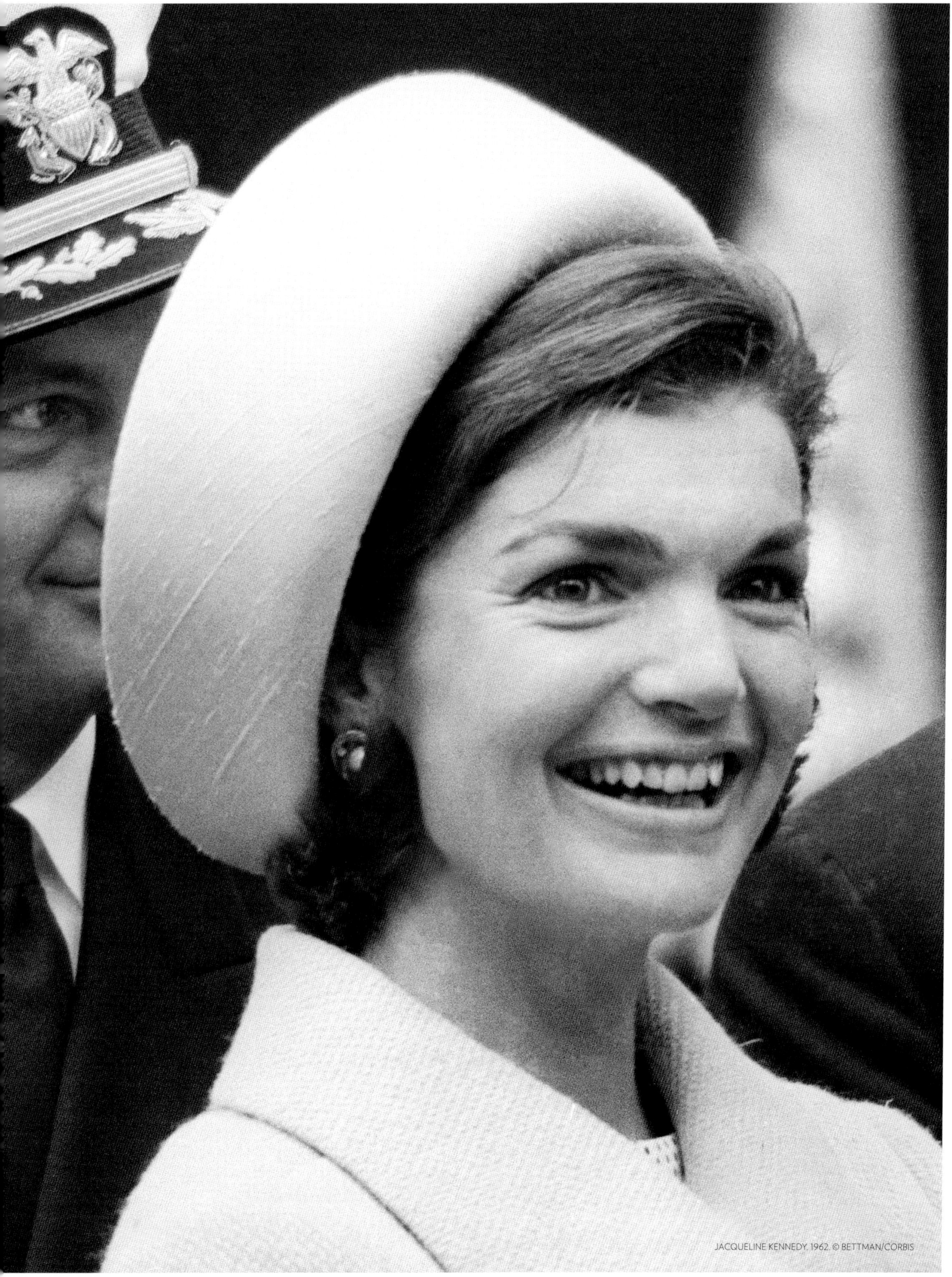
JACQUELINE KENNEDY, 1962. © BETTMAN/CORBIS

118

Robert Indiana

b. 1928

LOVE (RED/ BLUE)

stamped with signature, dated *1966-1999* and numbered *4/5*
polychromed aluminium
244 BY 244CM BY 122CM.; 96 BY 96 BY 48IN.

1,000,000-1,500,000 US$
3,640,000-5,460,000 QAR

In 1954, Robert Clark traded his life in New Castle, Indiana for a Coenties Slip loft with Ellsworth Kelly, Agnes Martin and Jack Youngerman and an art supply shop on West 57th Street. It was in Manhattan that Clark found his trademark artistic style and new surname to match. Drawing heavily on contemporary pop and commercial artists as well as the hard-edge and minimalist styles of his house-mates, Indiana developed an aesthetic characterized by a tension between pop and abstraction which seemed to anticipate the looming op-art movement.

Indiana's LOVE paintings are some of the most ubiquitous of Pop art culture. They have become a staple of the popular global lexicon appearing everywhere from U.S. postage stamps to rock album covers. The LOVE iconography, both formalist and sensitive, first appeared in a series of poems originally written in 1958, in which Indiana stacked LO and VE on top of one another. The first LOVE sculpture, carved out of a solid block of aluminum was made for the artist's show at the Stable Gallery in 1966. Shortly after, Indiana was commissioned to design a Christmas card for the Museum of Modern Art; three small paintings of the word love in red, blue and green.

But LOVE is not simply a cultural icon; it is a man's ground-breaking examination of the delicate abstractions in the written word. It is an exploration of language on an aesthetic visual level, a challenge to not only hear but *see* the expressive power of words in their lines, planes and geometric forms. Indiana is not only focused on the meaning of words but also the formal statement they make. By enlarging their letters and playing with the format in which we ordinarily see them, Indiana draws our attention to LOVE'S elegant linearity and form. He further highlights these subtleties by filling in the interiors of letters and the spaces between them with different colors. These works become visual melodies; each version of LOVE accentuating different notes, beats and harmonies. Sometimes his cool hues and formal equilibrium hum the melody of an aged romance; the peace that exists between old lovers and other times the violent staccatos, jutting forms and electric tonality sing a different tune. It is the tumultuous passion of new love- the clashing colours, the hot reds, the fights and the fire.

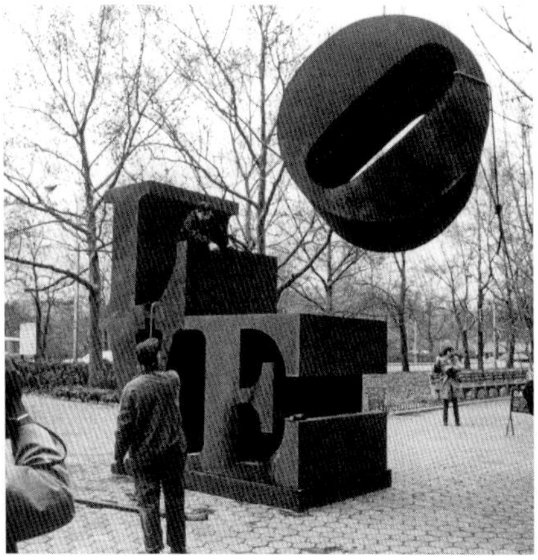

ERECTION OF THE 12-FOOT STEEL *LOVE* FOR TEMPORARY VIEWING CENTRAL PARK, NEW YORK, CHRISTMAS, 1971. PHOTOGRAPH BY TOM RUMMLER. © 2009 MORGAN ART FOUNDATION LTD. / ARTISTS RIGHTS SOCIETY (ARS), NEW YORK, DACS, LONDON.

The present work's bi-chromatic aesthetic seems to speak to a middle ground, a universal concept of love if you will. Its vibrant red facades are cooled by softer blue interiors. Like a strong relationship, it maintains an arduous spirit infused with the comfort and compassion of years. In this marriage of fire and water, Indiana depicts not only romantic love but the love we share with our brothers, mothers, and countrymen. It is a polarity only understood in bonds that are everlasting; the point where peace and chaos converge.

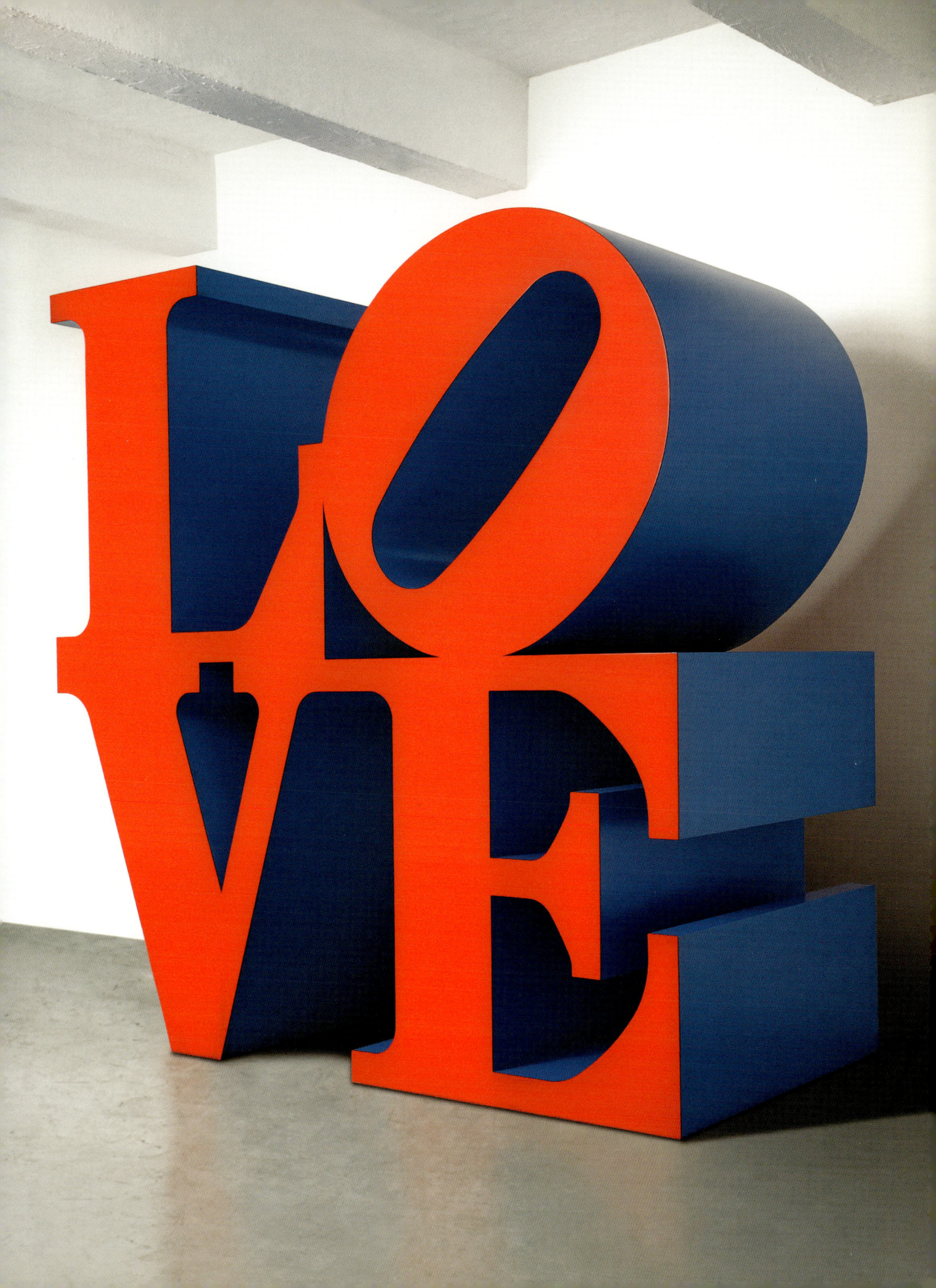
LO
VE

119

Gerhard Richter

b. 1932

HEU

signed, dated *1995* and numbered *831-1* on the reverse
oil on canvas
200 BY 140CM.; 78¾ BY 55⅛IN.

2,600,000-3,600,000 US$
9,470,000-13,110,000 QAR

PROVENANCE
Marian Goodman Gallery, New York
Acquired directly from the above by the present owner in 1997

EXHIBITED
Nîmes, Carré d'Art, Musée d'Art Contemporain, *Gerhard Richter - 100 Pictures*, 1996, p. 112, illustrated in colour

LITERATURE
Exhibition Catalogue, Düsseldorf, K20 Kunstsammlung Nordrhein-Westfalen, *Gerhard Richter*, 2005, no. 831-1, illustrated in colour

"Abstract paintings are fictitious models, because they visualize a reality which we can neither see nor describe but which we may nevertheless conclude to exist [...] This is not an artful game, it is a necessity; and since everything unknown frightens us and fills us with hope at the same time, we take these images as a possible explanation of the inexplicable or at least a way of dealing with it."

Gerhard Richter cited in: Exhibition Catalogue, Kassel, *Documenta 7*, 1982, Vol. 1, pp. 84-85

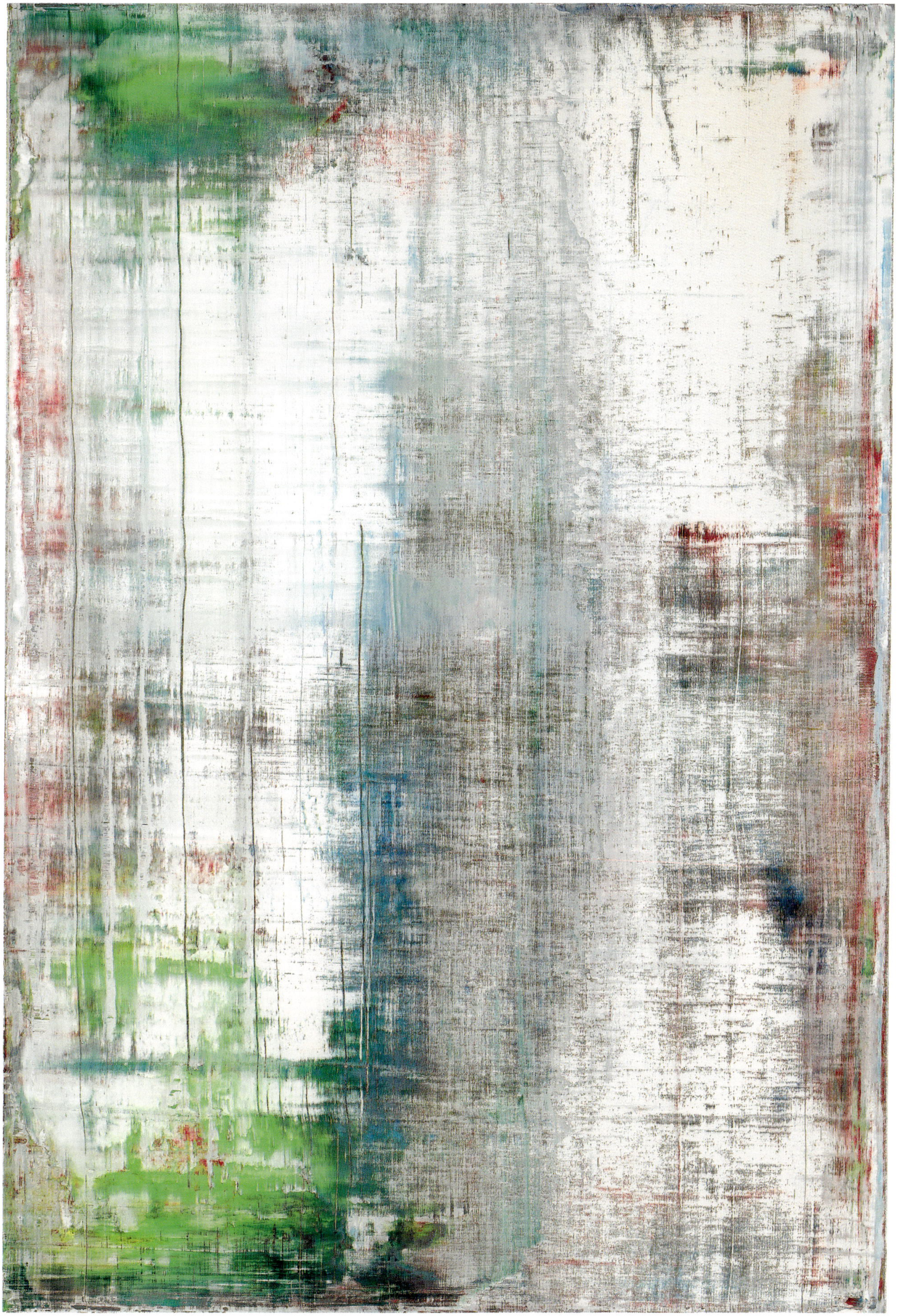

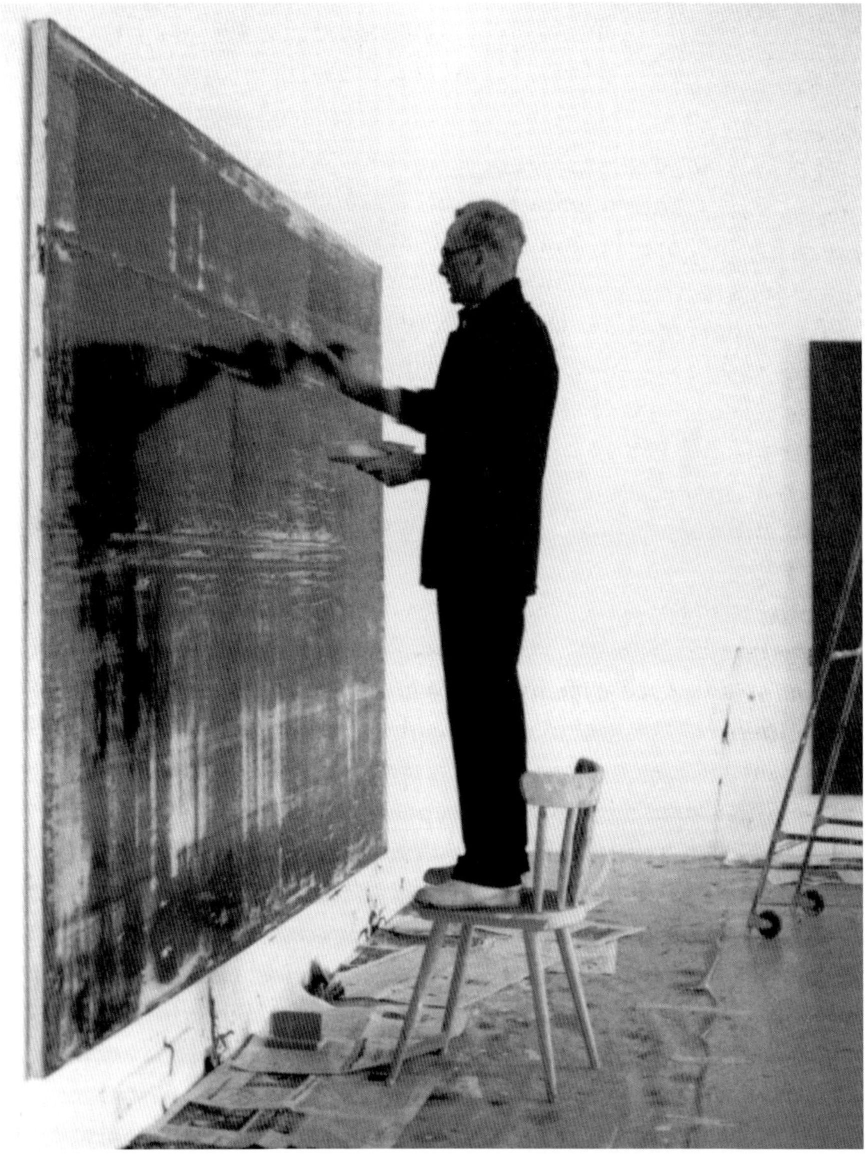

GERHARD RICHTER, STUDIO, COLOGNE, 1995. © SABINE RICHTER 2009.

A symphony of both chromatic and technical virtuosity, Gerhard Richter's *Heu* of 1995 brings together a lyrical composition, colouristic density and a certain aesthetic romance that is archetypal of his most illustrious 'Abstract Paintings'. It is a perfect example of the abstract painting technique that Richter had only perfected by the 1990s. In portrait format this magnificent work is two metres tall and nearly one and-a-half metres wide, thus belonging to a short sequence of five paintings he painted in this largest canvas format between the beginning of 1995 and the end of 1997. Indeed, its dimensions confront the viewer and reflect the human scale, filling our field of view and immersing us in Richter's painted vision. The rich and dense surfaces resonate with colouristic and architectural harmony. The interplay of hues and the complex layering of impasto both reveal and conceal at the same time, inviting us to look both at and through the laminas of paint material.

Contrary to the apparent immediacy of the painting's surface, this work is the result of Richter's systematic and remarkably methodical technique of scraping layers of paint across the canvas over an extended period of time. He begins by placing a number of primed white canvases around the walls of his studio, eventually working on several or all of them simultaneously. A soft ground of red, yellow, blue, or green is then applied only to be subsequently altered by large strokes: tracks of colour drawn out with the straight edge of a rubber squeegee. The painting undergoes multiple variations in which each new accretion brings colour and textural juxtapositions that are reworked until they are completely harmonized. *Heu's* glossy layers of whites, lilacs, blues, and greens have been smeared on the surface, squeezed into the perpendicular canvas weave, blended together before being partially scraped and scratched away.

Although initiated in the mid 1970s, it was not until the early 1990s that Richter's colossal project of gestural abstract painting developed out of an experimental exploration of visual communication into a more direct assertion of aesthetic principles. By this time the character of the *Abstraktes Bild* became invested with a confident legitimacy; the rigour of the prolific painter's flawless technique broadcasting something greater than mere painterly experimentation. Through an idiosyncratic combination of artistic instinct and technical dexterity, Richter created paintings of stunning beauty. As he has himself explained, "I want to end up with a picture that I haven't planned. This method of arbitrary choice, chance, inspiration and destruction may produce a specific type of picture, but it never produces a predetermined picture...I just want to get something more interesting out of it than those things I can think out for myself." (Gerhard Richter interviewed in 1990 in: Hubertus Butin, Stefan Gronert, and the Dallas Museum of Art, Eds., *Gerhard Richter: Editions 1965 – 2004: Catalogue Raisonné*, Ostfildern-Ruit 2004, p. 36). Indeed, with works such as *Heu* Richter's abstraction completely abandons all referents of the figurative world and affords the viewer a subjective sensory experience of phenomenological resonance.

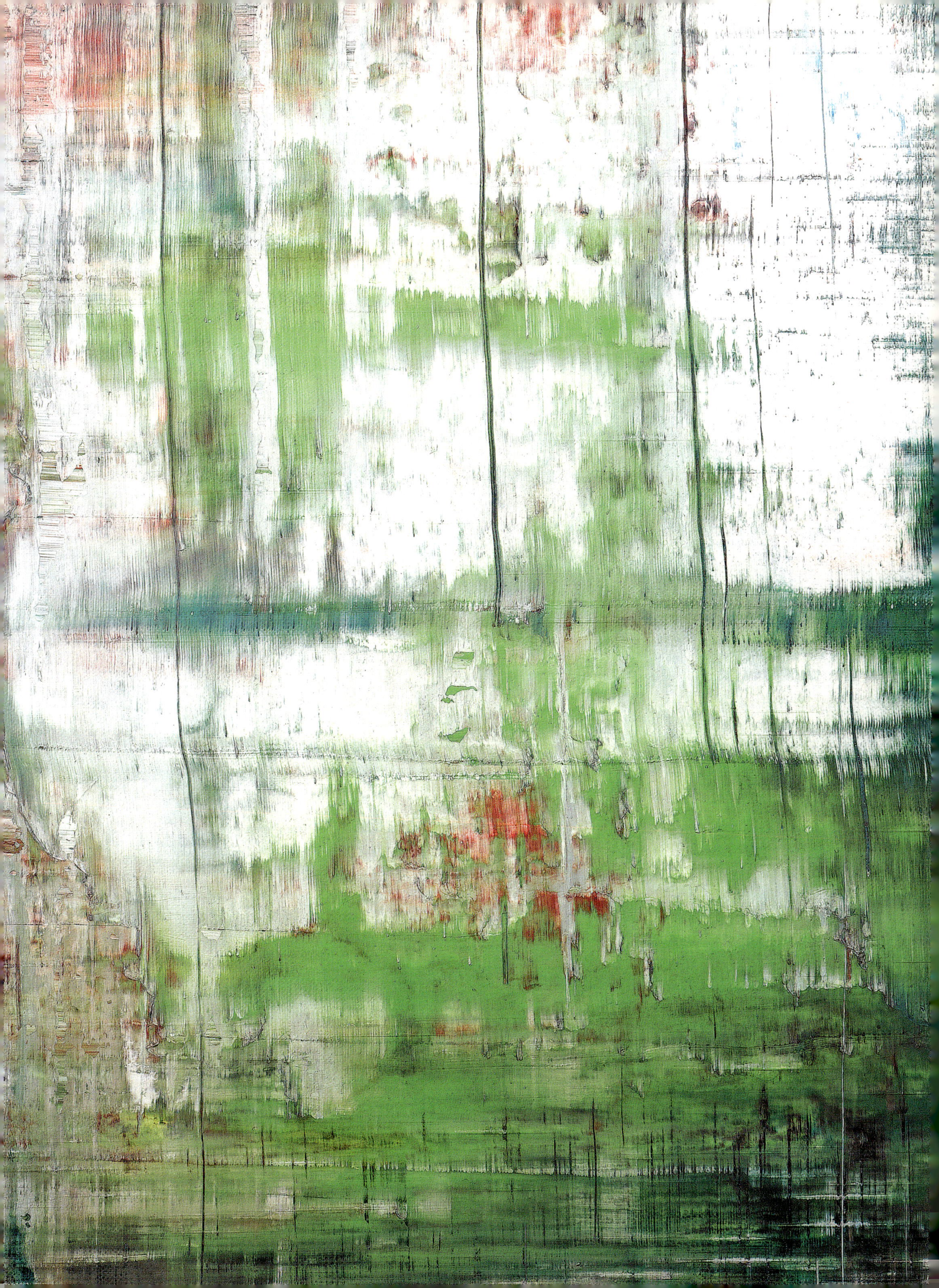

120

Anselm Reyle

b. 1970

UNTITLED

signed and dated *2006* on the overlap
acrylic and PVC foil on canvas
224 BY 189CM.; 88¼ BY 74⅜IN.

100,000-150,000 US$
364,000-550,000 QAR

PROVENANCE
Galerie Giti Nourbakhsch, Berlin
Acquired directly from the above by the present owner

Few contemporary artists have created as much of a stir in the art world as the German abstractionist Anselm Reyle. With a brilliant combination of unorthodox materials and fresh colors, the artist has breathed new life into abstract art; a genre some considered passé at best, wholly irrelevant at worst. An heir to the aesthetic structures of Barnett Newman, Ellsworth Kelly, Jackson Pollock and Kenneth Noland, Reyle deftly unites the rigorous restraint of nonfigurative art with the iconoclastic bombast of Pop. However, while many of his peers have looked to Pop's themes for inspiration, Reyle has turned a more nuanced eye to the movement by focusing on Pop's processes and materials.

On the surface, *Untitled* 2006 bears a strong resemblance to a stripe painting of Kenneth Noland. Both of their evenly spaced bars of color create visually arresting patterns of form and tonalities. However, unlike Noland's compositions, Reyle's painting is not concerned with the purification and totality of color and surface. Rather, by sampling the themes of another artist, like a disc-jockey samples from other musicians, the artist secularizes and democratizes the art-making process. This is further emphasized through the utilization of studio assistants and modern mass-produced materials such as mirrors and PVC foil.

Reyle's clever juxtaposition of art historical models, Pop philosophies of art production and Contemporary culture have propelled him to the forefront of art discourse. In a culture that obsesses over personality while ironically stressing conformity Reyle's work is a reflection of this clashing duality. As the artist has said, "I just take things that fascinate me, especially when I know they are deemed tasteless... that's where I get my energy." (Anselm Reyle in: Christopher Mooney, 'The New King of Kitsch', *Art Review*, Issue 28, December 2008, p. 63)

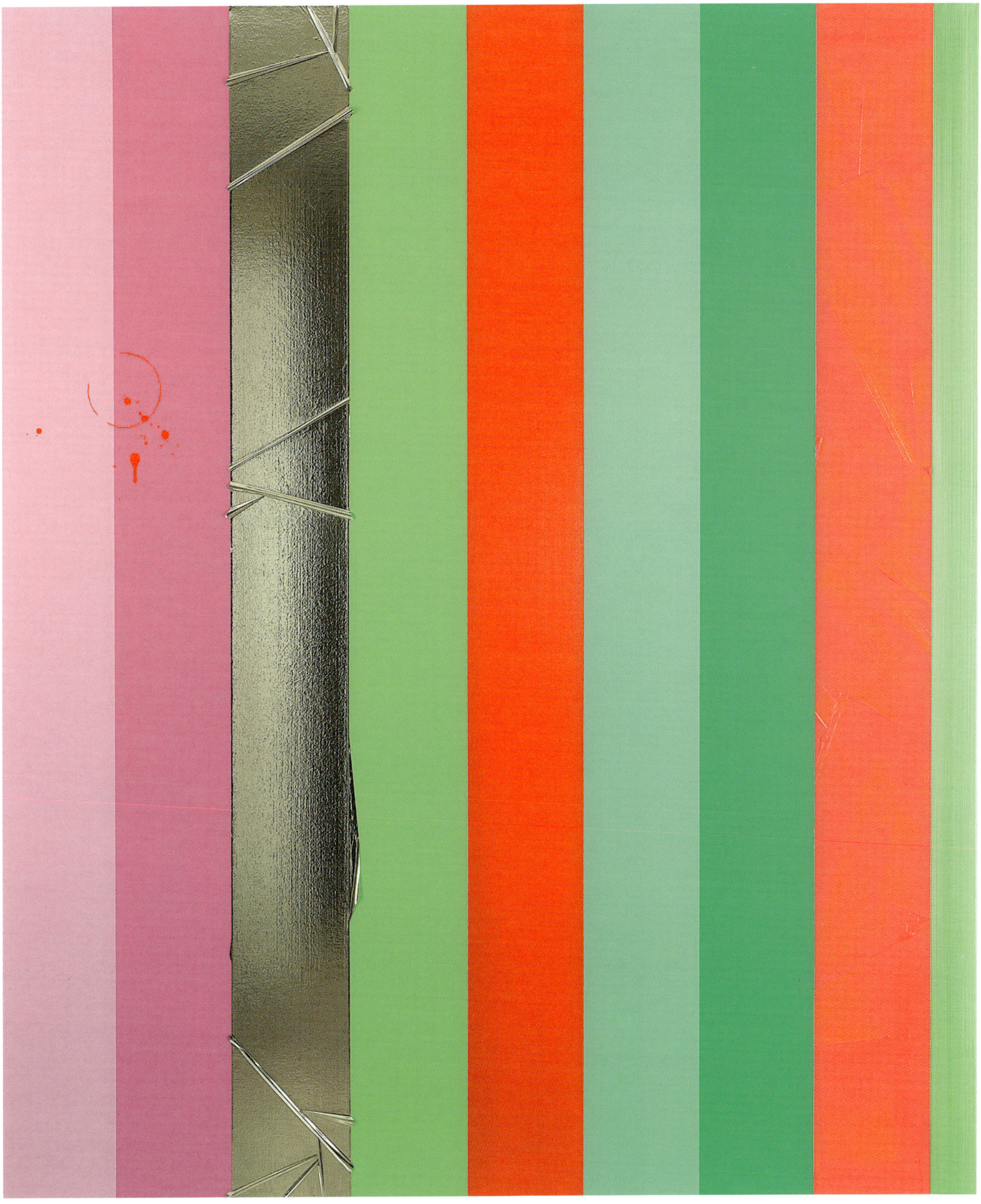

121

Banksy

b. 1975

SID VICIOUS

tagged; signed on the reverse; signed on the stretcher
acrylic, spraypaint stencil and diamond dust on canvas
91.8 BY 91.8CM.; 36⅛ BY 36⅛IN.

Executed *circa* 2000.

120,000-150,000 US$
437,000-550,000 QAR

PROVENANCE
Lazarides Gallery, London
Acquired directly from the above by the present owner

Authenticated by Pest Control Office

Executed nearly ten years ago during an early and highly formative period for the artist, *Sid Vicious* by Banksy is a unique canvas created in a one-off template configuration. There is only one further canvas depicting Sid Vicious, though this is a different composition. A consummate portrayal of one iconic bad-boy of British urban subculture by another, this is a brilliant summation of both post-Modernism and urban graffiti art, two of the most exciting trends in British art of the past two decades.

The composition consists of the multiple portrait of the subject, Sid Vicious, in a square, three-by-three grid format totalling nine repetitions. Achieved via the street artist's stencil, this multiplication is deliberately evocative of the work of Andy Warhol, whose repeated portraits of world-famous celebrities from Jackie Kennedy to Elvis Presley to Mick Jagger spearheaded the global omnipotence of Pop Art and have conditioned global visual culture ever since. The three-by-three compositional arrangement of nine heads is a direct reference to Warhol's 'Mao' and 'Marilyn' reversal series, executed from 1979,

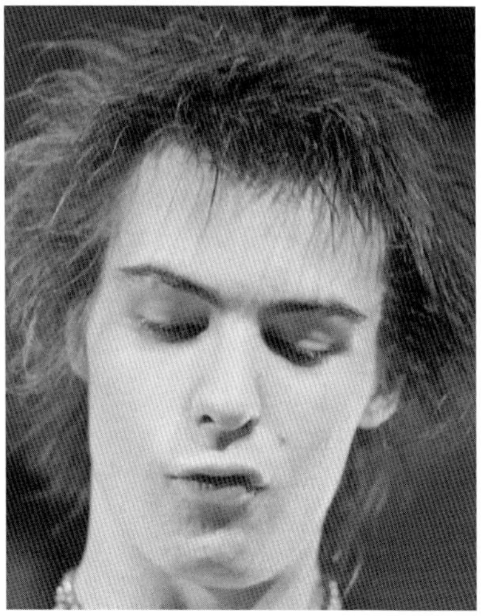

SID VICIOUS OF THE SEX PISTOLS, 1978. © CORBIS

in which nine representations appeared in a similar grid format. The use of diamond dust also quotes the work of Andy Warhol, who utilised the innovative material in a variety of portraits and 'Shadow Painting' works from the 1970s and 1980s.

The infamous bass guitarist for the *Sex Pistols* band, Sid Vicious remains the foremost embodiment of the Punk phenomenon. Punk aimed to revolutionise mundanity and indifference, railing against the desensitized apathy of mass-produced popular music and culture. Here Banksy brilliantly re-presents the literal personification of Punk – Sid Vicious – in Warhol's instantly recognizable dialect of Pop Art. The resolute individuality that stands at the heart of the Punk ethos is perfectly satirised by its desensitising multiplication. At the same time, the diamond dust portrait at the centre of *Sid Vicious* suggests Banksy's ultimate conviction in individuality and freedom of expression.

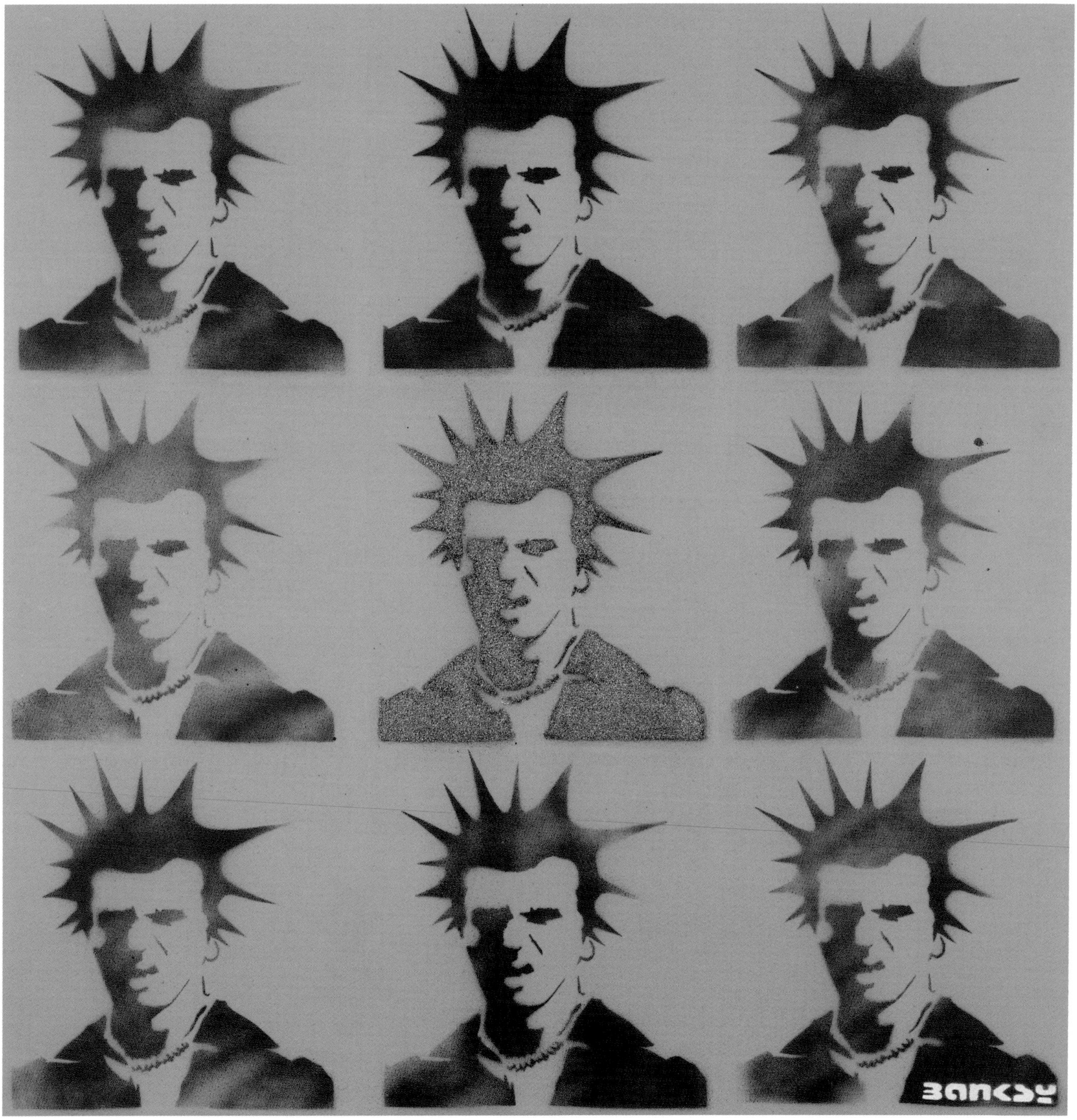
BANKSY

122

Farhad Moshiri

b. 1963

LORAZEPAM

signed, titled and dated *2007* on the overlap
acrylic and glitter on canvas
145.5 BY 175.3CM.; 57¼ BY 69IN.

150,000-200,000 US$
550,000-730,000 QAR

PROVENANCE

Daneyal Mahmood Gallery, New York
Acquired directly from the above by the present owner

EXHIBITED

New York, Daneyal Mahmood Gallery, *Sweet Dreams*, 2007

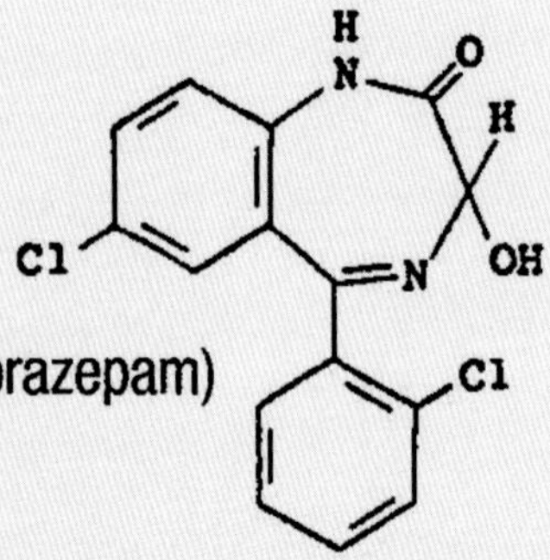

(lorazepam)

INDICATIONS AND USAGE

(lorazepam) is indicated for the management of anxiety disorders or for the short-term relief of the symptoms of anxiety or anxiety associated with depressive symptoms. Anxiety or tension associated with the stress of everyday life usually does not require treatment with an anxiolytic.

Physical and Psychological Dependence

The use of benzodiazepines, including lorazepam, may lead to physical and psychological dependence. The risk of dependence increases with higher doses and longer term use and is further increased in patients with a history of alcoholism or drug abuse or in patients with significant personality disorders. The dependence potential is reduced when lorazepam is used at the appropriate dose for short-term treatment. Addiction-prone individuals (such as drug addicts or alcoholics) should be under careful surveillance when receiving lorazepam or other psychotropic agents.

In general, benzodiazepines should be prescribed for short periods only (e.g. 2-4 weeks). Extension of the treatment period should not take place without reevaluation of the need for continued therapy. Continuous long-term use of product is not recommended. Withdrawal symptoms (e.g. rebound insomnia) can appear following cessation of recommended doses after as little as one week of therapy. Abrupt discontinuation of product should be avoided and a gradual dosage-tapering schedule followed after extended therapy.

Abrupt termination of treatment may be accompanied by withdrawal symptoms. Symptoms reported following discontinuation of benzodiazepines include headache, anxiety, tension, depression, insomnia, restlessness, confusion, irritability, sweating, rebound phenomena, dysphoria, dizziness, derealization, depersonalization, hyperacusis, numbness/tingling of extremities, hypersensitivity to light, noise, and physical contact/perceptual changes, involuntary movements, nausea, vomiting, diarrhea, loss of appetite, hallucinations/delirium, convulsions/seizures, tremor, abdominal cramps, myalgia, agitation, palpitations, tachycardia, panic attacks, vertigo, hyperreflexia, short-term memory loss, and hyperthermia. Convulsions/seizures may be more common in patients with pre-existing seizure disorders or who are taking other drugs that lower the convulsive threshold such as antidepressants.

There is evidence that tolerance develops to the sedative effects of benzodiazepines.

Lorazepam may have abuse potential, especially in patients with a history of drug and/or alcohol abuse.

LORAZEPAM: DIRECTIONS FOR USE

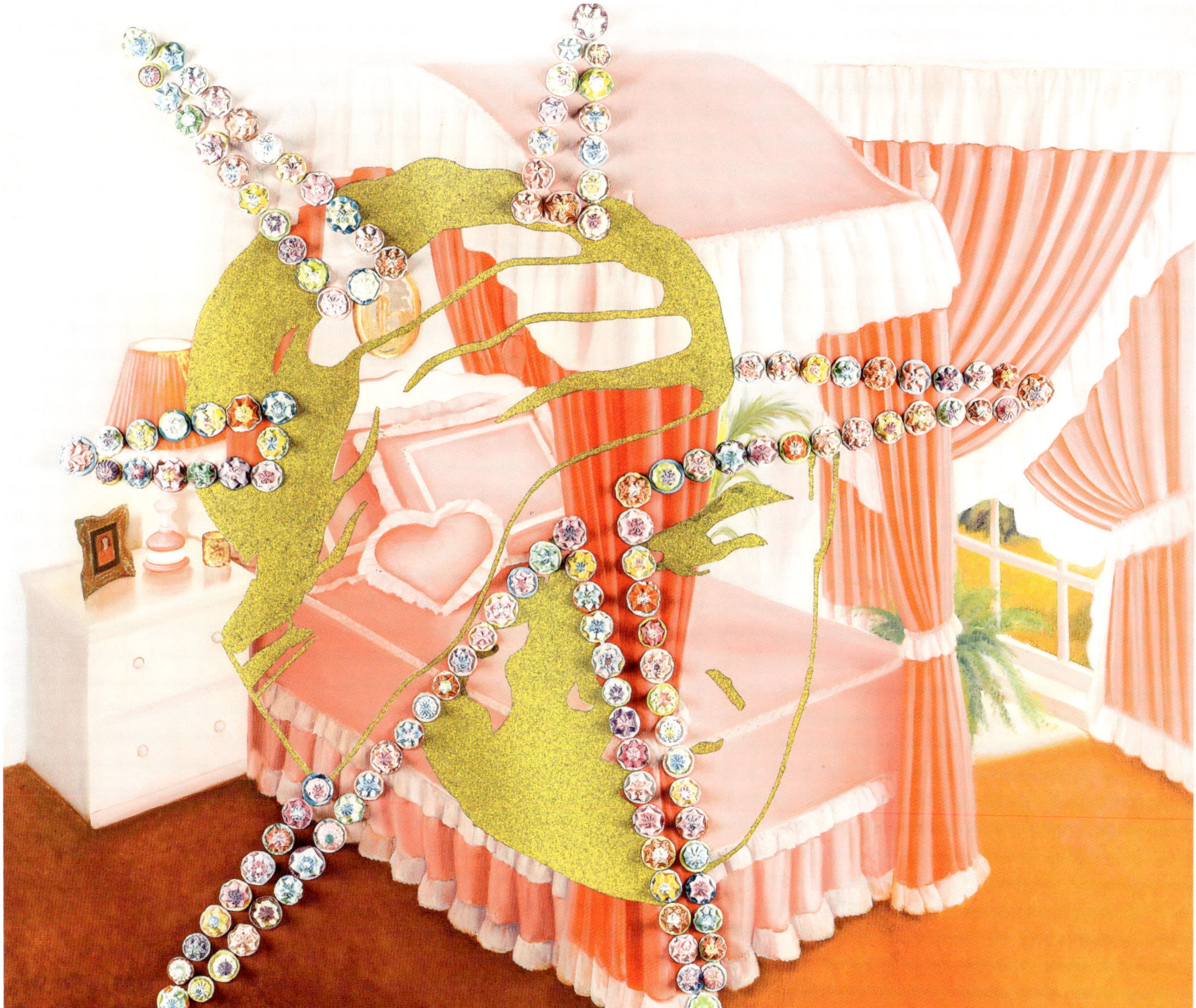

123

Hossein Zenderoudi

b. 1937

GANJE PAINDJOM

signed and dated *81*; signed in farsi; signed, titled and dated *81* on the reverse
acrylic on canvas
205 BY 90CM.; 80¾ BY 35½IN.

300,000-400,000 US$
1,100,000-1,460,000 QAR

PROVENANCE
Acquired directly from the artist by the present owner in 1983

EXHIBITED
Châteauroux, Centre d'Art Contemporain, *Ecrits Célestes*, 1995

"Water, Air, Earth, Fire…and Soul. Is there any treasure more precious than these five?" Hossein Zenderoudi in conversation with Sotheby's, 2008

Ganje Paindjom is a consummate testament to the artist's unique ability to sustain the depth and spirituality of Iranian artistic tradition whilst maintaining its contemporary relevance. As one of the central fore-runners of Iranian neo-traditionalism, and the founding father of its principal movement, the Saqqa-Khaneh, Zenderoudi's works are both emblematic and inimitable.

Tireless in his visual evolution, Zenderoudi's oeuvre has experienced several stylistic transitions. At the beginning of his career he principally worked with intricate talismanic depictions, filling his canvas densely with minutely rendered calligraphic charts and numerological symbols, but in the 1980's Zenderoudi developed a new-found interest in the scale and architecture of painted letter-forms, as exemplified in the present work.

Ganje Panjom highlights Zenderoudi's shifting interest away from complex talismanic calligraphy towards a distinctly elegant painterly style. Giving more attention to the compositional aspects of his depiction, and the monumental structure of his letter-forms, Zenderoudi's works from this period explore the architecture of calligraphy in its pure form as opposed to its ritual application. In the current work Zenderoudi weaves a harmonious visual interplay between bulbous compressed, rounded letters squeezed together in the top half of the composition, and flowing, reed-like strokes that are draped over the bottom section of the canvas, interlocking the playful, buoyant two-eyed Ha letter forms in the centre.

Whilst the use of vivid fluorescent hues, and lively, playful characters evokes a distinctly pop sensation within the composition, the present work is imbued with the same intellectual gravity that characterises Zenderoudi's oeuvre. Ganje Panjom, or "Fifth Treasure", points towards the highly symbolic nature both of Zenderoudi's paintings, and of the Islamic mysticism he is fascinated with. The Fifth Treasure is a testament to the sanctity of the number five in Islamic tradition, not only referring to the five pillars of Islam but also to the Ahl-e Bayt, or five inner circle of the prophets family, considered particularly holy in Iranian tradition. This is further reflected in the five central *Ha* letters which occupy the centre of the composition, under which a row of *Meem* forms drape downwards; interestingly the letters *Ha Meem* prefix several Sourah's of the Quran and act as a shorthand for the divine name Al-Hakim, or the 'All Wise'.

Whilst aesthetically progressive and visually sophisticated, the present work is re-enforced by perceptive and illuminating elements of Iranian tradition and is therefore a monumental, refined demonstration of Zenderoudi's ability to the combine the visual and the spiritual in perfect artistic harmony.

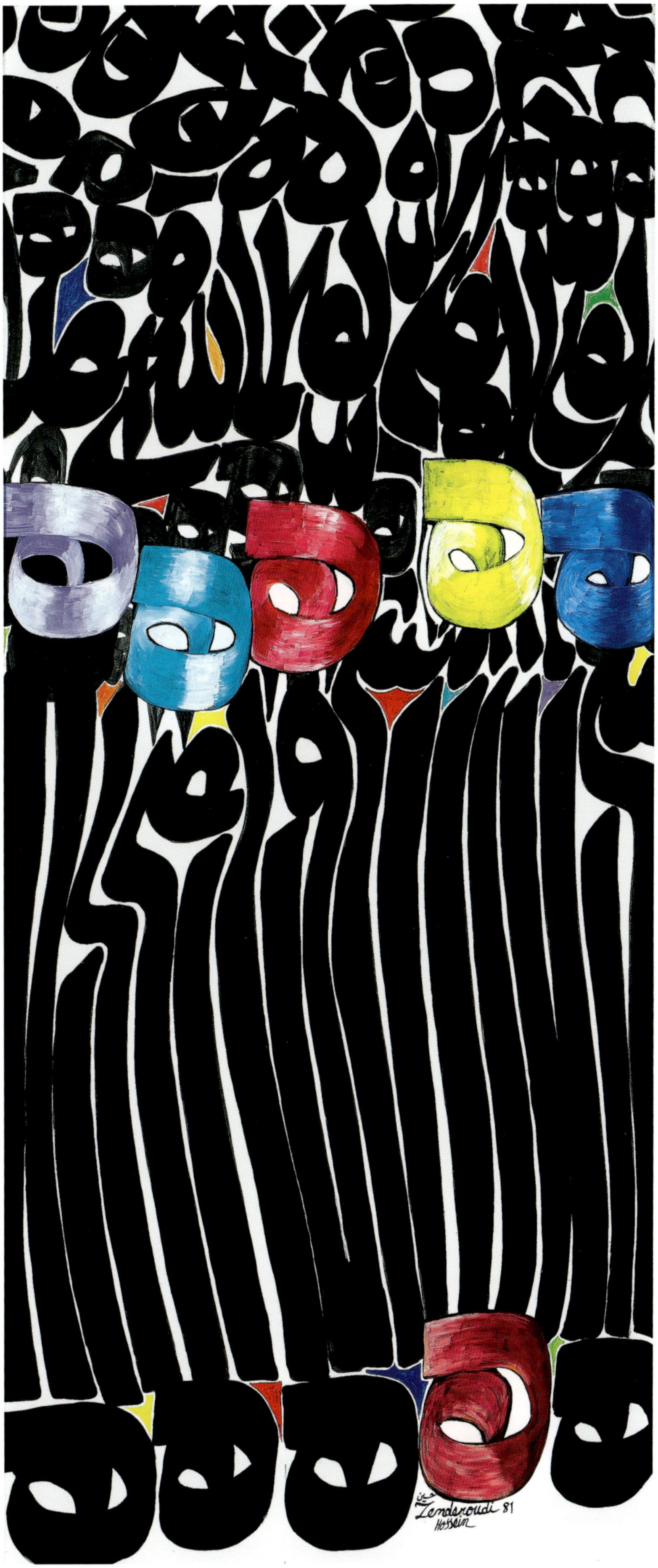
حسین
Zenderoudi 81
Hossein

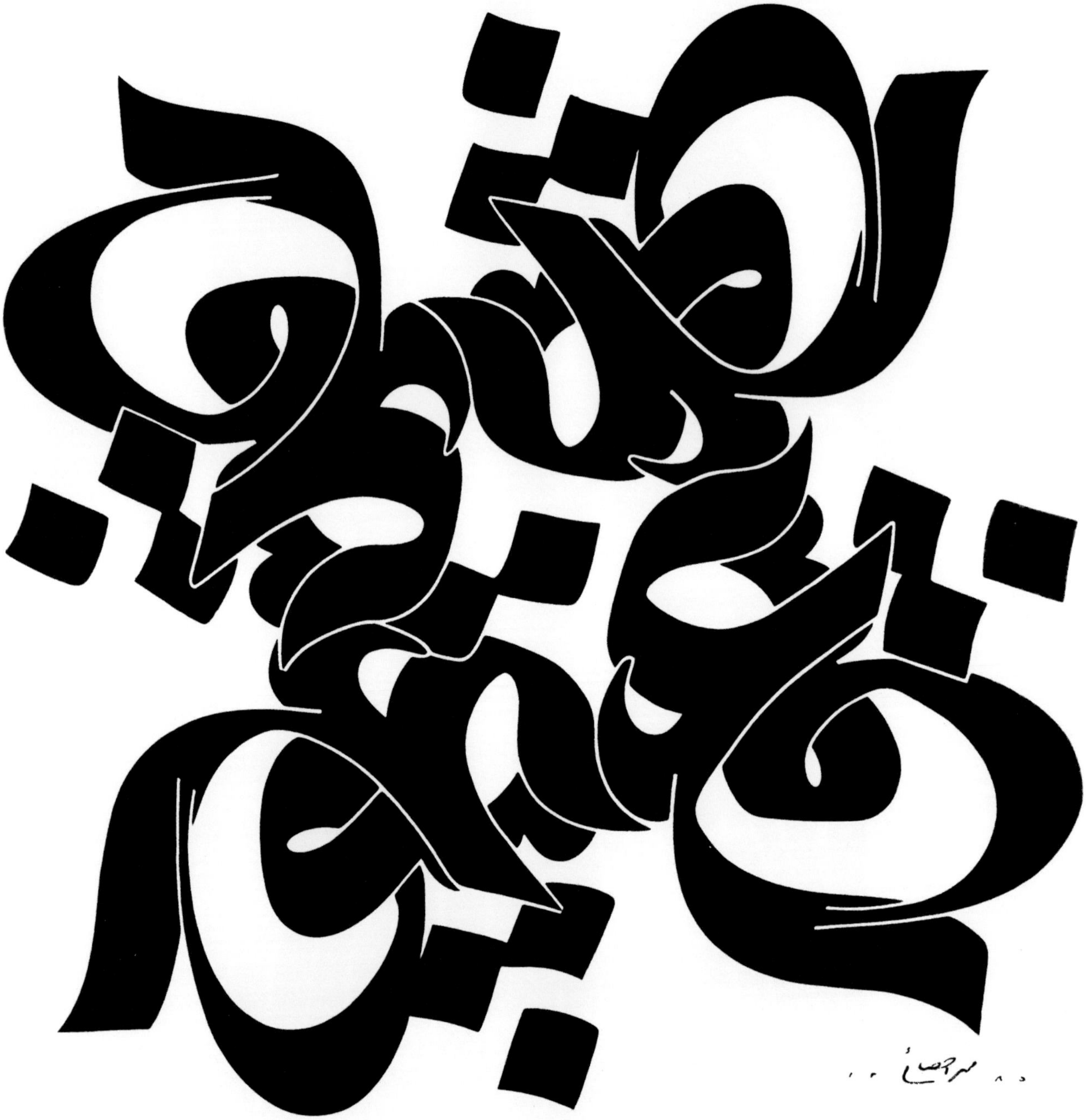

124

Mohammad Ehsai

b. 1939

ESHGH (LOVE)

signed twice
acrylic on canvas, in two parts
EACH 130 BY 130CM.; 51⅛ BY 51⅛IN.

Executed in 2006.

PROVENANCE
Acquired directly from the artist by the present owner in 2006

200,000-300,000 US$
730,000-1,100,000 QAR

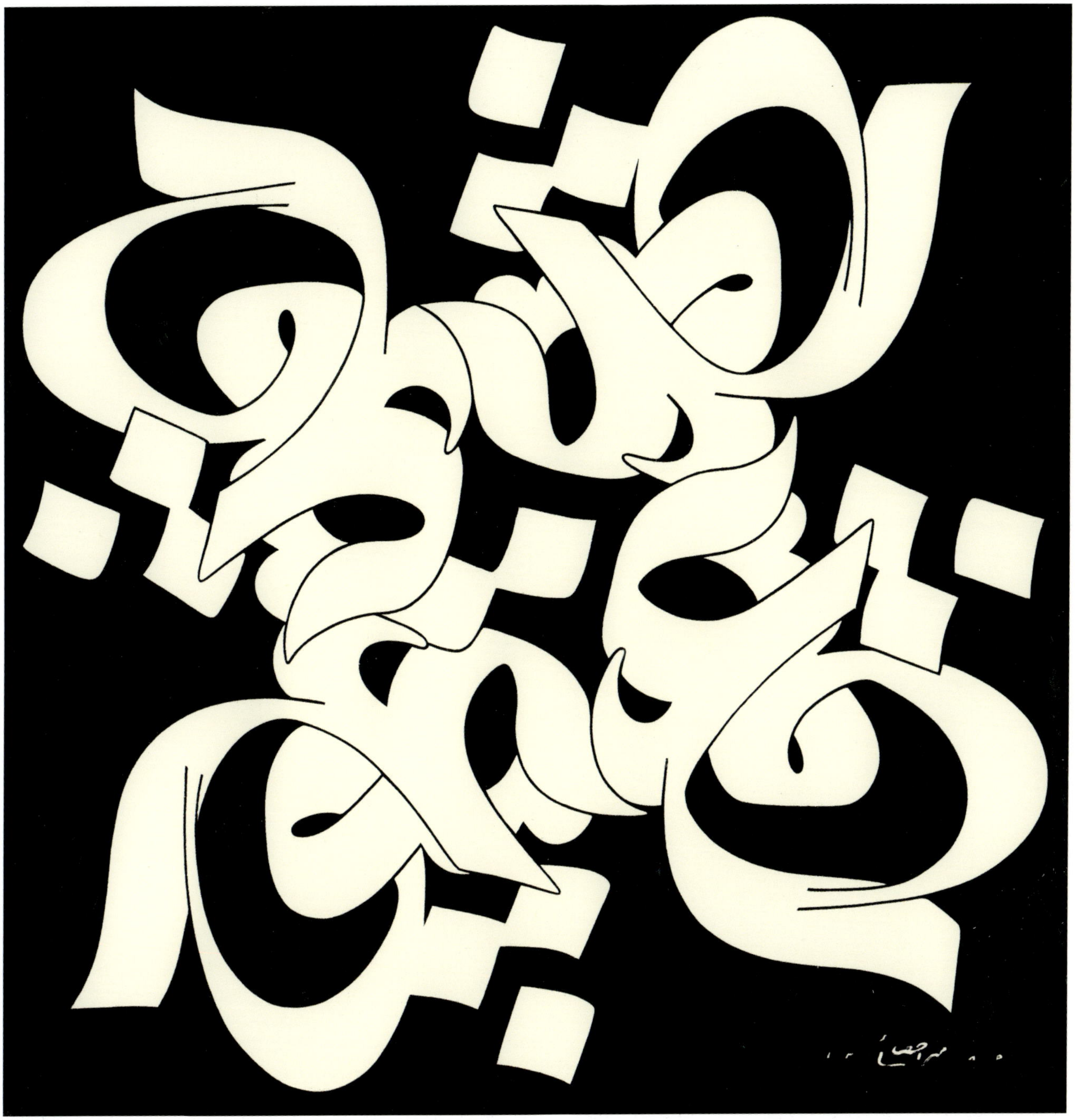

125

Chafic Abboud

1926-2004

UNTITLED

signed and dated *61*; signed and dated *1961* on the reverse
oil on canvas
195 BY 300CM.; 76¾ BY 118⅛IN.

150,000-200,000 US$
550,000-730,000 QAR

PROVENANCE
Galerie Cazenave, Paris
Acquired directly from the above by the present owner

EXHIBITED
Paris, Musée d'Art Moderne de la Ville, 2ème *Biennale de Paris*, 1961

This exceptionally large and complex composition is considered as one of Chafic Abboud's masterpieces of the early 1960s. The painting, two meters high and three meters wide, is the largest single panel canvas the artist created between the beginning of 1960 and the end of 1977. Its intricate brightness is an exquisite example of the artist's innovative expression of form and place through a complex—yet harmonious use of colour.

In 1947, having graduated from the Académie Libanaise des Beaux Arts, Abboud moved to Paris, where he quickly became a part of the city's vibrant art scene. Throughout Europe, the end of World War II had precipitated a move towards Abstract Expressionism that would slowly draw a young Abboud away from the figurative art on which his education was firmly rooted. Working under André Lhote and Fernand Léger at the École Nationale Supérieure des Beaux Arts, the artist adopted the particularly lively abstraction that now distinguishes his technique. As wonderfully put forth by the leading French art critic Patrick Waldberg, "it might be said in a rather drastic way, that [Abboud] does not perceive reality but that he dives into it, wallows in it, merges with it, to such an extent that, when he brings it back to us filtered through his desire, it has simultaneously been dissolved and reconstituted according to harmonic laws inside which... perfumes, colours and sounds answer each other" (Patrick Waldberg in: *Shafic Abboud*, Claude Lemand, (Ed.), Paris, pp. 349-350).

Despite his imminent embrace of abstraction, Abboud did not turn away from his Lebanese roots. Born in the small village of Bikfaya, during a time when the coast of central Lebanon was still considered the 'Riviera' of the Middle East, his childhood and adolescence, blissfully spent between bustling Beirut winters and the summer tranquillity of Mount Lebanon, would have a long-lasting influence on the artist's style. Indeed "despite [his] continuous absence from Lebanon... [memories of Beirut] fused into his abstract canvases through a poetic harmony of colours" (Frieda Howling, *Art in Lebanon 1930-1975*, 2005, p. 110). The present lot, beautifully expressive, is a superlative affirmation of this trend.

Untitled is a true masterpiece of chromatism and an unmistakable product of the artist's original interpretation of the trend towards abstraction in Post War 20th Century Art. The interlacing treatment of blues, purples and lilacs come together to draw the viewer into an unfathomable, deeply lyrical composition. The warm shades of yellow, green, and white soften the painting, creating an exceptional vividness which allows the materialization of a puzzling narrative

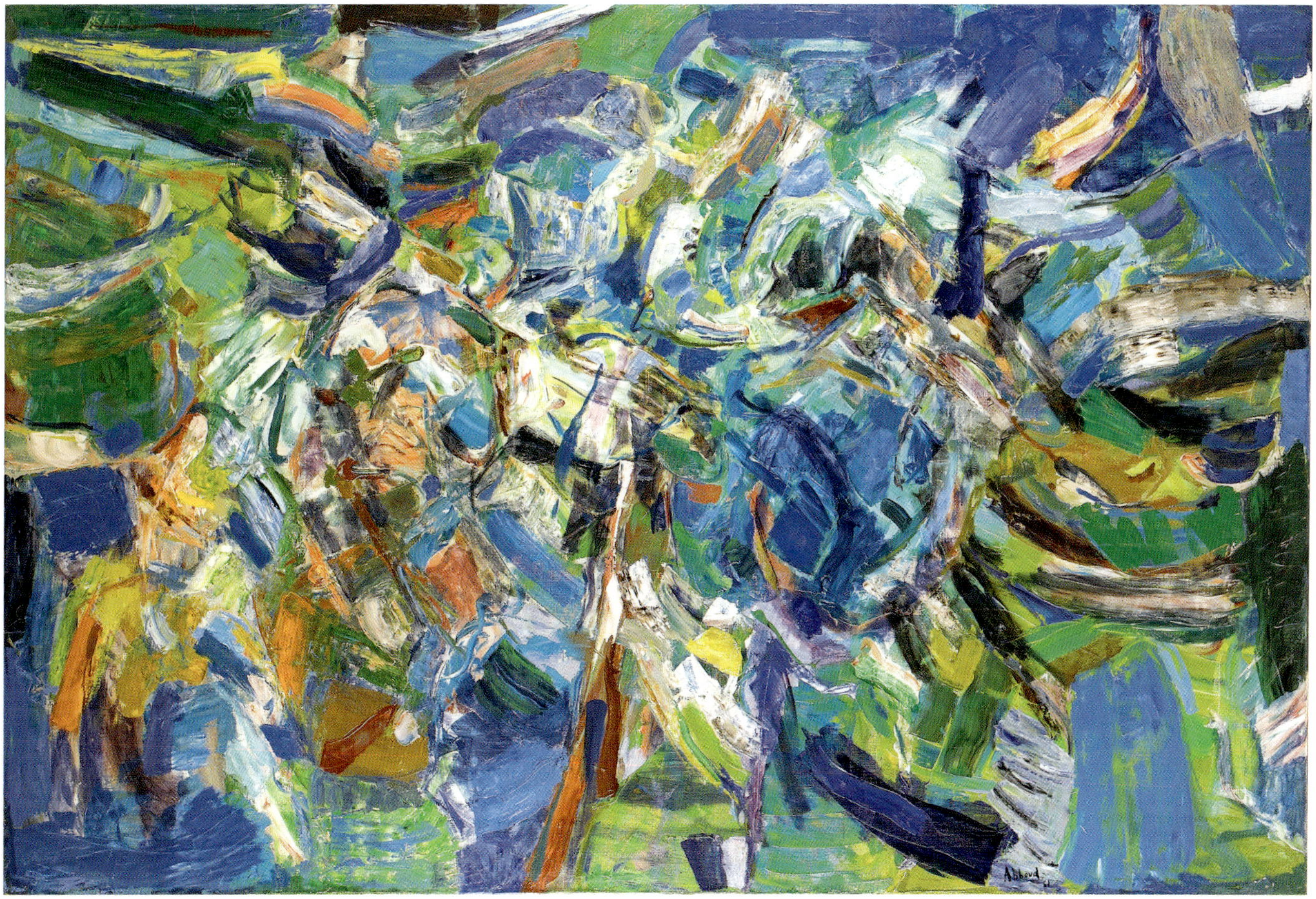

PROPERTY FROM A FRENCH PRIVATE COLLECTOR

126

Abdallah Benanteur

b. 1931

LES NOSTALGIQUES NO.4

signed twice; signed, titled and dated *2000* twice on the reverse
oil on canvas, in two parts
OVERALL: 200 BY 240CM.; 78¾ BY 94½IN.

80,000-120,000 US$
292,000-437,000 QAR

PROVENANCE
Acquired directly from the artist by the present owner

LITERATURE
Claude Lemand, Ed., *Benanteur, Paintings*, 2002, pp. 202-203, illustrated in colour

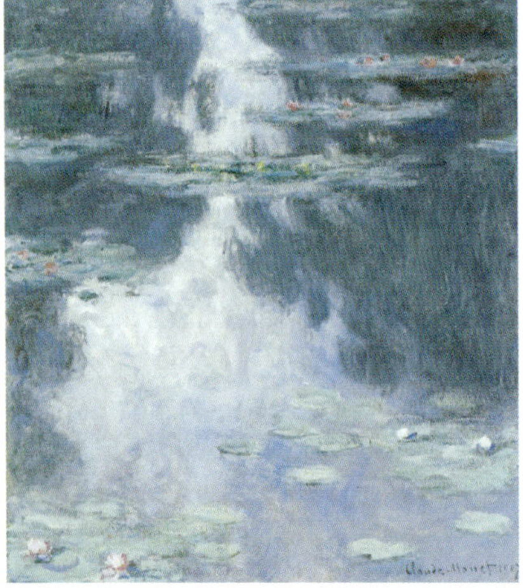

CLAUDE MONET, *NYMPHÉAS*, 1907. THE MUSEUM OF FINE ARTS, HOUSTON, GIFT OF MRS. HARRY C. HANSZEN

"Benanteur's paintings have formal and sensitive beauty, with a strong visual impact, being neither figurative, insofar as the image could replace a photographic object, nor abstract , because they are always rooted within the elements of a deeply observed and felt nature [...] Lyrical landscapes, in which the imaginary struggles with deeply buried memories. A floating world, close to that of Chinese painting, in which top and bottom are interchangeable within a limitless space."

Marc Hérissé, *Prologue* in Galerie Claude Lemand, Ed., *Benanteur, Volume 1, Paintings*, Paris 2002, p. 7

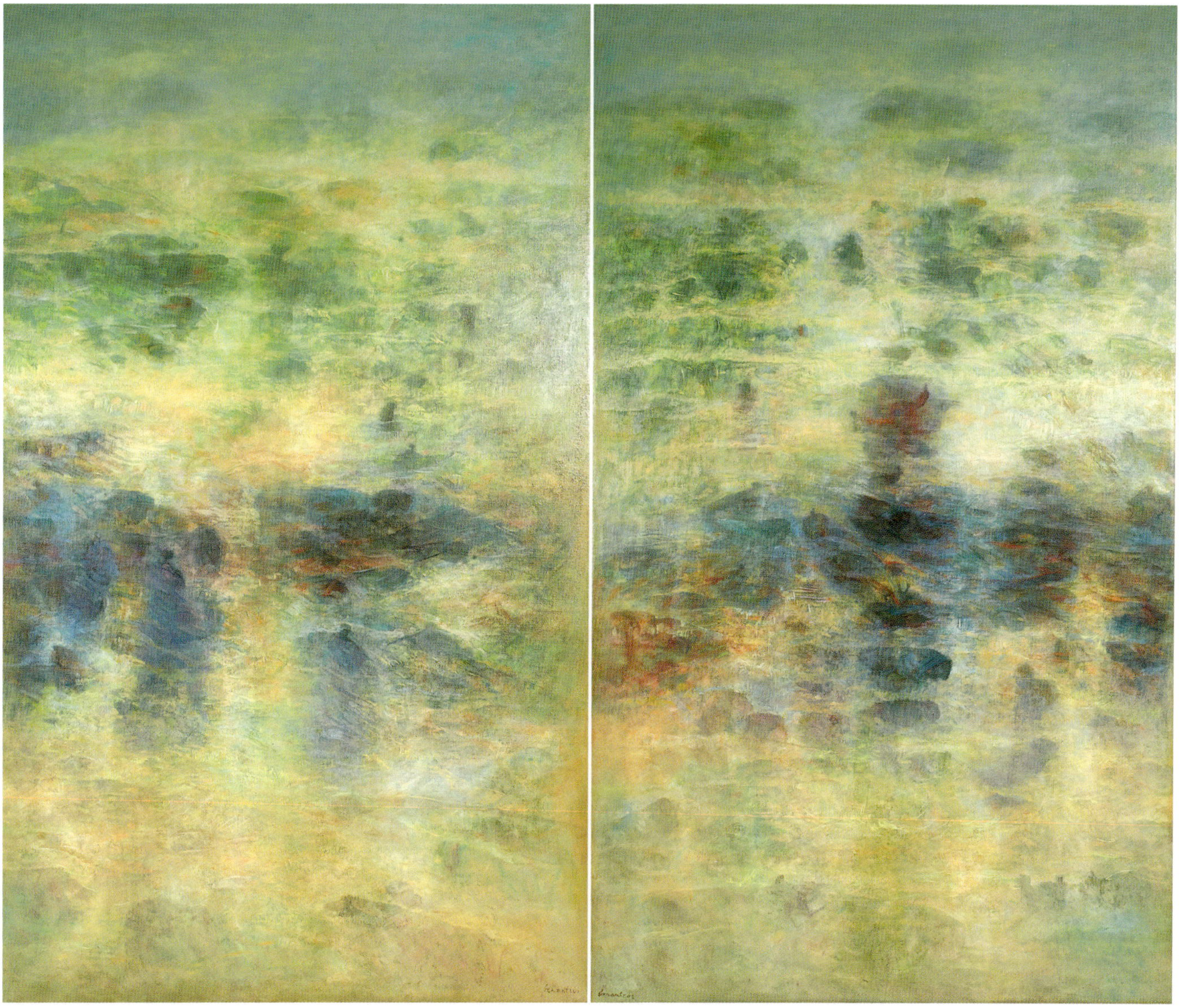

PROPERTY FROM A FRENCH PRIVATE COLLECTOR

127

Chafic Abboud

1926-2004

A LA BELLE POLONAISE

signed, dated *1978* and titled on the reverse
oil on canvas
100 BY 81CM.; 39⅜ BY 31⅞IN.

100,000-150,000 US$
364,000-550,000 QAR

PROVENANCE
Acquired directly from the artist by the present owner

LITERATURE
Claude Lemand, Ed., *Shafic Abboud*, 2006, p. 141, illustrated in colour

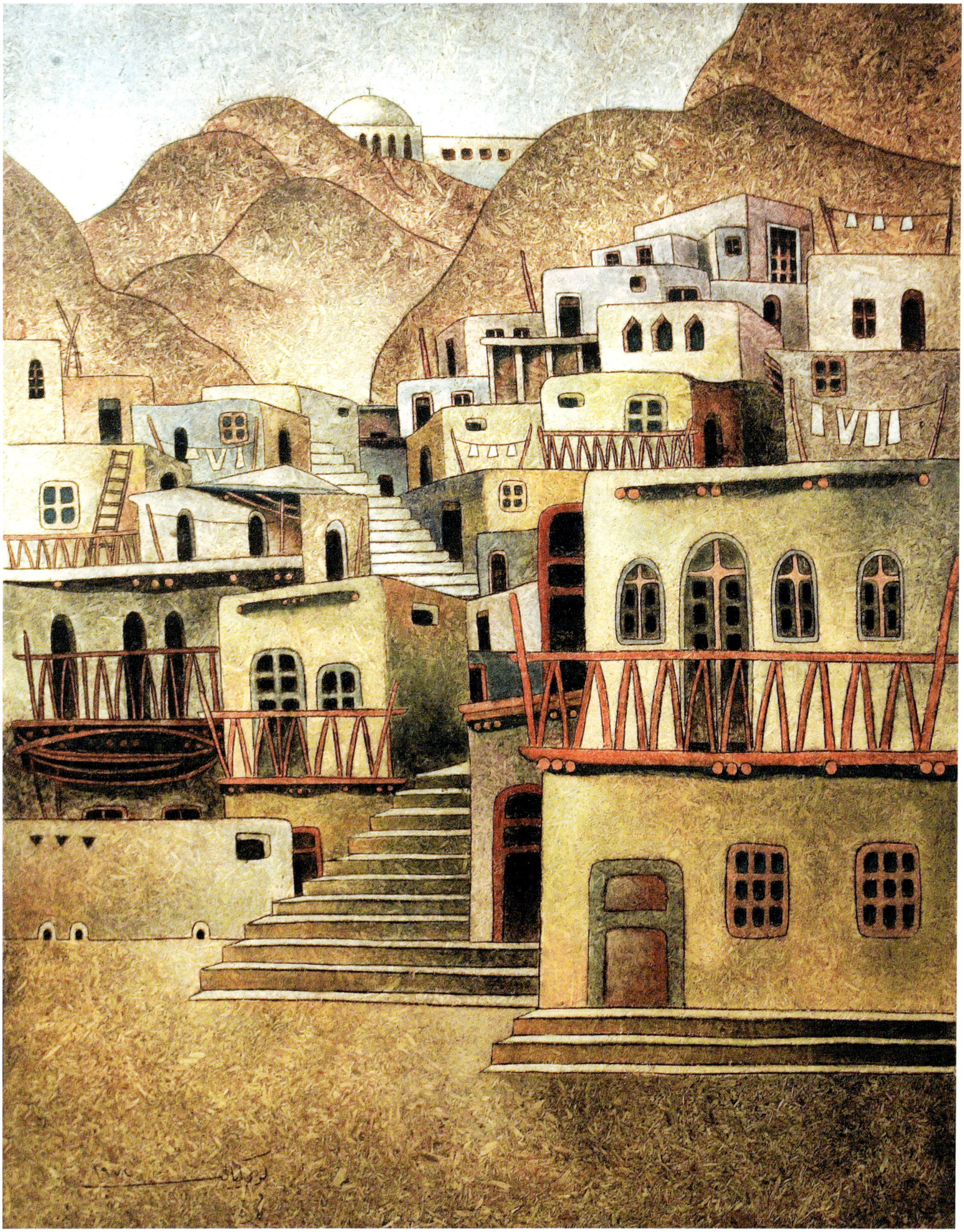

129

Louai Kayyali

1934-1978

UNTITLED (WAITER)

signed and dated *1974* in Arabic
oil on masonite
95 BY 75CM.; 37⅜ BY 29½IN.

70,000-100,000 US$
255,000-364,000 QAR

PROVENANCE
Acquired directly from the artist by the present owner in the 1980's

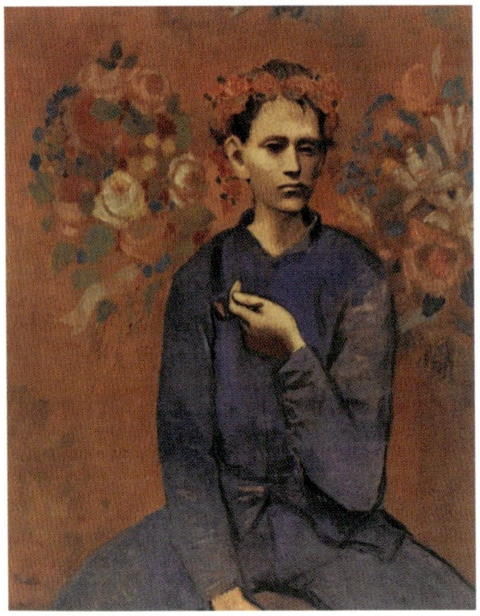

PABLO PICASSO, *BOY WITH A PIPE*, 1905, PRIVATE COLLECTION.
© SUCCESSION PICASSO/DACS 2009

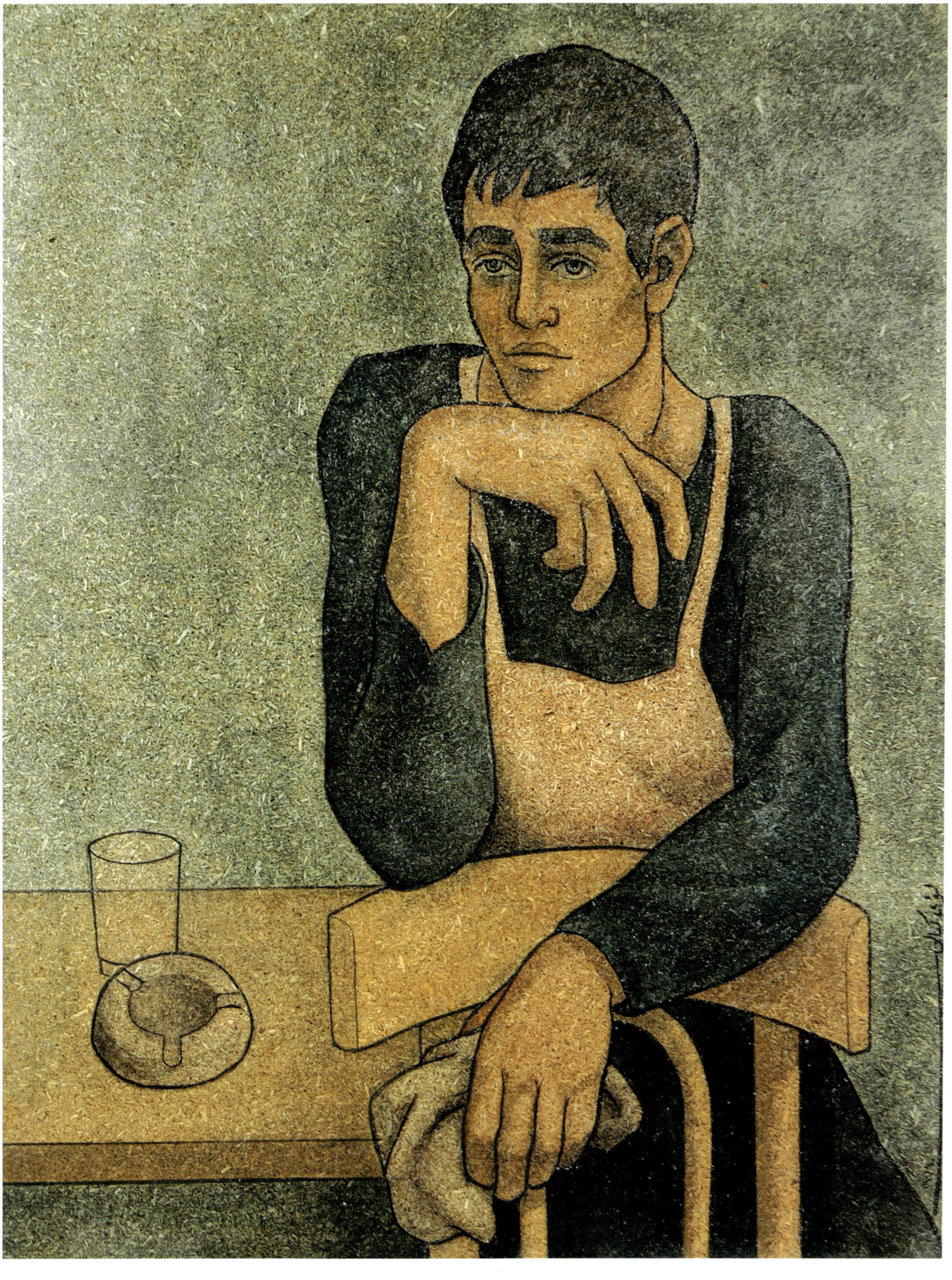

130

Paul Guiragossian

1926-1994

AL-HIJRA (MIGRATION)

signed
oil on canvas
60.5 BY 120CM.; 23¾ BY 47¼IN.

Executed *circa* 1962.

70,000-100,000 US$
255,000-364,000 QAR

Paul Guiragossian's life and art has been heavily impacted by the dislocation and migration of his family. Born in Jerusalem to survivors of the Armenian genocide, Guiragoissian and his family left for Lebanon in the late 1940s, initially settling down at a refugee camp in Bourj Hammoud. Consequently, in paintings such as the present work, the artist actively draws on his heritage and migratory experience for inspiration. These, along with the artist's unique perception of the strength of human cohesion, come together wonderfully to create the unusual and intricate narrative of *Al-Hijra*.

Throughout his artistic career, Guiragossian worked towards establishing a particular style that would bring out the essence of his subject matter. This process led him to take a step away from the figurative protagonists of his early works, reducing them to simple albeit powerful elements in a manner that could effectively be described as essentialist. *Al-Hijra* captures this effort to portray the essence, providing critical insight of the artist's transition towards the strong vertical minimalism that would distinguish his later paintings.

As suggested by the title, *Al Hijra* depicts a group of people enduring the pain and suffering of being forced into flight. With traces of his representational past, Guiragossian implies movement by presenting the viewer with the subtle yet unmistakable forms of a donkey and a cart. However, the emotion that the artist wants to allude to—that mixture of despair and surrender which an exodus connotes—is not rendered by recognizable shapes, but rather infused into the canvas by the curving mass of seemingly bleak bodies disappearing into the horizon.

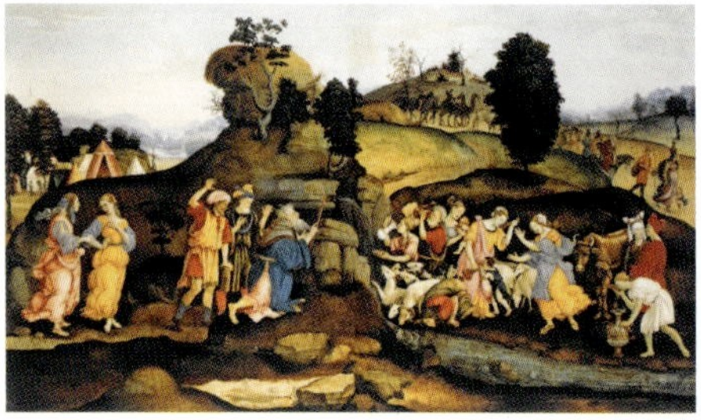

FILIPPINO LIPPI AND THE MASTER OF MEMPHIS, *MOSES BRINGS FORTH WATER OUT OF THE ROCK*, CIRCA 1500. THE NATIONAL GALLERY, LONDON.

Through a most fascinating technique, Guiragossian skillfully contrasts the darker vertical brushstrokes that represent the human and animal figures against the brighter tones of the horizontal foreground and the flat sky. This colour scheme, saturated with the oppressive intensity of an unforgiving terracotta orange, allows Guiragossian to encapsulate the dejected crowd, insinuating that in distress, one's instinctive fight for survival brings them so close together that an individual becomes almost unrecognizable within the mass. The distinctive minimal elements—those solitary vertical souls that he projects onto his work—are clustered into a collective body, finding protection and security in the midst of their isolation... the apparent perpetual pain of living a constant exodus.

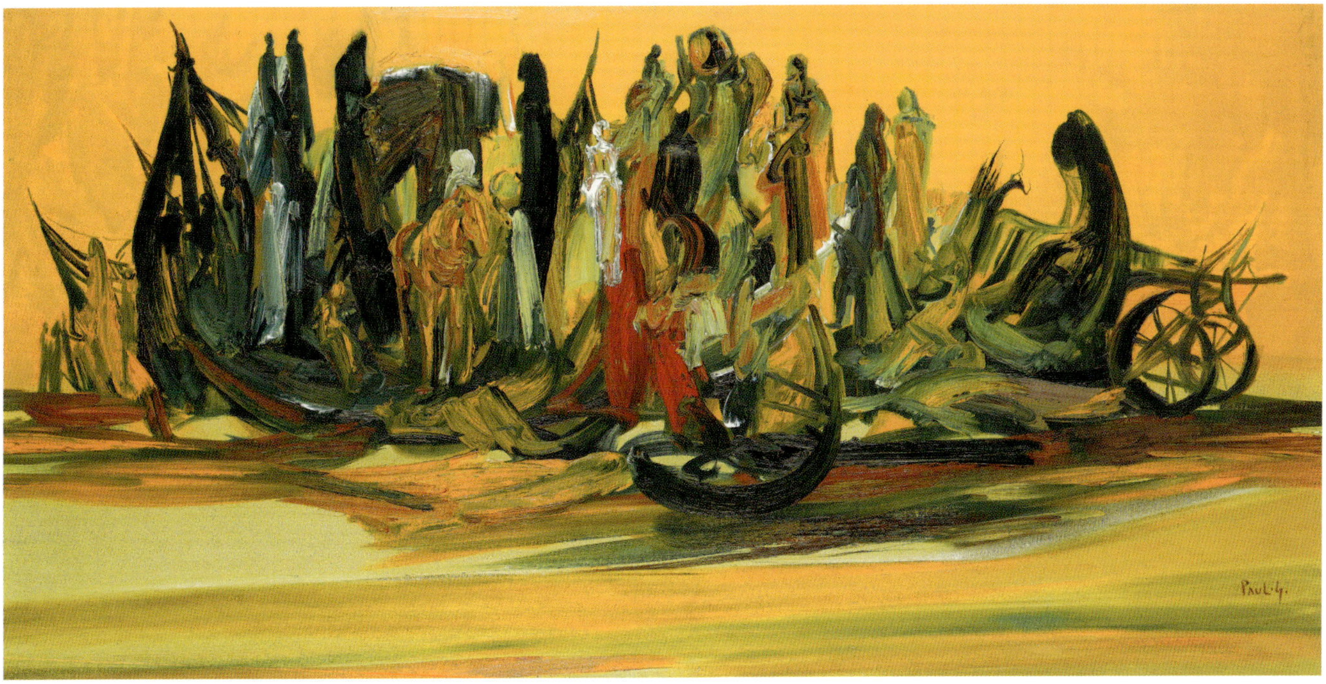

131

Georges Hanna Sabbagh

1877 - 1951

BANYAN TREE

signed and dated *1940*
oil on canvas
115 BY 135CM.; 45¼ BY 53⅛IN.

80,000-120,000 US$
292,000-437,000 QAR

PROVENANCE

Private Collection, Egypt (acquired directly from the artist in 1950's)
Acquired directly from the above by the present owner

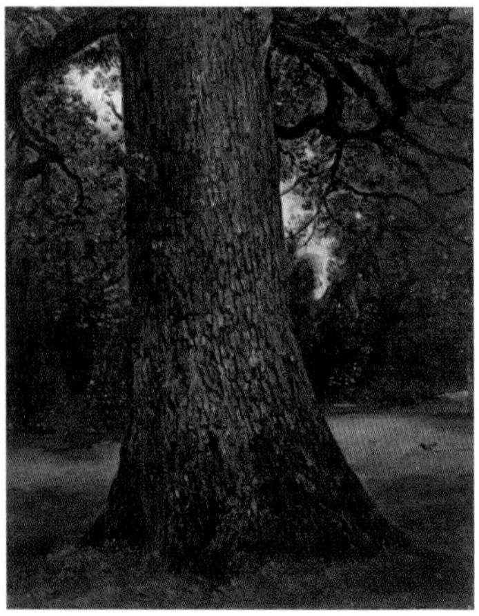

JOHN CONSTABLE, *STUDY OF THE TRUNK OF AN ELM TREE*, CIRCA 1821. VICTORIA AND ALBERT MUSEUM, LONDON, GIFT OF MISS ISABEL CONSTABLE

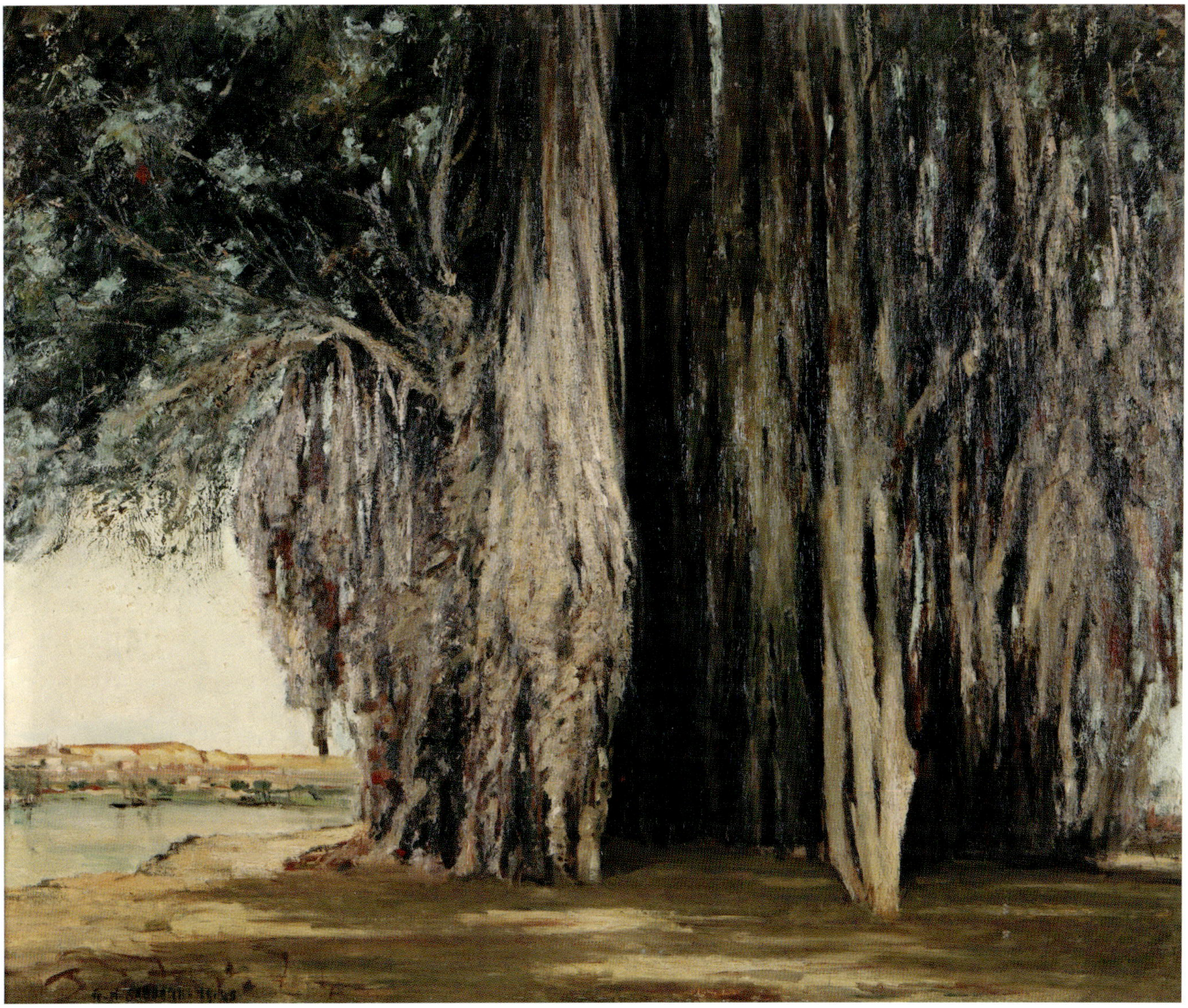

132

Hossein Zenderoudi

b. 1937

UNTITLED

signed and dated *85*
oil, felt-tip pen, acrylic and silver leaf on canvas
75 BY 100CM.; 29½ BY 39¾IN.

40,000-60,000 US$
146,000-219,000 QAR

PROVENANCE
Private Collection, New York (acquired directly from the artist)
Private Collection, Milan
Acquired directly from the above by the present owner

Hossein Zenderoudi is one of the founding fathers of Iranian neo-traditionalism and undoubtedly one of its most talented protagonists. Captivated and inspired by the overt, spiritual imagery of urban, Islamic landscapes, Zenderoudi has extracted the salient elements of Islam's popular religious aesthetic and given it stylistic uniformity, synthesising centuries long sacred concepts into a mature artistic language.

Whilst famous for his deftly executed, vibrant calligraphic depictions and earlier highly symbolic talismanic imagery, *Untitled* is rare and remarkable in that it contains both of these stylistic hallmarks balanced in an ideal visual harmony.

Intricately rendered scrolling talismans, astrological charts, numeral sequences and benedictory couplets, dominate the canvas, revealing Zenderoudi's deep connection with Muslim spirituality. For centuries, Islamic scholars have held that the structure of the Holy Quran contains complex mathematical relationships that shed light on the nature of divine perfection. Giving Arabic letterforms isopsephic numeral values – by assigning numeric values to individual letters- medieval mystics formed a divine language rooted in mathematical harmony and sacred attributes. It is this language which Zenderoudi weaves effortlessly into his composition, expressing with aesthetic exuberance what was otherwise fashioned for worship and devotion.

Combined with his use of talismanic imagery, *Untitled* overlays the bold, classical calligraphic characteristic of Zenderoudi's later work on the four corners of the composition with the use of Persian words 'thought' (Goman), 'life' (Jaal), 'world' (Glam) and 'appearance' (Jamal). All of which are carriers of strong Sufi concepts, namely those that implore the soul to pierce through the transient appearance of the material world and reach a meditative unity with the divine.

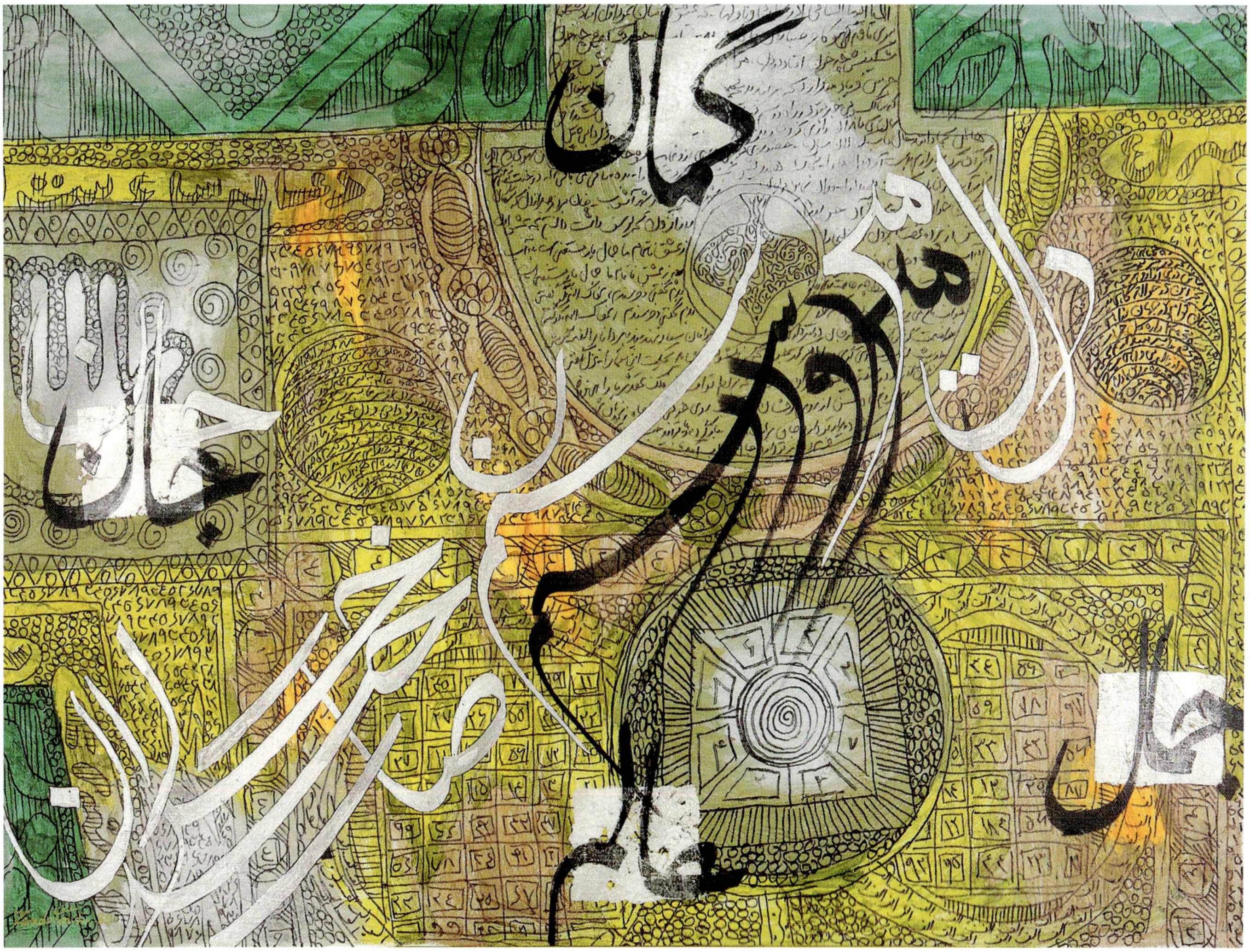
گمان
جمال

133

Shirin Neshat

b. 1957

ON GUARD

signed, titled, dated *1997* and numbered *3/3* on the reverse
ink on gelatin silver print
101 BY 150CM.; 39¾ BY 59⅛IN.

80,000-120,000 US$
292,000-437,000 QAR

PROVENANCE
Annina Nosei Gallery, New York
Cotthem Gallery, Brussels
Acquired directly from the above by the present owner

"I see my work as a visual discourse on the subjects of feminism and contemporary Islam – a discourse that puts certain myths and realities to the test, claiming that they are far more complex than most of us have imagined."

Shirin Neshat cited in: Exhibition Catalogue, Vienna, Kunsthalle Wien, *Shirin Neshat*, 2000, p. 13

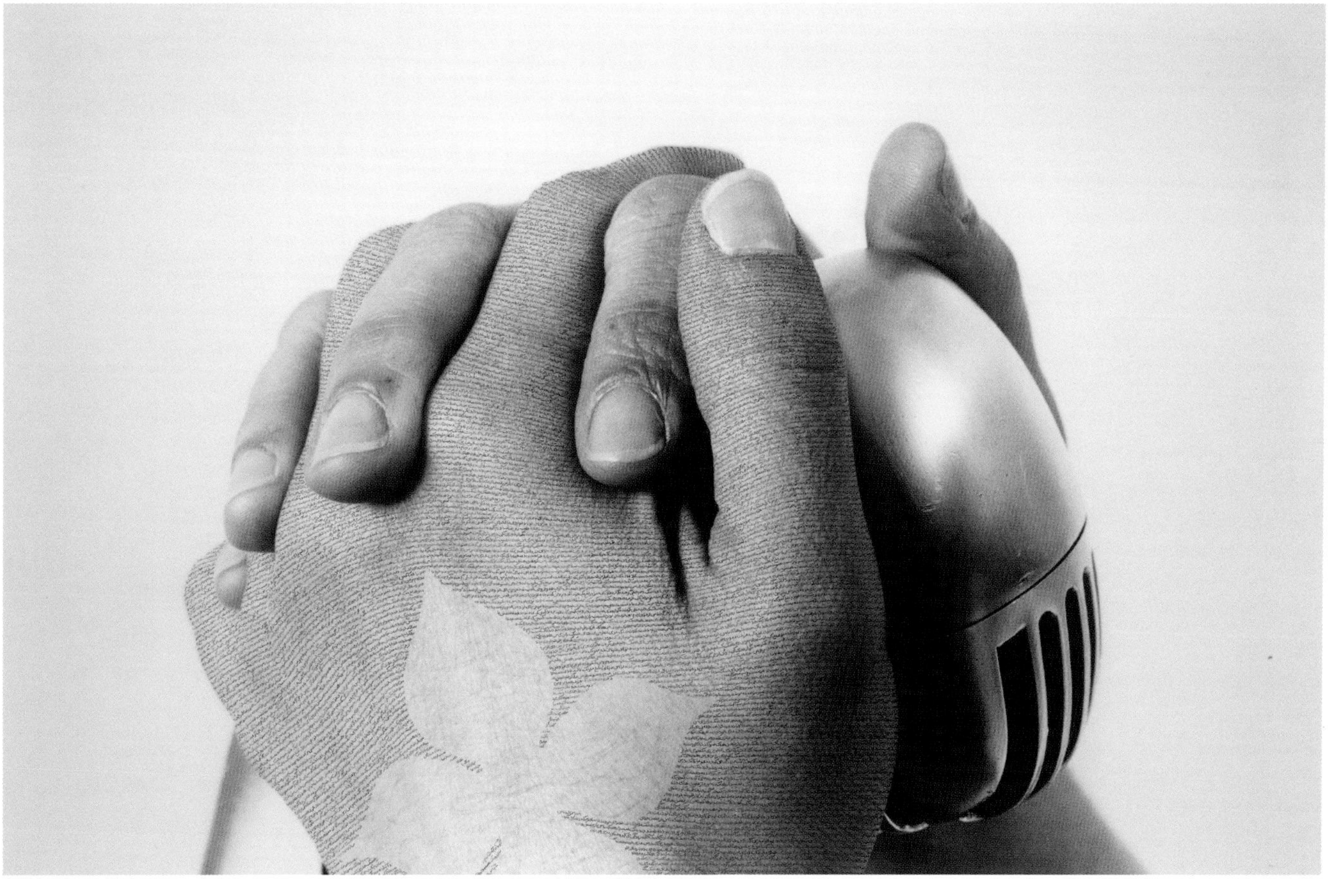

Celebrated for her investigations into the social, cultural and religious codes of contemporary Muslim society, Shirin Neshat is an Iranian artist who lives and works in New York. Arguably the most well known and influential Persian artist within the Western artistic sphere, Neshat's unique contribution to Contemporary artistic practice was recognized in 1999 when she won the International Award of the XLVIII Venice Bienniale. Her oeuvre crosses boundaries of nationality, culture, and artistic medium, addressing the collision of tradition and modernity in the East and West and the concurrent social, political and psychological dimensions of women's experience in contemporary Islamic societies. Nowhere is this complex marriage of conflicting forces more profoundly explored than in her iconic *Women of Allah series* (1994-1997) in which photographic portrait images of Muslim women are overlaid by enchanting and intricate arabesques of Persian calligraphy.

The present lot, *On Guard*, is one of the most technically accomplished and poetic images from this pre-eminent body of works. Focusing upon the hands of an unseen woman clasped around a microphone, its soft contours and grisaille tones light up as Farsi motifs and script spread over the image. As the icon absorbs the word, the skin becomes an ambiguous book in which the viewer's interpretations are projected, absorbed and reflected. The rich interplay of textures between the overlaid calligraphic swirls and the photographic background prompts a range of interpretations which reflect the complex intellectual and religious forces shaping the identity of Muslim women throughout the world.

Although Neshat actively rejects stereotypical or cliched representations of Islam in her work, her artistic objectives are not explicitly polemical. Rather, her work provides an expression of her own experiences that began with her birth in 1957 to an upper middle-class westernized Iranian family whose household adored the Shah of Iran and his ideologies of modernization. "He fantasized about the west," states Neshat about her father, "romanticized the west, and slowly rejected all of his own values; both my parents did. What happened, I think, was that their identity slowly dissolved, they exchanged it for comfort. It served their class." As a part of Neshat's own "Westernization" she was enrolled in a Catholic boarding school in Tehran - an environment she found cold and hostile in comparison to that of her caring family. Neshat's father encouraged his daughters to "be an individual, to take risks, to learn, to see the world." Through this came an exposure to Western ideologies and a form of western feminism. Keen to further her own education, shortly before the Iranian Revolution began, Neshat left Iran to study art in Los Angeles and she eventually enrolled in UC Berkeley. After graduate school, she moved to New York where she worked for an organization called Storefront Art and Architecture - a multidisciplinary, non-profit organization that exposed her to many different ideologies and concepts that would later become integral to her work as an artist.

In 1990, she returned home to Iran and found the country transformed by the political restructuring of the revolution. Her father, who had previously been financially secure and about to retire, was left without benefits and a meager salary. Iran's society had been rebuilt as a traditional Islamic nation and her family was no longer able to enjoy the comfortable, liberal life to which they had grown accustomed. As a way of coping with the discrepancy between the culture that she returned home to and that of the pre-revolution Iran in which she was raised, she began her first mature body of work, the *Women of Allah*, of which the present work is an outstanding example . Symbolic of her personal grief, anxiety and the pain of separation from her home country, these works engage in an inquiring but ultimately humanistic investigation into the conflicted nature of contemporary identity in an increasingly globalized world.

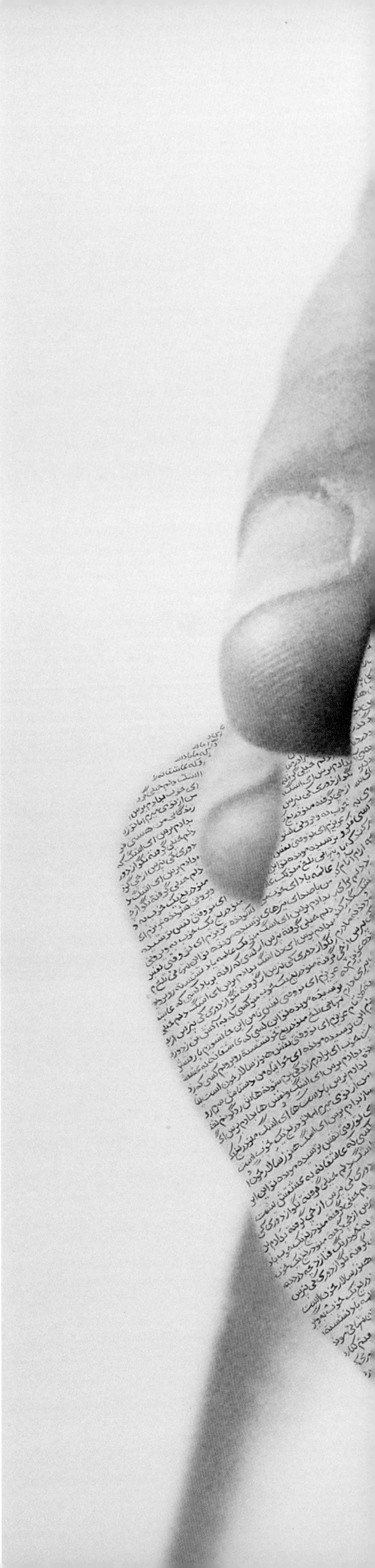

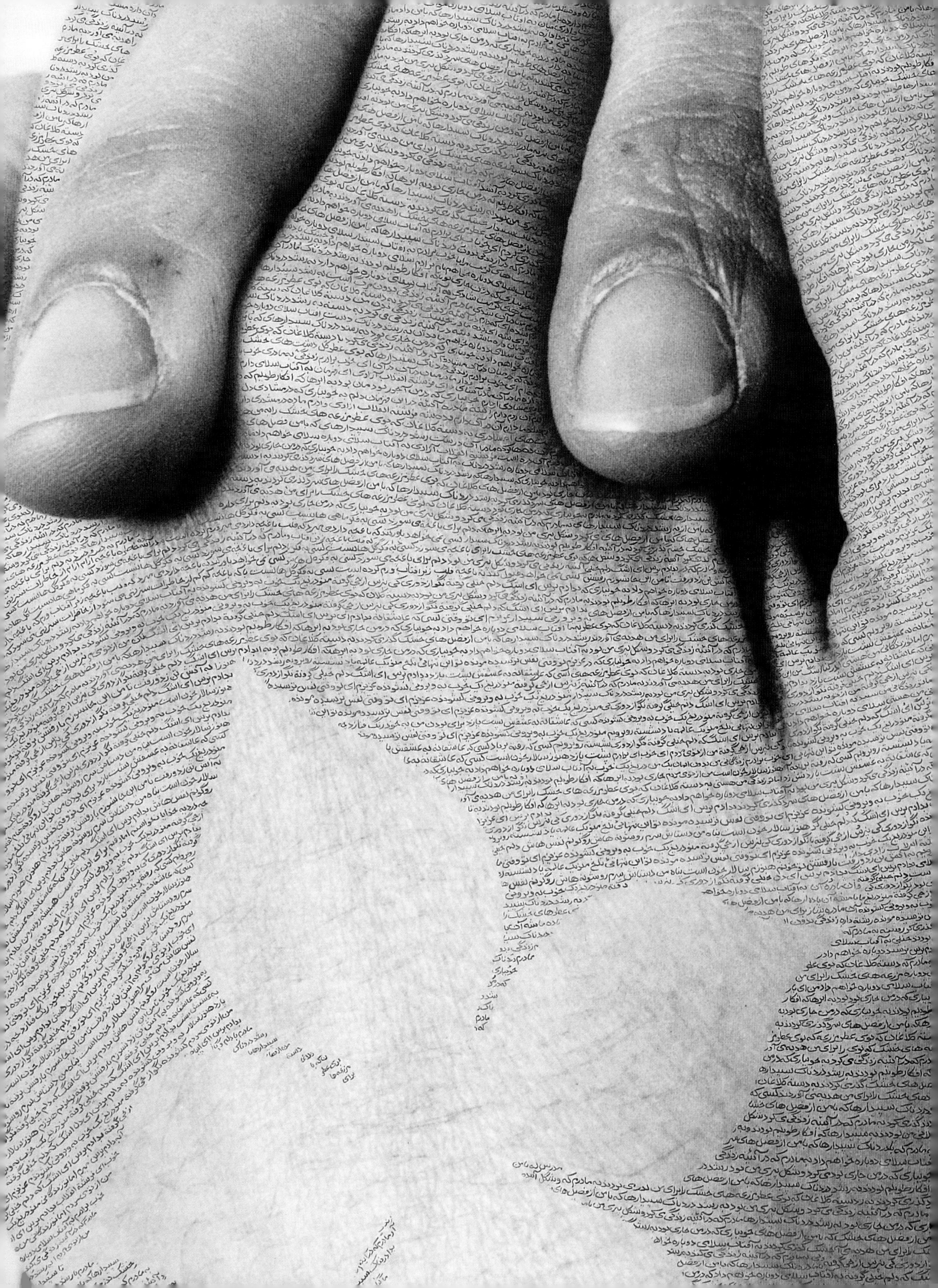

134

Hossein Zenderoudi

b. 1937

LALM + LALM

signed and dated *70*; signed, titled and dated *1970* on the reverse
oil on canvas
130 BY 97CM.; 51⅛ BY 38¼IN.

70,000-100,000 US$
255,000-364,000 QAR

PROVENANCE
Collection Michel Tapié de Céleyran, Paris (acquired directly from the artist in 1970)
Acquired directly from the above by the present owner in 1984

EXHIBITED
Teheran, Iran America Society, *Hossein Zenderoudi, A Retrospective*, 1970, no. 16, illustrated in colour

"His abstract and skillful black and white compositions, owing to their plastic characteristics, lose their original meanings. Signs in a nervous graphism, such as commas, bows, and interlaces and interwoven lines are patterned orderly or expand like stormy sea waves."

Genevieve Breerette cited in: Ed., Ruyin Pakbaz and Yaghoub Emdadian, *Hossein Zenderoudi, Pioneers of Iranian Modern art*, Tehran 2001, p. 39

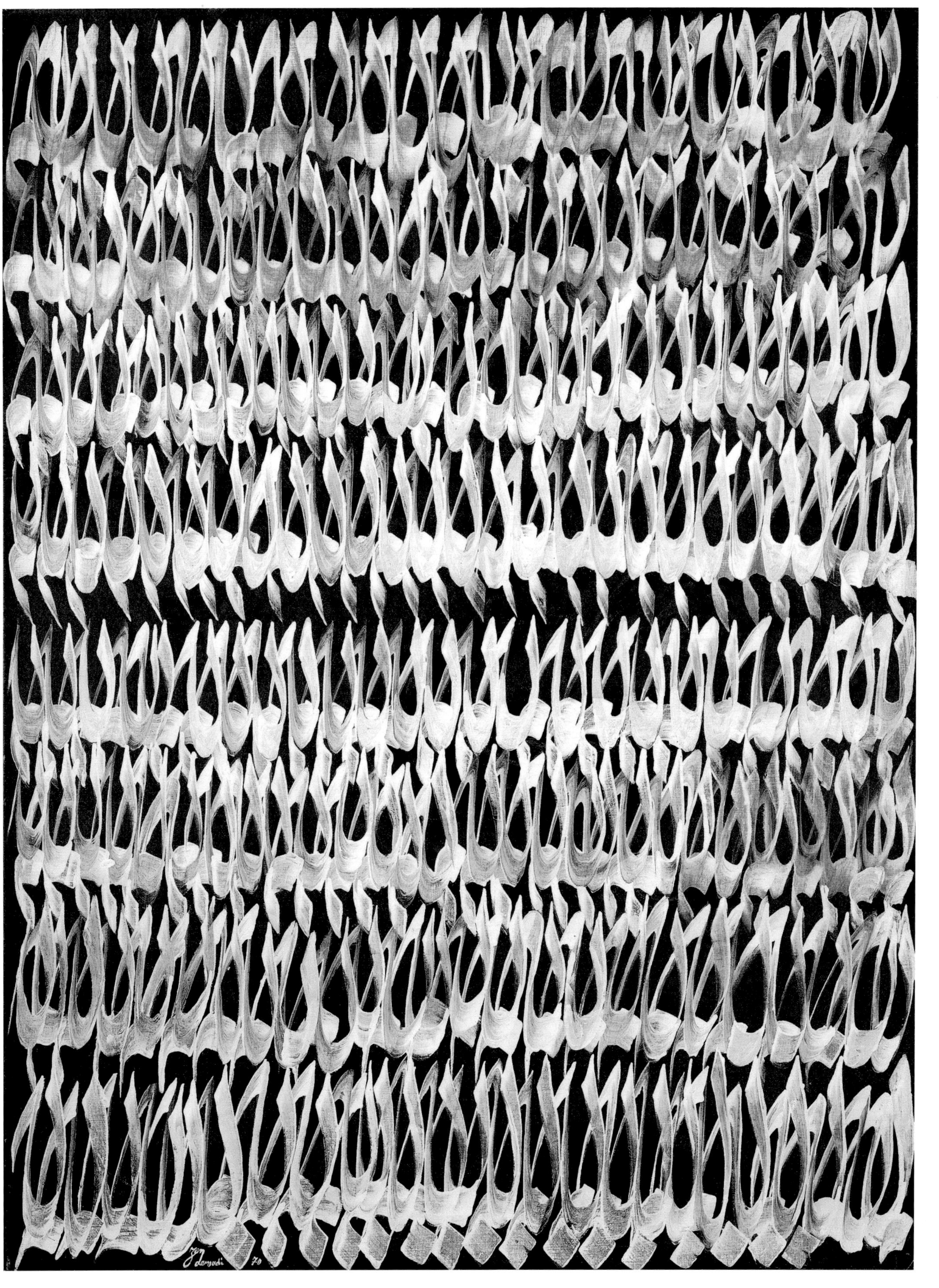

135

Mona Hatoum

b. 1952

DOORMAT II

stainless steel, nickel plated pins, canvas and glue

3 BY 75.5 BY 42CM.; 1¼ BY 29¾ BY 16½IN.

Executed in 2000-2001, this work is number 2 from an edition of 3.

80,000-120,000 US$

292,000-437,000 QAR

PROVENANCE

White Cube, London,

Sale: Christie's, London, *Contemporary Art*, 1 July 2008, Lot 315

Acquired directly from the above by the present owner

LITERATURE

Michael Archer, Guy Brett & Catherine de Zegher, Ed., *Mona Hatoum*, London 1997, p. 14, illustration of another example in colour

Exhibition Catalogue, London, Tate Britain, *Mona Hatoum: The Entire as a Foreign Land*, 2000, p. 16, illustration of another example in colour

Exhibition Catalogue, Santiago de Compostela, Centro de Arte de Salamanca; Centro Galego de Arte Contemporánea, *Mona Hatoum*, 2000, p. 36, illustration of another example

"An object from a distance might look like a carpet made out of lush velvet, but when you approach it you realize it's made out of stainless steel pins, which turns it into a threatening and cold object rather than an inviting one. It's not what it promises to be. So it makes you question the solidity of the ground you walk on, which is also the basis on which your attitudes and beliefs lie."

Mona Hatoum cited in: Exhibition Catalogue, Salamanca, Centro de Arte de Salamanca, Mona Hatoum, p. 123

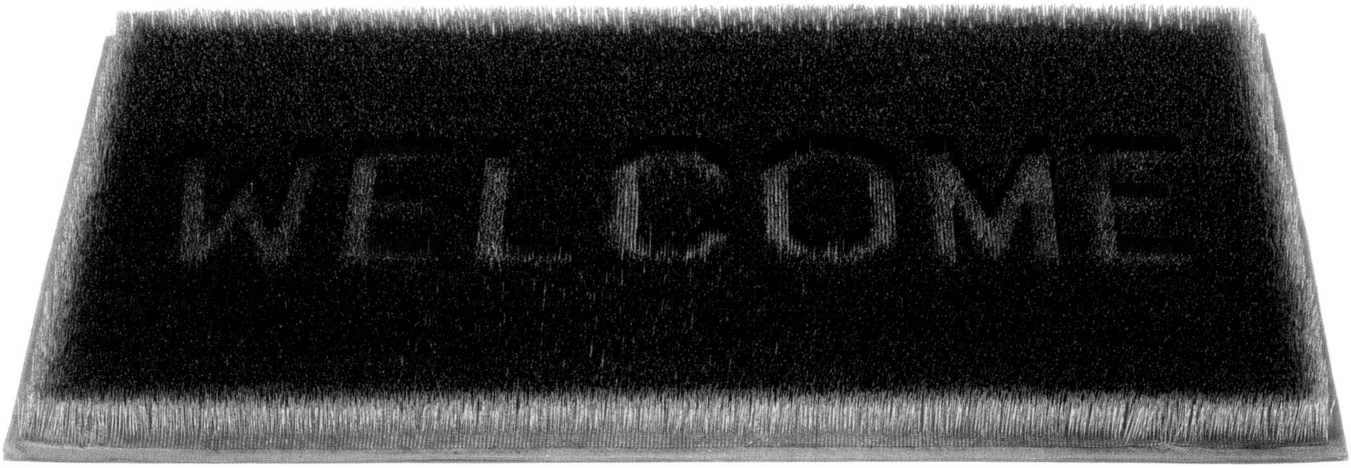
WELCOME

PROPERTY FROM THE COLLECTION OF JANE HOLZER, NEW YORK

136

Yayoi Kusama

b. 1929

INFINITY NETS

signed, titled and dated *2002* on the reverse
acrylic on canvas
80.3 BY 100CM.; 31⅝ BY 39⅜IN.

150,000-200,000 US$
550,000-730,000 QAR

PROVENANCE
Ota Fine Arts, Tokyo
Private Collection, Tokyo
Sale: Sotheby's, New York, *Contemporary Art*, 16 May 2007, Lot 349
Acquired directly from the above by the present owner

Yayoi Kusama moved to New York in 1958, attracted by the energy of the city and the avant-garde artists established there. Indeed, Mark Rothko, Barnett Newman and Jackson Pollock, among others, each explored the critical subject of space and brought to abstract art a new psychological, philosophical, and formal depth. Like them, Kusama transcends and "declares the space" in her most acclaimed series, *Inifinity Nets,* which she began during that period. Not only do the impasto weaving patterns create dots that seem to drift across the plane, but the play between the negative and positive actually suggests a deep void, the vastness of the universe beneath the painted net.

The inspiration for the series stems from her childhood, a time spent constantly envisioning proliferations of dots and nets. Kusama still seems to be subject to these haunting hallucinations, which, as she describes, return her to "the infinity of eternal time and absolute space." To Kusama, this was not an illusion, "but realty." (Yayoi Kusama, quoted in *Yayoi Kusama*, New York 2000, p. 36)

There is no doubt that these dreams affected her repetitive technique portrayed in the *Infinity Nets*. According to her 1998 "Across the Water" interview with Damien Hirst, it is actually a disease she refers to as "obessional neurosis" which she has been suffering from for over 60 years. Painting is her cure.

Constantly reproducing this same subject matter also demonstrates Kusama's focus on spreading her vision like the nets in her painting. "I must work very hard to be internationally active in an avant-garde manner" Kusama wrote in 1966 to a European gallerist. Her ambition for recognition as an innovative international artist drove her to break away from the still dominating Abstract Expressionist movement. The artist's application of pure white paint to the canvas in delicate patterns demonstrates a retort to the established gesturalism of much of the art at the time.

This 2002 passionate example of the *Infinity Nets* perfectly justifies why Yayoi Kusama is currently considered the most renowned and acclaimed post-war Japanese artist.

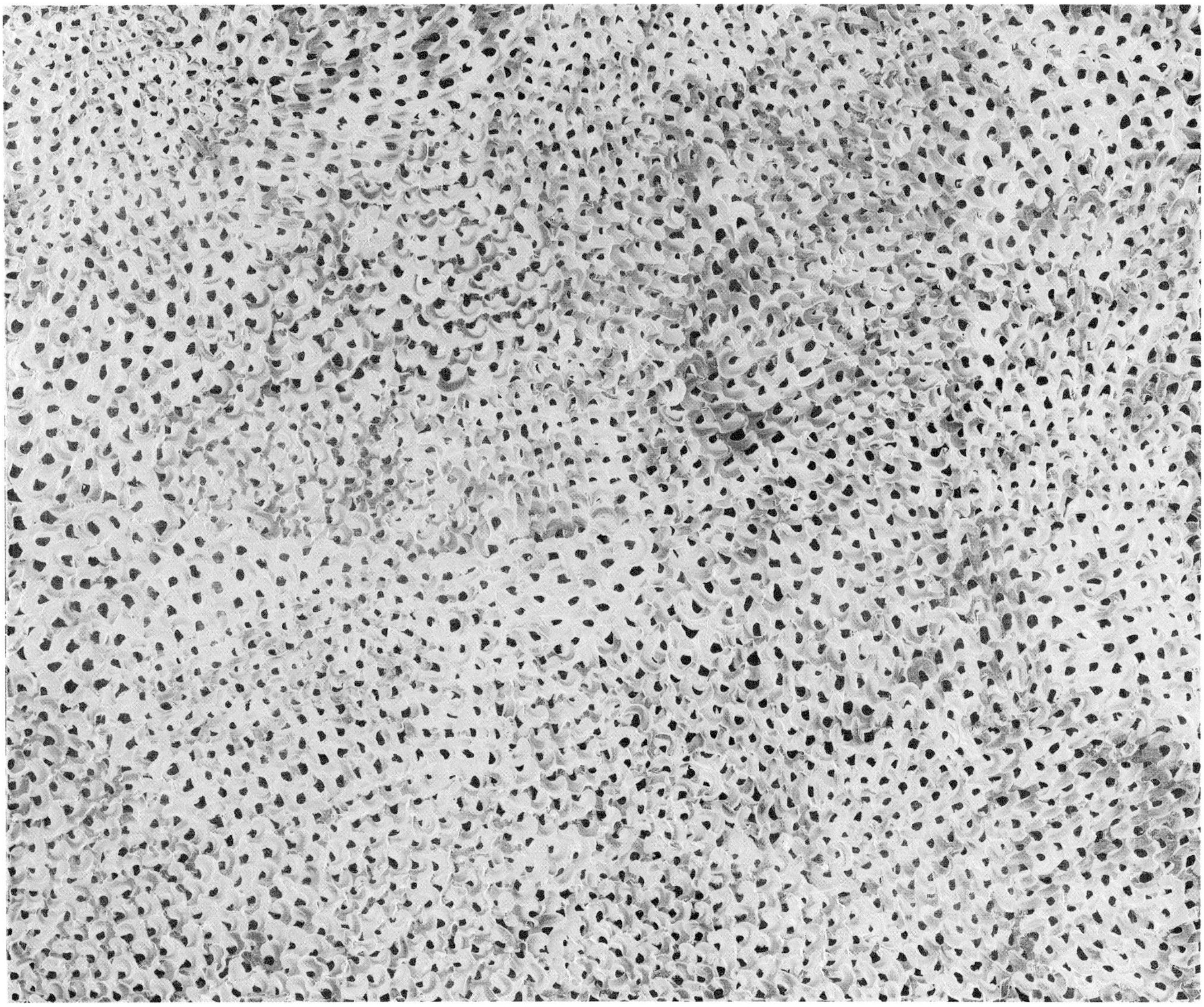

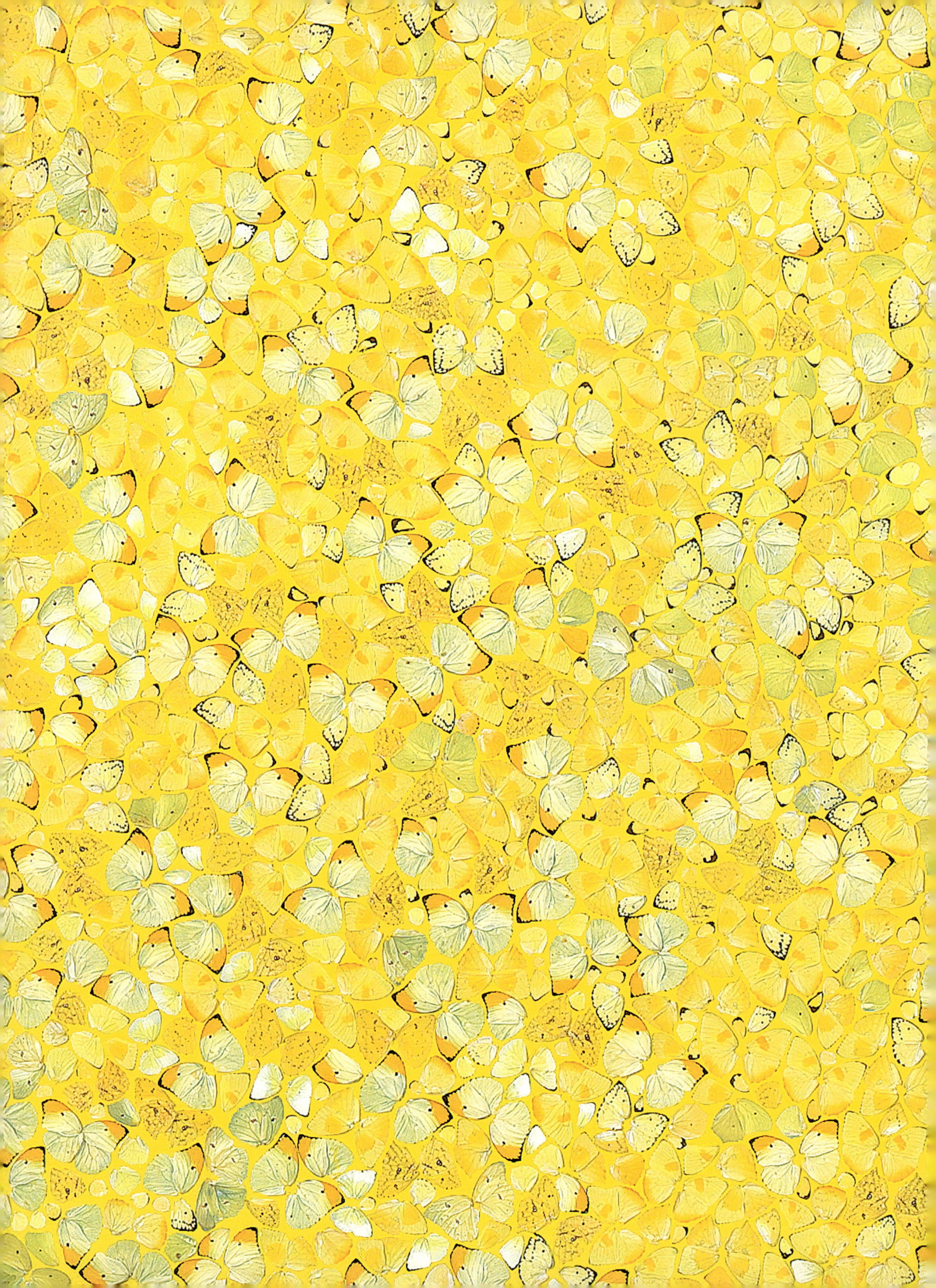

137

Damien Hirst

b. 1965

TEMPTATION

signed, titled and dated *2008* on the reverse
butterflies and household gloss on canvas
DIAMETER: 243.8CM.; 96IN.
DIAMETER INCLUDING FRAME: 261 BY 14CM.; 102¾ BY 5½IN.

800,000-1,200,000 US$
2,920,000-4,370,000 QAR

PROVENANCE
The Artist

"You have to find universal triggers, everyone's frightened of glass, everyone's frightened of sharks, everyone loves butterflies."

Damien Hirst cited in: Damien Hirst, *I want to spend the rest of my life everywhere, with everyone, one to one, always, forever, now*, London, 1997, p. 132

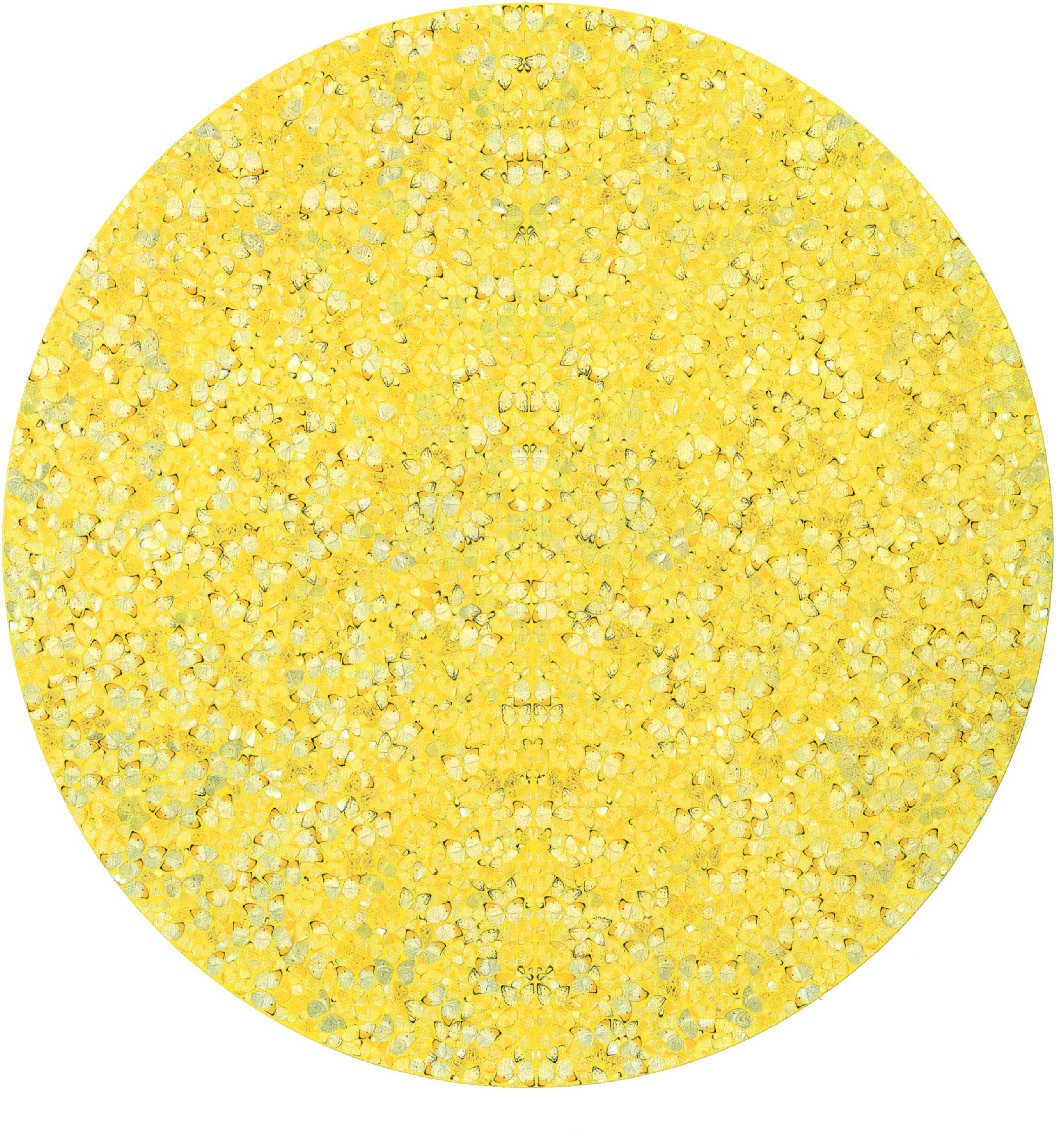

138

Andy Warhol

1928-1987

SHADOW

signed and dated *1978* on the overlap
synthetic polymer paint and silskcreen ink on canvas
198 BY 125CM.; 78 BY 49¼IN.

Executed in 1978.

600,000-800,000 US$
2,190,000-2,920,000 QAR

PROVENANCE
Thomas Ammann Fine Arts, Zurich
Private Collection, New York
Skarstedt Gallery, New York
Sale: Phillps de Pury & Company, London, *Contemporary Art*, 28 February 2008, Lot 138
Acquired directly from the above by the present owner

Shadows had long been a fascination of Andy Warhol's before he exclusively concentrated on them in a series of powerfully haunting iconic images constructed out of seemingly nothing – a series which marked the artist's foray into the world of abstraction. By this point in his career, Warhol had dissociated himself from the Pop commercial subject matter that had consumed him for much of his earlier work. This departure began with his *Oxidation* paintings and ended with his *Rorschachs* and *Camouflage* works of the 1980s. While the *Shadow* paintings were novel in their use of the shadow as the prime subject matter, much of Warhol's body of work, from his celebrity portraits to the *Death and Disaster* paintings, exhibits his continuing fascination with the shadowy underside of modern life. In the 1970's this fascination was manifested in Warhol's deliberate and mounting use of lengthening shadows until the enigmatic shadow became the sole subject in its own right.

Warhol remarked on the origin of this series, "I called them *Shadows* because they are based on the shadow of my office." Each painting represents the enigmatic silhouette of a shadow cast by a cardboard maquette leaning against the wall. Ronnie Cutrone, Warhol's assistant, had specially made these maquettes so that they would form ambiguous shapes, reiterating the shadow's ability to exist on the edge between the form and formless. Throughout his career, Warhol's art embraced the ambiguity of images, their inability to truly convey information; their limitations are his strength. With an affinity to Warhol's earlier work, the shadow is ultimately an abstract two dimensional projection of a three dimensional form. Warhol was intrigued by the shadow's dual-nature; while it is physically perceptible, it is equally ephemeral and insubstantial. For a shadow is a trick of the light, a subtle tangential implication of an object's presence. As Donna de Salvo notes of the *Shadow* paintings, "no essence is revealed, no single truth asserts itself. The experience is one of a late twentieth century landscape, everything is surface and nothing but surface." (Exhibition Catalogue, London, Tate Gallery, *Andy Warhol*, 2002, p. 51)

Shadow is filled with an abstract interplay of darkness and light that allows Warhol to cleverly balance his own sense of foreboding with his sense of humor. In the *Shadow* paintings, Warhol's painted surface is broadly handled; his energetic brushwork irregularly fills the canvas with a technique that visually mimics the brushstrokes of the Abstract Expressionists such as Franz Kline and Willem de Kooning. Warhol's desire to engage with the tenets of the Abstract Expressionist was deliberate and offers an element of parody, an element that mocks the Abstract Expressionist's lofty declarations of using abstraction as a means to the spiritual.

Despite such references, Warhol's primary pre-occupation in the creation of these works was with the creation of an enigma, drawing the viewer in and ultimately refusing all perceptual analysis so as to reveal that in reality they are nothing but a painted surface - a striking image on a pure surface. *Shadow* depicts a complex and subtle interplay with issues of representation, mainly of reality versus illusion and presence versus absence. The series presents a blatant, concretized depiction of nothingness that does not assert to be anything other than itself. Lynn Cook writes that, "Thematically, the shadow has a seminal role in the originary accounts of both painting and photography as art forms. In Warhol's variants, reduced to essentials, it assumes a paradigmatic identity, devoid of identifiable origin or source, detached from its maker or creator, it exists in and of itself, a purposefully made image of 'nothing,'" (Lynne Cooke, "Andy Warhol Shadows", see www.diachelsea.org). Chiefly dark, ostensibly abstract and intriguingly enigmatic, Warhol's *Shadows* not only form one of his most significant bodies of work, but also remain at the heart of his oeuvre.

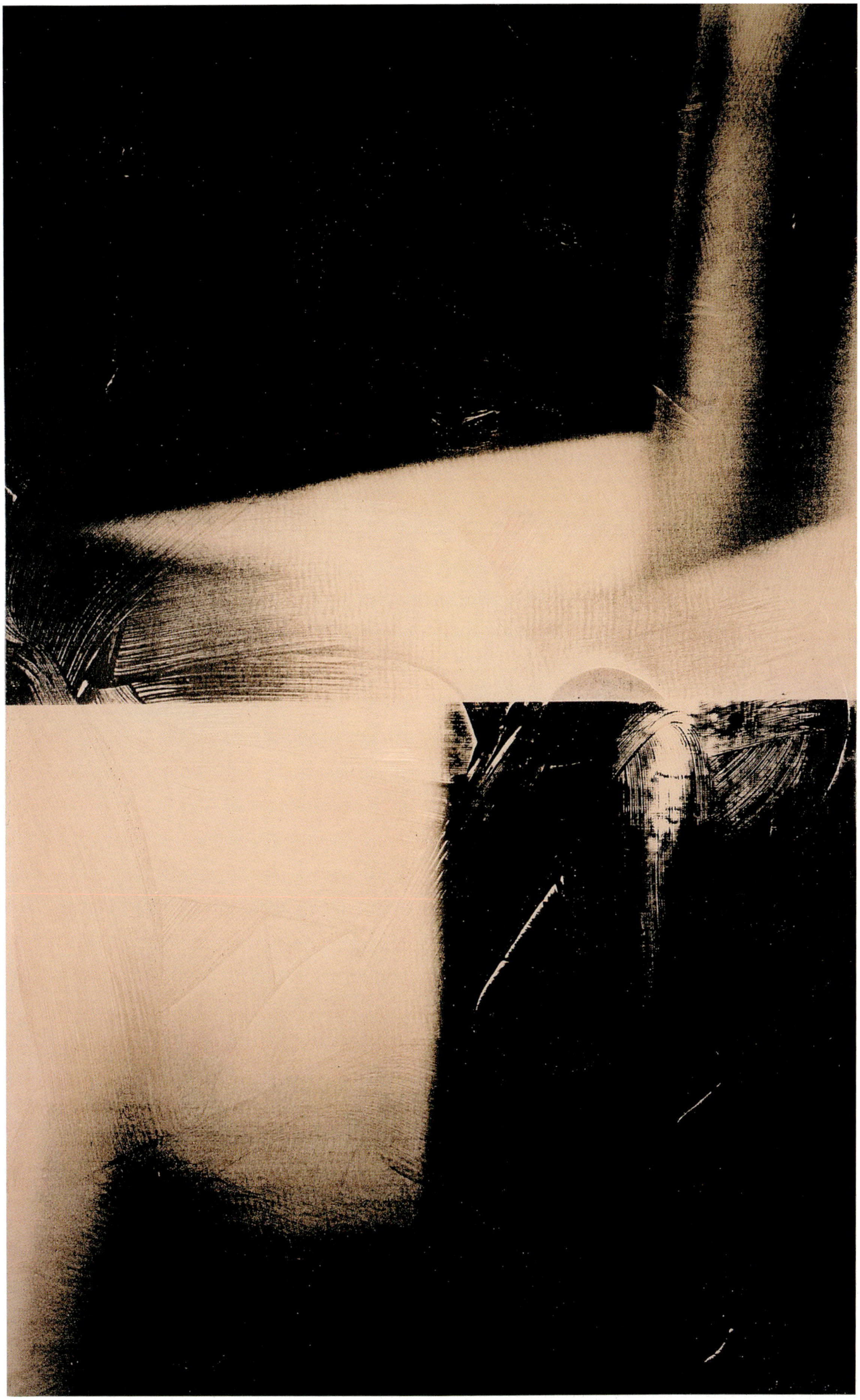

139

Arman

1928-2005

LE LUTH DE SYRIE

incised with the artist's signature, dated *2001* and numbered *EA II/IV*
sliced lute and bronze
83.2 BY 49.5 BY 27.9CM.; 32¾ BY 19½ BY 11IN.

Executed in 2001, this work is the second artist's proof from an edition of 8 plus 4 artist's proofs.

50,000-70,000 US$
182,000-255,000 QAR

PROVENANCE
Private Collection, France
Sale: Paris, Massol, *Art Contemporain*, 10 December 2007, Lot 242
Acquired directly from the above by the present owner

This work is registered as number 9647 in the archives of Madame Denyse Durand-Ruel.

Beginning in the late 1950's and early 1960's, Arman accumulated troves of everyday household goods, refuse, toys, tools and musical instruments, systematically arranging, slicing, burning and destroying them then displaying them on an artistic platform. The gathering of the objects reflected an attempt to understand society as if their accumulation granted sanctuary and control; toys and trash to regulate mass consumerism, gasmasks and swords to restrain conflict and angst. The obliteration and preservation of the objects reflected a desire to slow down the fast pace of our existence and observe, learn and adapt to the lessons we can take away from their presence. As the artist noted, "I believe that in the desire to accumulate there is a need for security and that in destruction, in cutting up, can be found the wish to stop time." (Houston, Museum of Fine Arts, *Arman 1955-1991: A Retrospective*, 1991, p. 41)

One of the most frequent muses for Arman has been musical instruments. In addition to his friendships with experimental musicians such as Pierre Schaeffer, it has been noted that the artist, "whose father played the cello, whose first wife was a composer, and whose own deepest concerns are visual, was especially drawn to the violin for its intimate connection with harmony, and [...] its graceful, ageless, and physically perfect shape." (Jan van der Marck, *Arman*, New York, 1984, p. 31) For the artist, the musical instrument represented the ideal object to comprehend the present via a direct continuity with the past: "Traditional subject matter for figurative artists [...] has a certain quality of permanence, and it allows the artists to develop his style trough a subject that is always recognizable; in time, it becomes the platform for his style. I discovered that musical instruments [...] express this kind of permanence [...] They are very good props for an artist, because you can do a great deal with them, and their identity will survive." (Houston, Museum of Fine Arts, *Arman 1955-1991: A Retrospective*, 1991, p. 92)

The present work perfectly exemplifies Arman's desire to connect with the past while remaining relevant to the present. Predecessors to the Luth de Syrie, called an "Oud" emerged as long as 5000 years ago and to this day, remains a popular instrument throughout the world. The instrument itself, finely inlayed, represents the history of the arts and the highest achievements of man; humanity's ability to convert chaos to a finer and higher purpose. However, by dividing the Oud, Arman strips it of its potential energy. Ironically, in its new state, the work becomes infinitely more powerful. Without an ability to produce sound, we are left only with the image. Yet, dramatically sliced and displayed in bronze, the instrument becomes not only a tangible link to the past, but a hope for man's potential greatness in the future.

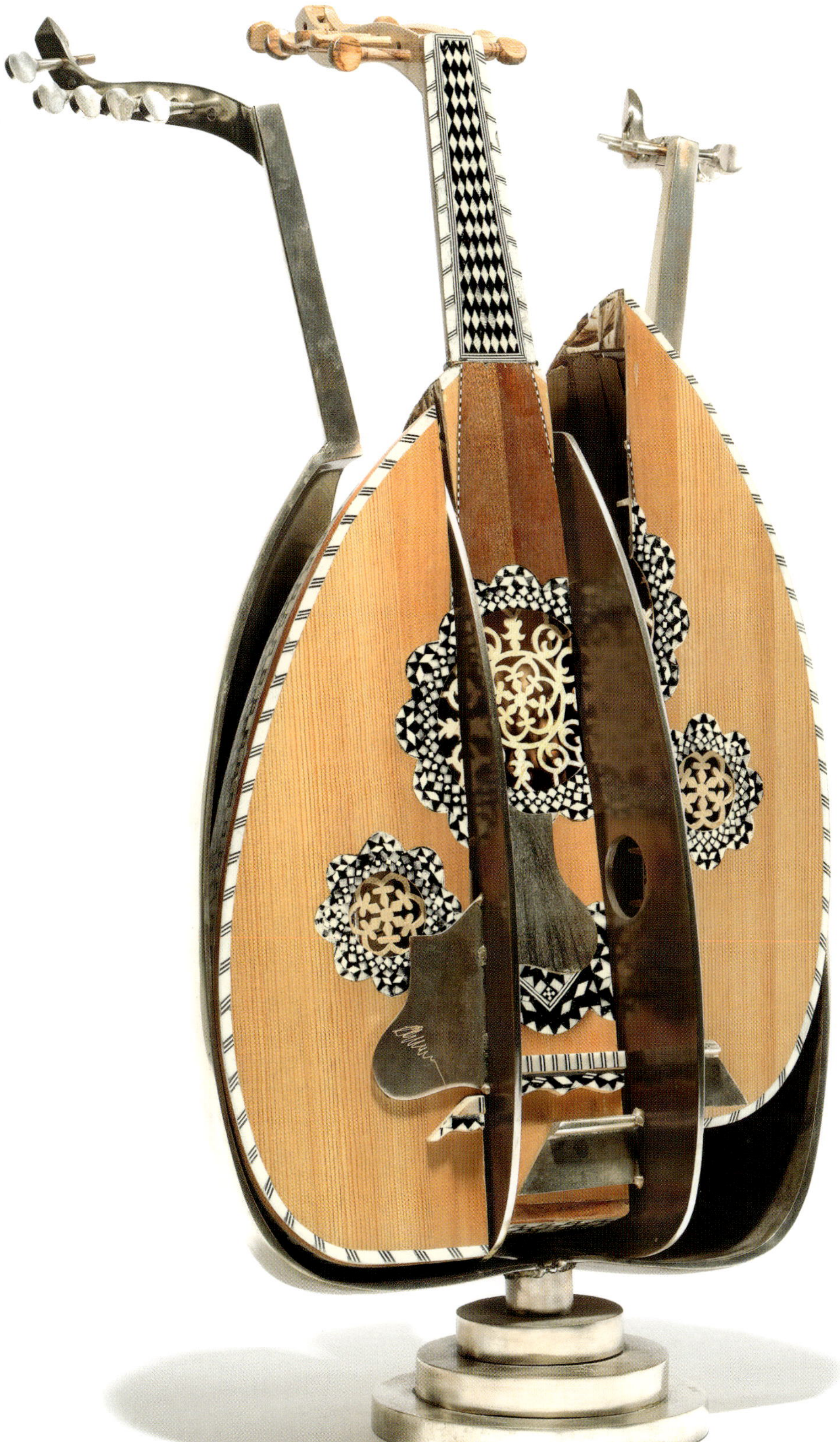

140

Arnaldo Pomodoro

b. 1926

ROTANTE MASSIMO I

bronze

DIAMETER: 10.2CM.; 4IN.

Executed in 1968, this work is from an edition of 2 plus 1 artist's proof.

20,000-30,000 US$

73,000-110,000 QAR

PROVENANCE

Private Collection, Italy

Marisa del Re Gallery, New York

Acquired directly from the above by the present owner

LITERATURE

Gabriele Mazotta, Ed., *Libro per le sculture di Arnaldo Pomodoro*, Milan 1974, p. 162, illustrated

Flaminio Gualdoni, Ed., *Arnaldo Pomodoro, Catalogo Ragionato della Scultura, Tomo II*, Milan 2007, p. 548, no. 475

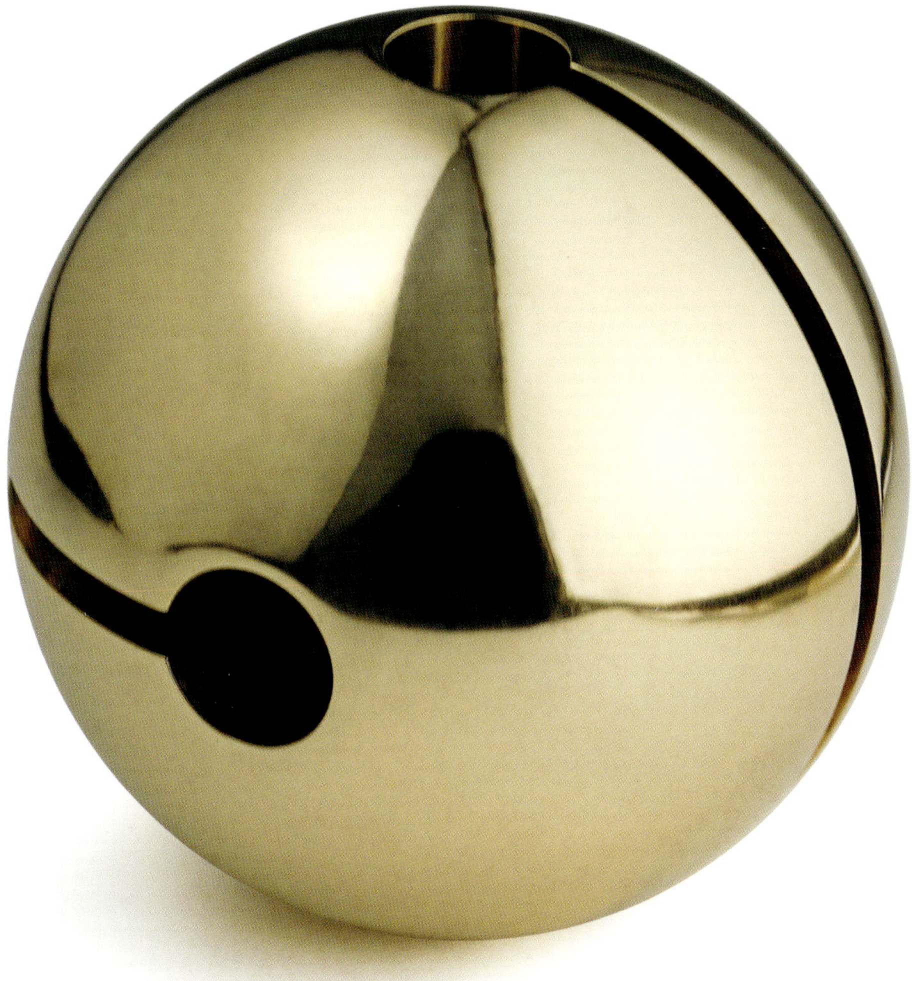

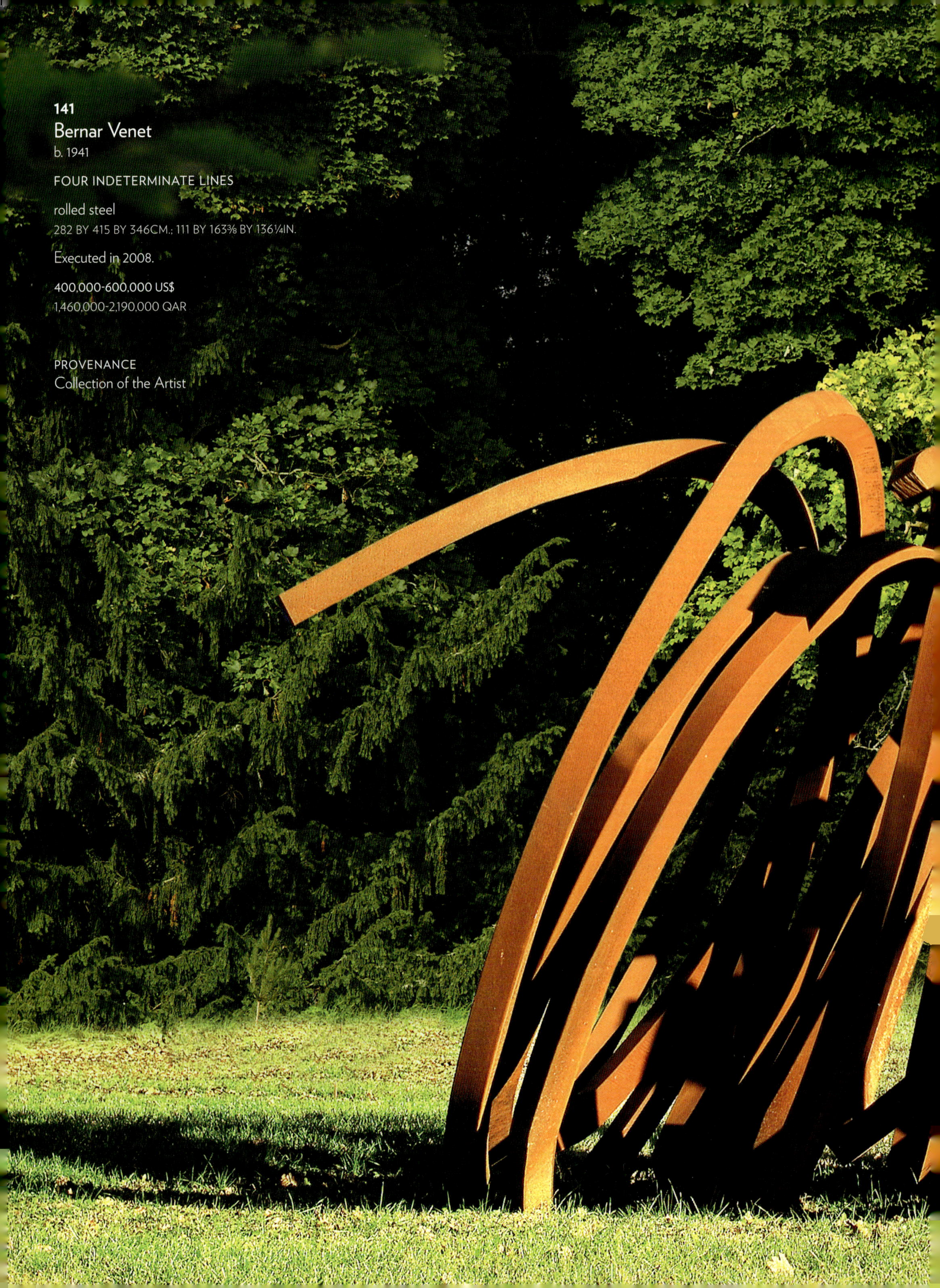

141

Bernar Venet

b. 1941

FOUR INDETERMINATE LINES

rolled steel

282 BY 415 BY 346CM.; 111 BY 163⅜ BY 136¼IN.

Executed in 2008.

400,000-600,000 US$

1,460,000-2,190,000 QAR

PROVENANCE

Collection of the Artist

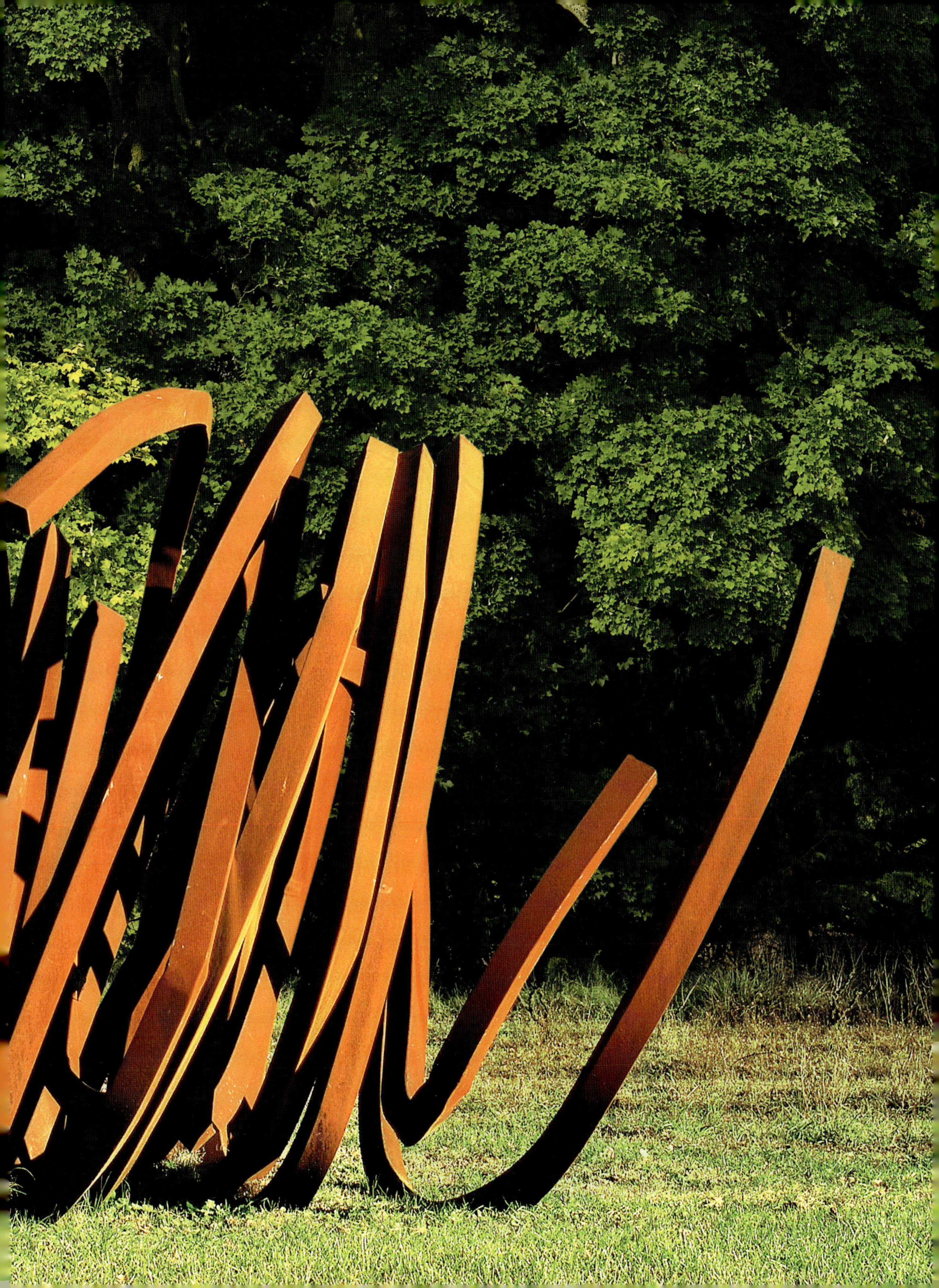

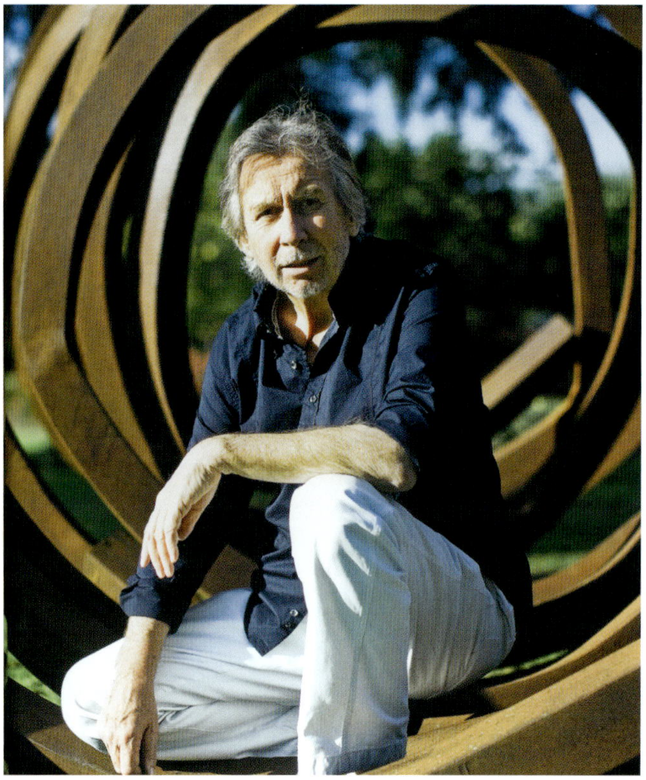

BERNARD VENET, SOTHEBY'S AT ISLEWORTH

Four Indeterminate Lines, 2008 represents an important example of Bernar Venet's dynamic oeuvre. After over 30 years, the artist has perfected the challenging technique of using an over-head crane to bend and twist long square steel poles. Today his abstract works are increasingly monumental and imposing with the lines becoming denser.

Despite the commanding scale, these colossal rods strangely resemble delicate calligraphy. The "scribbles" of the piece have been linked by some to handwriting. While the nonsensical twirls may seem to focus on the purely aesthetical nature of the work in the same way that many calligraphers often exercise in their own art, Venet's intent was, in fact, to avoid the aesthetic and focus on the impersonal mathematics and laws of physics which he studied at Columbia University during the 60s. The artist hoped to be freed of the aesthetic by science, similar to the American minimalists and conceptualists, and based on the doctrine of the French semiologist, Jacques Bertin, who believed that art was a code rather than a language.

Thus, there is a clear dichotomy that prevails in Venet's art. The *Indeterminate Lines* series he began in 1982 demonstrates the conflict between the artist's wish to obey set rules as opposed to succumbing to the unconscious flow of expression, or rather, to the medium's will. Indeed, steel is an extremely difficult material to forge. One can clearly observe the traces of the struggle between the artist and his creation.

Venet became increasingly conscious of the human incapability to enforce a predeterminate order. This awareness lead him to allow chance to intervene in his art. Venet calls his relationship with his matter a game, fighting the limitations of the metal against his intentions to mold it to his will.

This physical struggle is the essence of the *Indeterminate Line* sculpture. Consequently, no mathematical formula is applicable to the process: it is as fickle and uncontainable as life itself.

In fact, he does not make preparatory drawings rather resigning to the unpredictable nature of the steel. He then randomly combines these rods together forming the final sculpture. *Four Indeterminate Lines* portrays an exceptional and rare example of such a large number of poles assembled together to convey a sense of visual poetry gracefully defying nature's gravity.

The artist displays his works in open spaces juxtaposing the loops with the cubic buildings surrounding them, in addition to the hardness of the steel compared to soft grass or sand. Venet's remarkable art works are now collected by the most important institutions such as the Museum of Modern Art, NY and Paris which clearly acknowledge the artist's mastery.

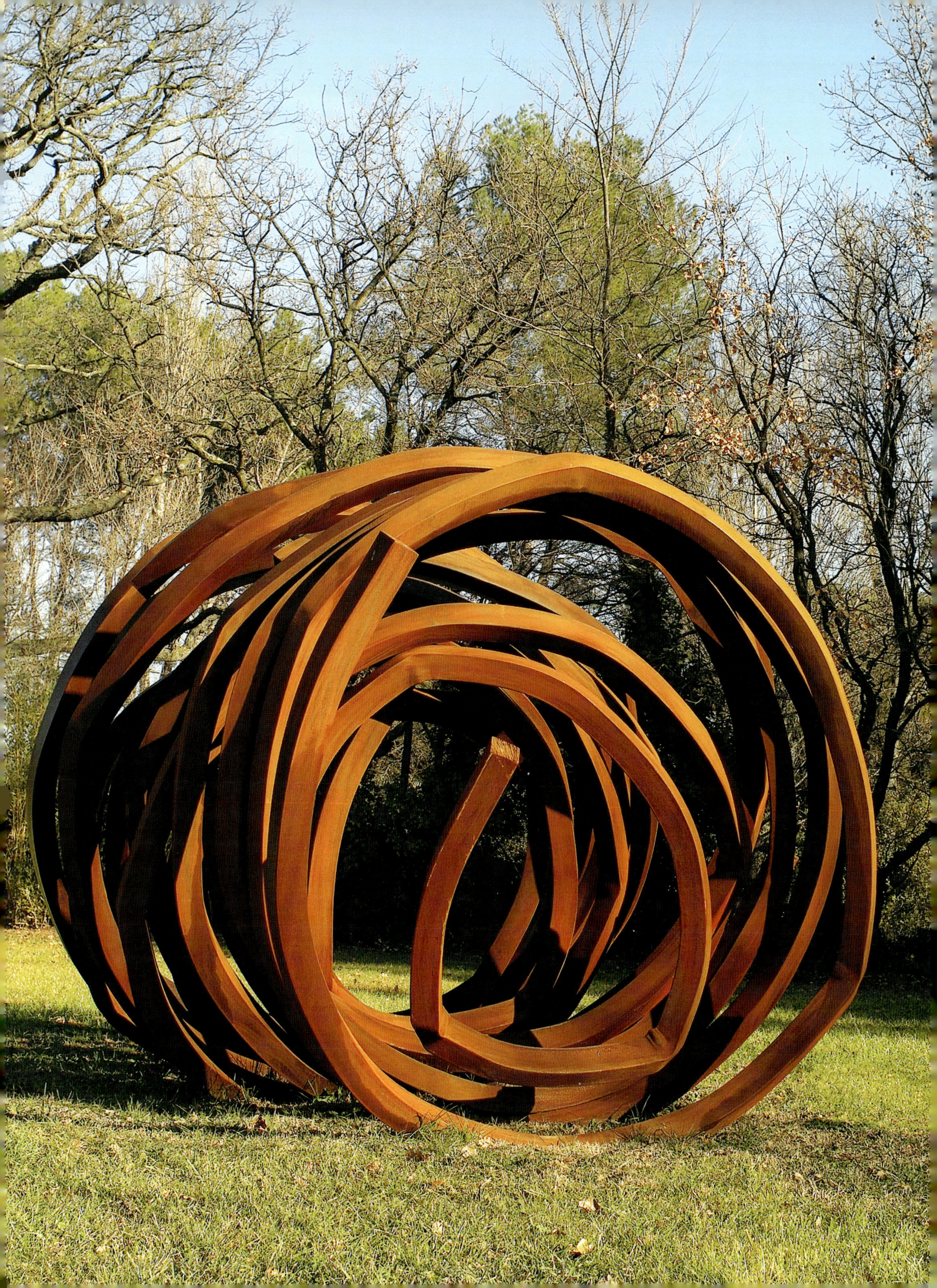

142

Josef Albers

1888-1976

STUDY FOR HOMAGE TO THE SQUARE: RECIPROCAL

signed with the artist's monogram and dated *68*; signed, titled and dated *1969* on the reverse

oil on masonite
40.2 BY 40.2CM.; 16 BY 16IN.

120,000-180,000 US$
437,000-660,000 QAR

PROVENANCE
The Estate of the Artist
Private Collection, Zürich
Acquired directly from the above by the present owner

EXHIBITED
Zürich, Haus für Konstruktive und Konkrete Kunst, *Josef Albers. Arbeiten auf Papier und "Homage to the Square"*, 1994
Zürich, Galerie Orlando, *Das Bauhaus: Weimar, Dessau, Berlin und The New Bauhaus Chicago*, 2005

This work will be included in the *Catalogue Raisonné of Paintings by Josef Albers* currently being prepared by the Josef and Anni Albers Foundation

Pure statements of visual logic, the paintings in Joseph Albers's iconic 'Homage to the Square' series have a feeling of the absolute and timeless. Sotheby's is delighted to be offering the following three superb examples of Albers's most celebrated and emblematic representation that consistently investigated the psychological effects of colour and space. Mathematically related to each other in size, the square is the perfect character for superimposition. But it is also a shape that never occurs in nature, which validated its necessarily man-made quality. The square thus became Albers ultimate research ground to assess the dialogue initiated between colours and its impact on the human eye. Indeed as the artist wittily puts it: 'I am not paying 'homage to the square'. It's only the dish I serve my craziness about colour in.' (Josef Albers cited in: Getulio Alviani, Ed., *Josef Albers*, Milan 1988, p. 235)

Executed with exceptional diligence, his technique favoured the restrained, systematic and ergonomic use of paint, thus opposing the wild freedom of Abstract Expressionism. Albers first applied one primary coat to masonite, a support favoured for its intrinsic durability. The unmixed paint was then squeezed and laid directly from the tubes onto the composition starting from the centre square, applied evenly with a knife palette in the thinnest fashion to recreate a so-called human order.

Born to a family of artisans in Bottrop Germany, Josef Albers inherited a tradition of careful, exact workmanship. He studied art in Berlin and Munich, but the milestone of his education took place in Weimar, Germany at the Bauhaus, where he subsequently became lecturer. Albers taught furniture design, drawing, and calligraphy, moving away from expressionism towards a constructivist art in the service of architecture. At the forefront of design innovations associated to the Bauhaus, Albers defended the idea that mass-production could be reconciled with individual artistic expression.

Functionality and rationality were therefore no longer incompatible with true creativity, instead Bauhaus unified art, craft and technology and proved to have an incommensurable impact on art and architecture trends of twentieth century Western Europe. Albers is believed to have influenced the movements of Geometric Abstraction and Minimalism, believing in the extreme reduction of form to a geometric idiom.

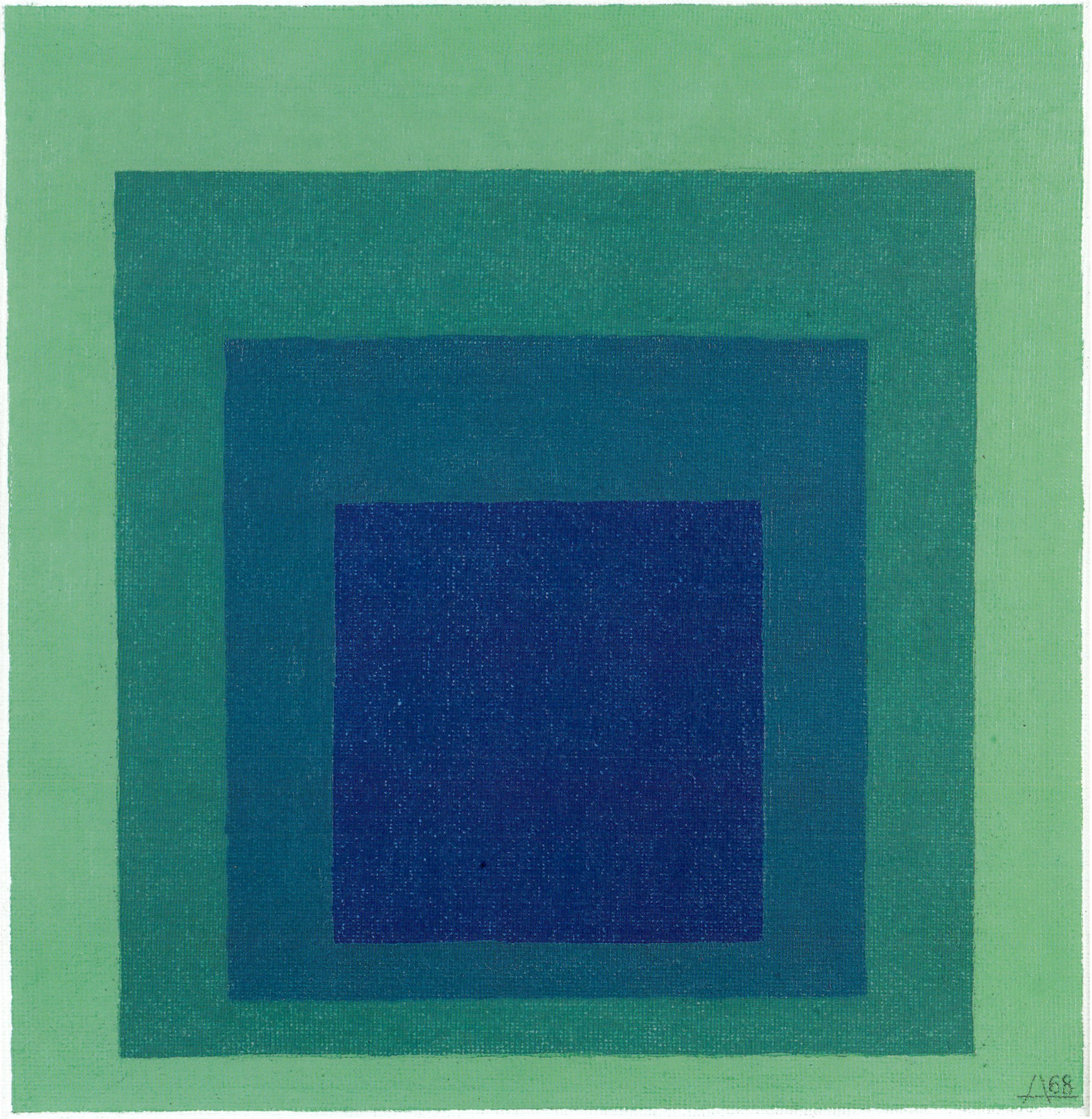

143

Josef Albers

1888-1976

STUDY FOR HOMAGE TO THE SQUARE: GLAD

signed with the artist's monogram and dated *69*; signed, titled and dated *1969* on the reverse
oil on masonite
40.2 BY 40.2CM.; 16 BY 16IN.

120,000-180,000 US$
437,000-660,000 QAR

PROVENANCE
The Estate of the Artist
Private Collection, Zürich
Acquired directly from the above by the present owner

EXHIBITED
Zürich, Haus für Konstruktive und Konkrete Kunst, *Josef Albers. Arbeiten auf Papier und "Homage to the Square"*, 1994
Zürich, Galerie Orlando, *Das Bauhaus: Weimar, Dessau, Berlin und The New Bauhaus Chicago*, 2005

This work will be included in the *Catalogue Raisonné of Paintings by Josef Albers* currently being prepared by the Josef and Anni Albers Foundation

ON MY "HOMAGE TO THE SQUARE"

Seeing several of these paintings next to each other
makes it obvious that each painting
is an instrumentation in its own.

This means that they all are of different palettes,
and, therefore, so to speak, of different climates.

Choice of the colors used, as well as their order, is
aimed to an interaction – influencing and changing
each other forth and back.

Thus, character and feeling alter from painting to
painting without any additional "hand writing"
or, so-called, texture.

Though the underlying symmetrical and quasi-
concentric order of squares remains the same in all
paintings – in proportion and placement –
these same squares group or single themselves,
connect and separate in many different ways.

In consequence, they move forth and back, in and out,
and grow up and down and near and far, as well as
enlarged and diminished.
All this, to proclaim color autonomy
as a means of a plastic organization.

Josef Albers cited in: Exhibition Catalogue, New York, Museum of Modern Art, *Josef Albers: Homage to the Square*, 1964

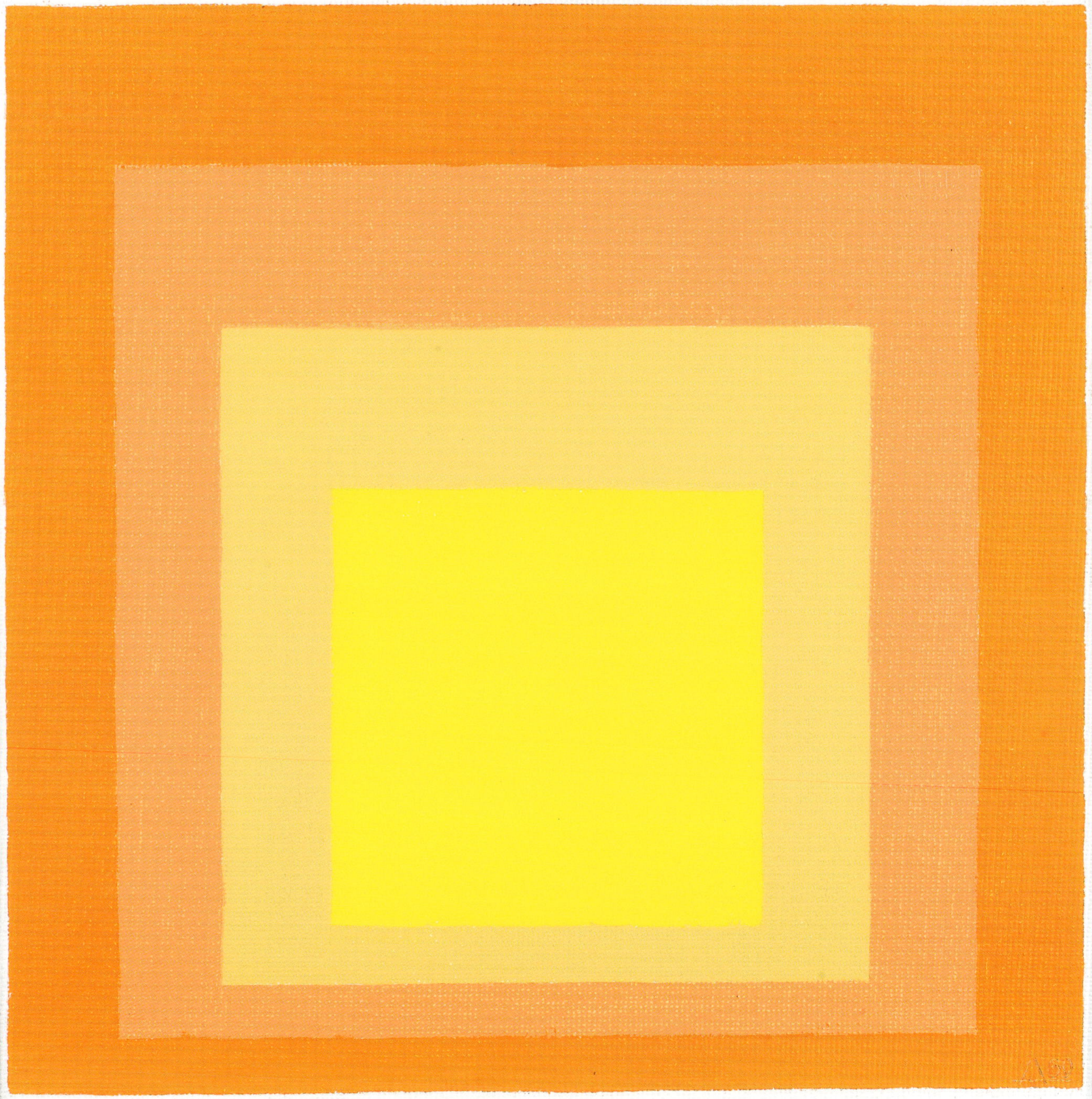

144

Josef Albers

1888-1976

STUDY FOR HOMAGE TO THE SQUARE: TRUE EARTH

signed with the artist's monogram and dated *65*; signed, titled and dated *1965* on the reverse
oil on masonite
40.2 BY 40.2CM.; 16 BY 16IN.

100,000-150,000 US$
364,000-550,000 QAR

PROVENANCE
The Estate of the Artist
Private Collection, Zürich
Acquired directly from the above by the present owner

EXHIBITED
Zürich, Haus für Konstruktive und Konkrete Kunst, *Josef Albers. Arbeiten auf Papier und "Homage to the Square"*, 1994
Zürich, Galerie Orlando, *Das Bauhaus: Weimar, Dessau, Berlin und The New Bauhaus Chicago*, 2005

This work will be included in the *Catalogue Raisonné of Paintings by Josef Albers* currently being prepared by the Josef and Anni Albers Foundation

"We are able to hear a single tone. But we almost never (that is without special devices) see a single colour unrelated to changing neighbours and changing conditions."

Josef Albers cited in: Josef Albers, *Interaction of Color*, New Heaven 1971, p. 5

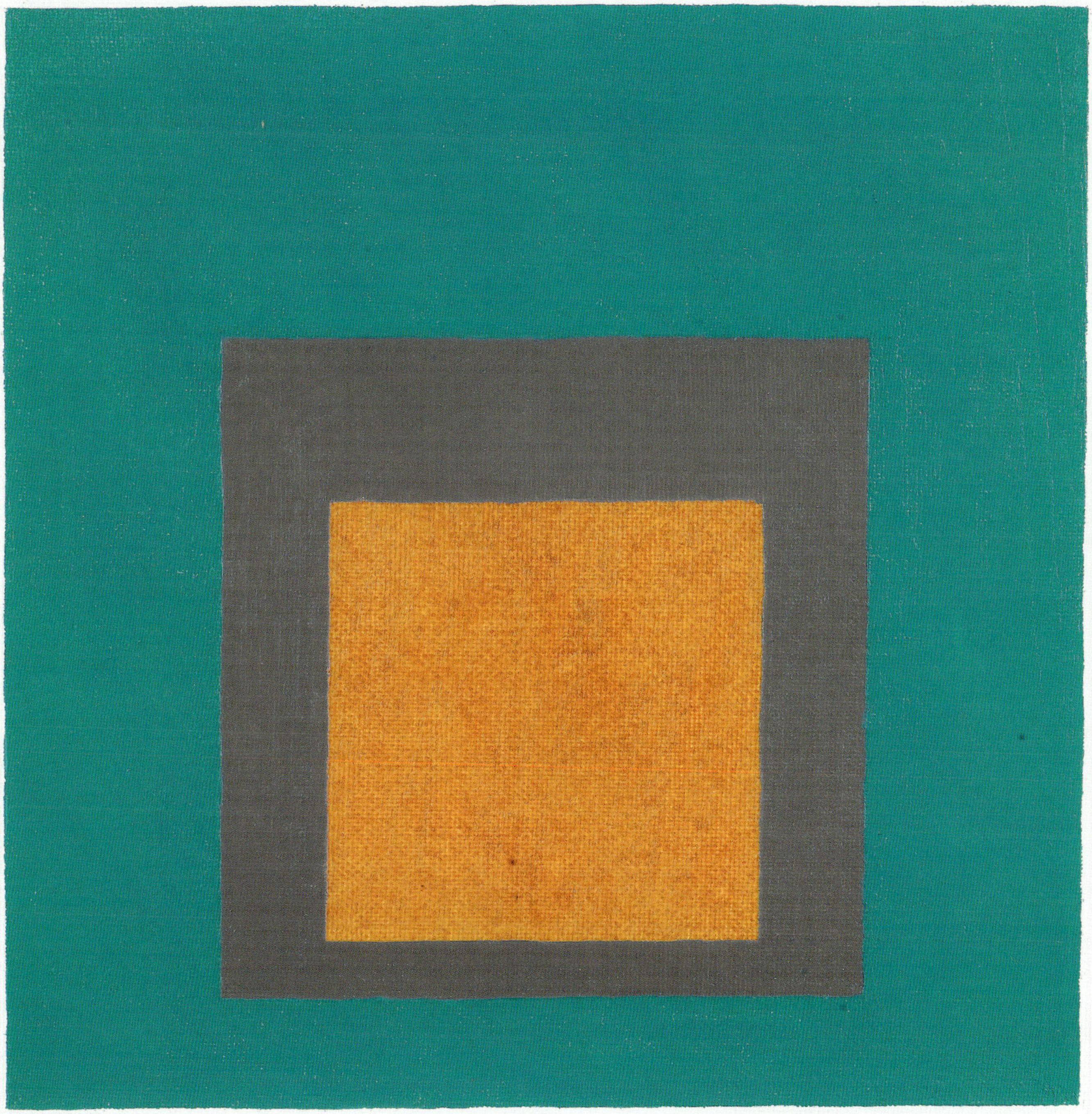

145

Mona Hatoum

b. 1952

UNTITLED (CRUTCHES)

rubber

EACH: 122 BY 21CM.; 48 BY 8¼IN.

Executed in 1991- 2001, this work is number 4 from an edition of 6.

60,000-80,000 US$

219,000-292,000 QAR

PROVENANCE

White Cube, London

Sale: Christie's, London, *Contemporary Art*, 1 July 2008, Lot 314

Acquired directly from the above by the present owner

LITERATURE

Exhibition Catalogue, Santiago de Compostela, Centro de Arte de Salamanca; Centro Galego de Arte Contemporánea, *Mona Hatoum*, 2000, p. 112, illustration of another example in colour

"It is so moving because it brings me to the fragility of the body, or a kind of disappointment when the body has failed you."

Mona Hatoum cited in: Exhibition Catalogue, Salamanca, Centro de Arte de Salamanca, Mona Hatoum, p. 125

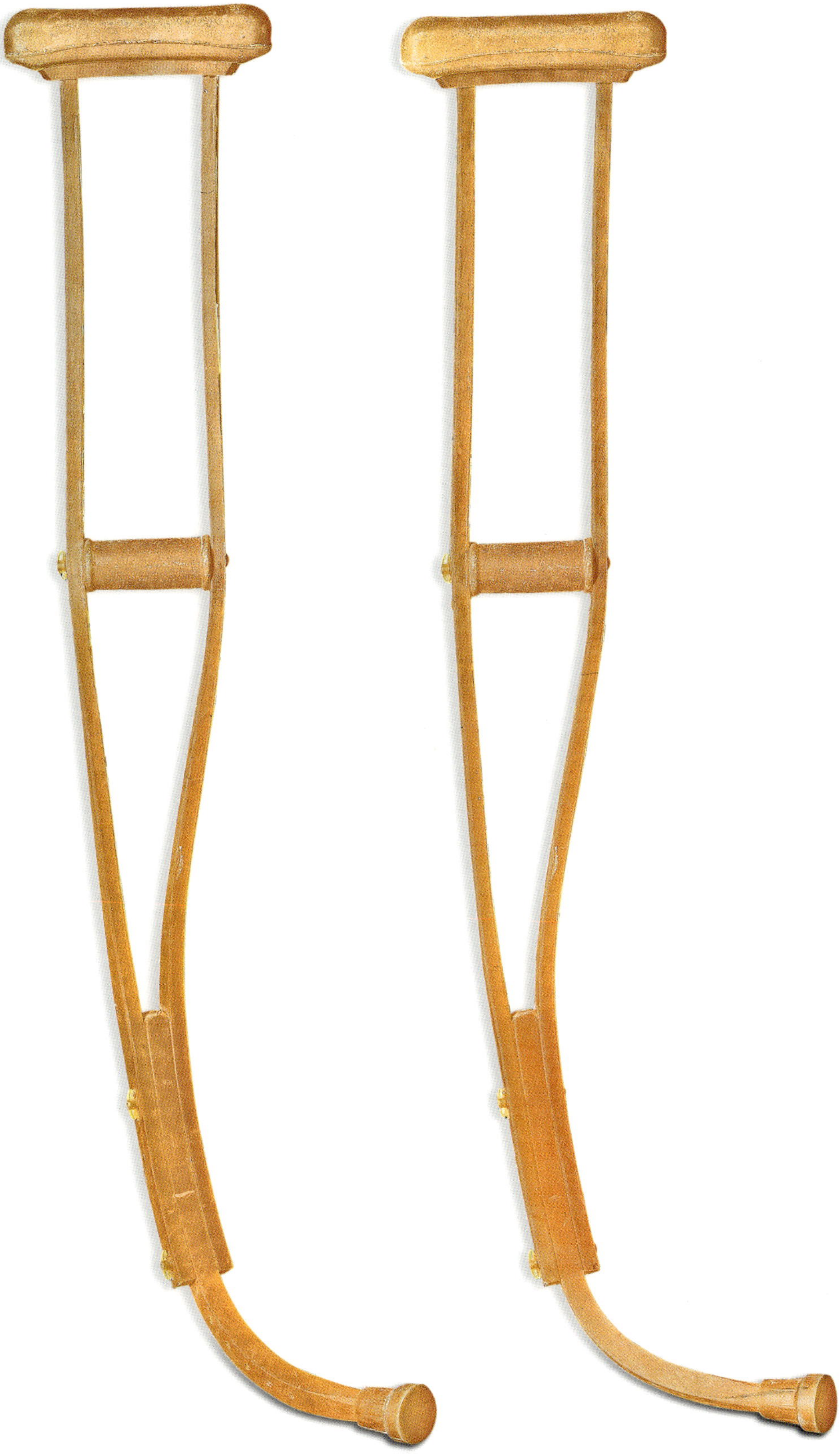

146

Faraj Daham

b. 1956

COORDINATE

signed and dated *08*
oil and mixed-media on wood
150 BY 120CM.; 59 BY 47¼IN.

10,000-15,000 US$
36,400-55,000 QAR

PROVENANCE
Collection of the Artist

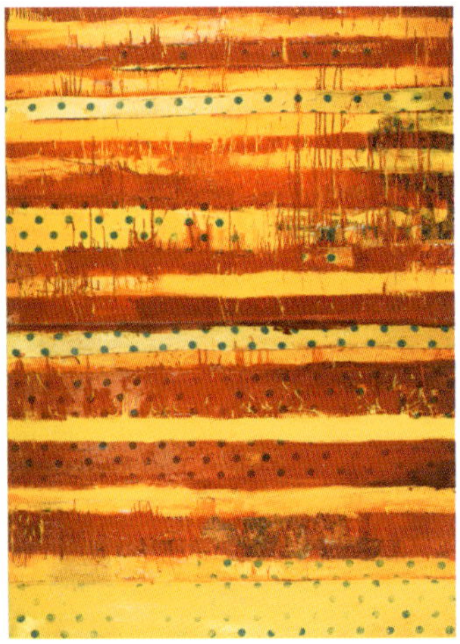

ROBERT RAUSCHENBERG, *YOICKS*, 1954. WHITNEY MUSEUM OF AMERICAN ART, GIFT OF THE ARTIST. © ESTATE OF ROBERT RAUSCHENBERG /DACS, LONDON/VAGA, NEW YORK 2009.

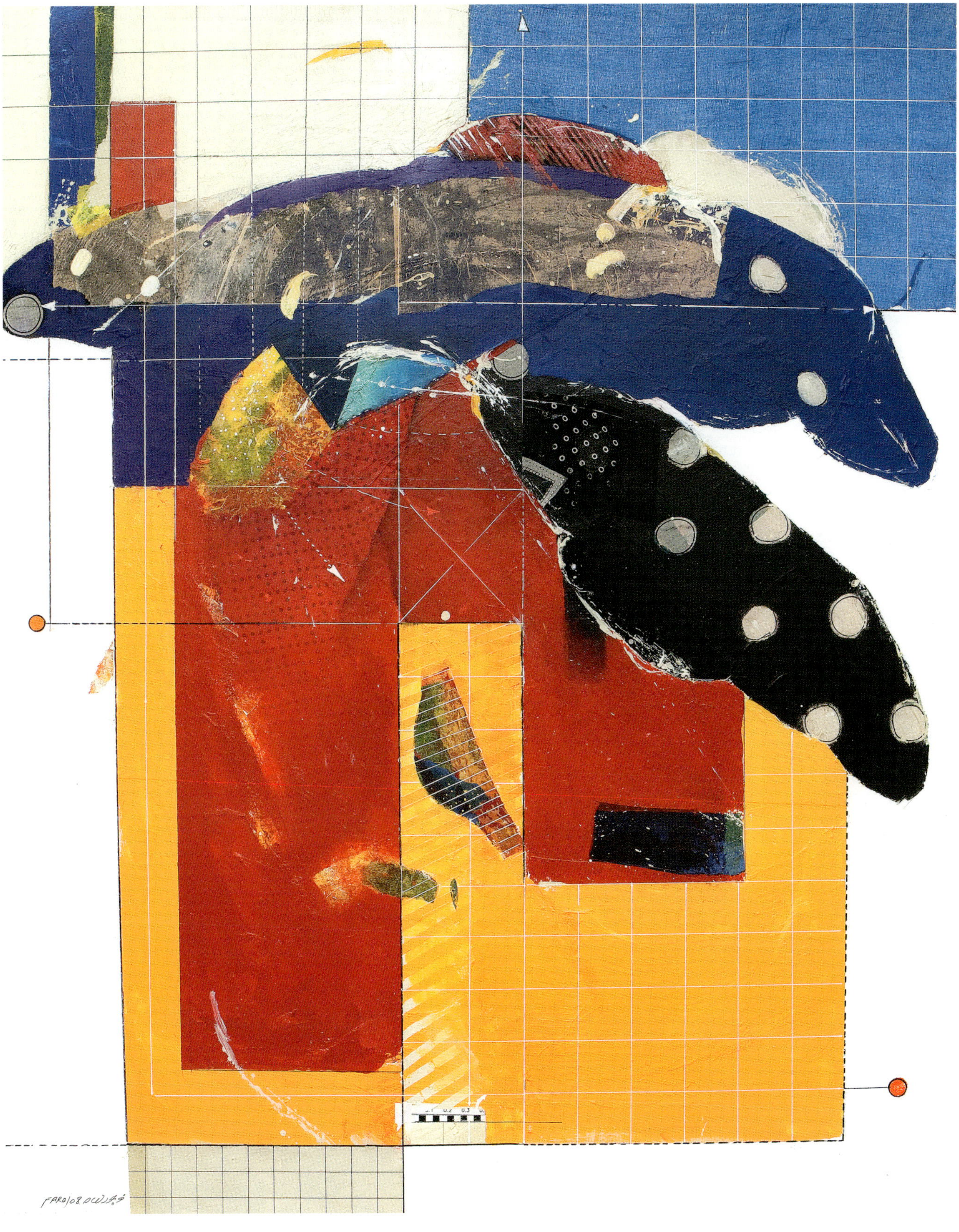

147

Salman Al Malik

b. 1958

FAMILY

signed and dated *08*; signed on the reverse
acrylic on canvas
80 BY 100CM.; 31½ BY 39⅜IN.

10,000-15,000 US$
36,400-55,000 QAR

PROVENANCE
Collection of the Artist

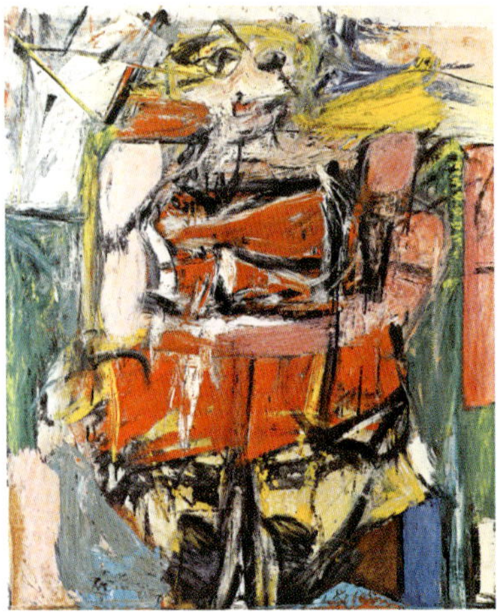

WILLEM DE KOONING, *WOMAN VI*, 1953, CARNEGIE INSTITUTE, MUSEUM OF ART, PITTSBURGH. © THE WILLEM DE KOONING FOUNDATION, NEW YORK/ ARS, NY AND DACS, LONDON 2009

"My paintings reveal my suffering and dreams that I hold within... by using my skills, I express the concept of the woman as being a home, a dream, and an active part in the progress of society."

Salman Al-Malik cited in: Mohammed Mahdi Hameeda, *Salman Al Malik And The Rhetorical Expression*

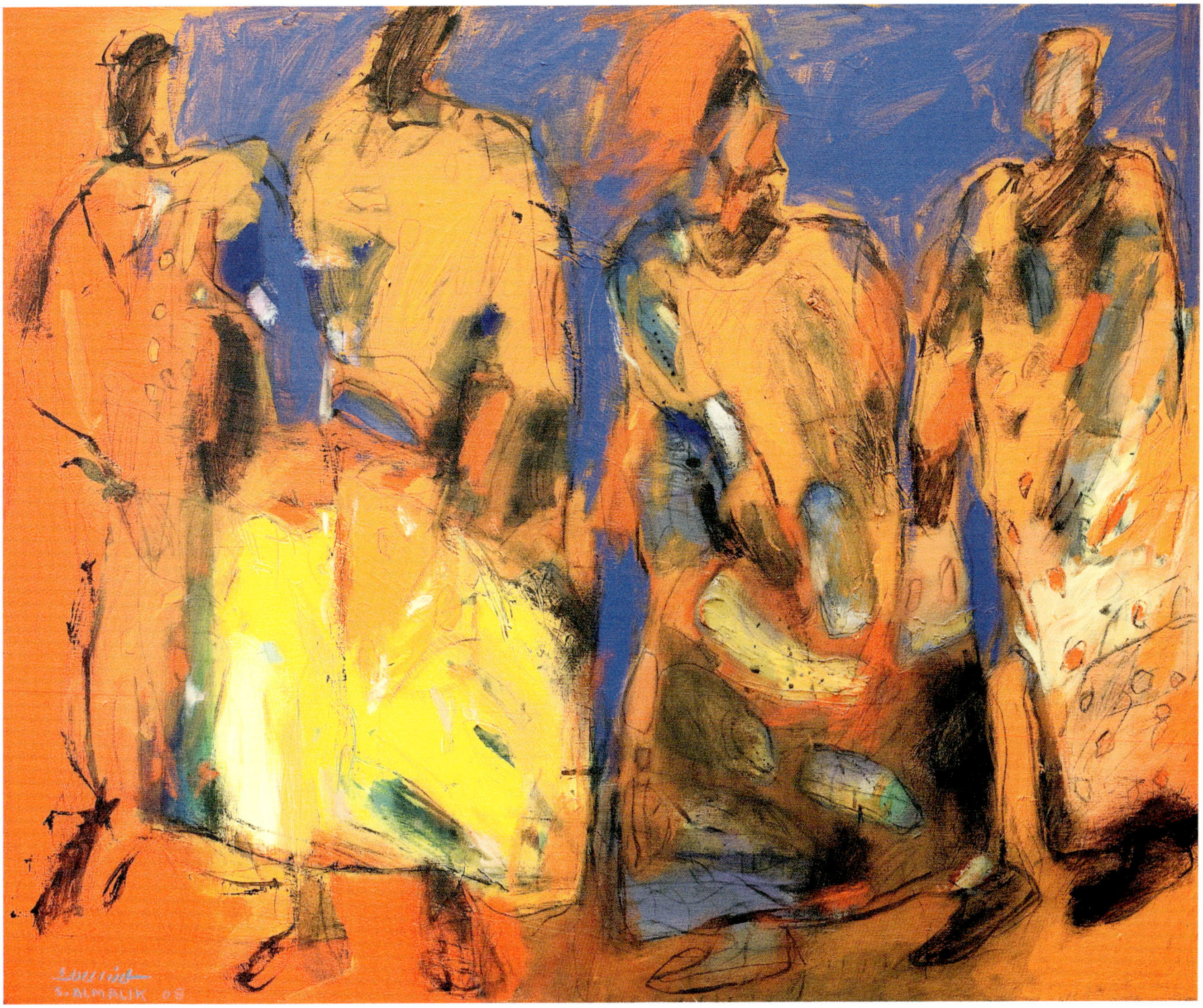
S. ALMALIK 08

148

Rachid Koraïchi

b. 1947

UNTITLED

signed
wool and silk
388 BY 228CM.; 152¾ BY 89¾IN.

Executed in 1989.

20,000-30,000 US$
73,000-110,000 QAR

PROVENANCE
Mutuelles du Mans, Le Mans
Private Collection, Paris

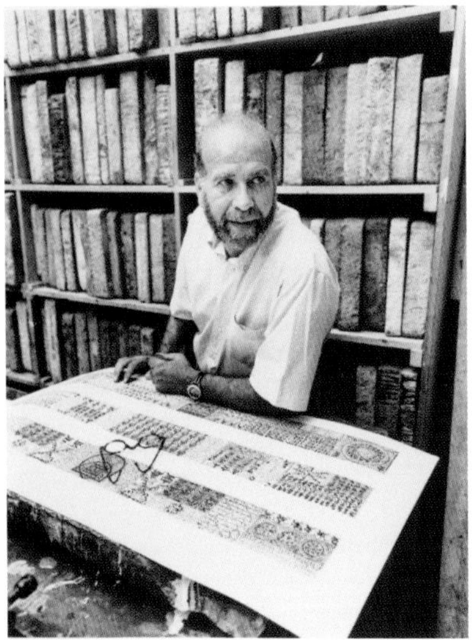

RACHID KORAICHI, COURTESY OF THE ARTIST

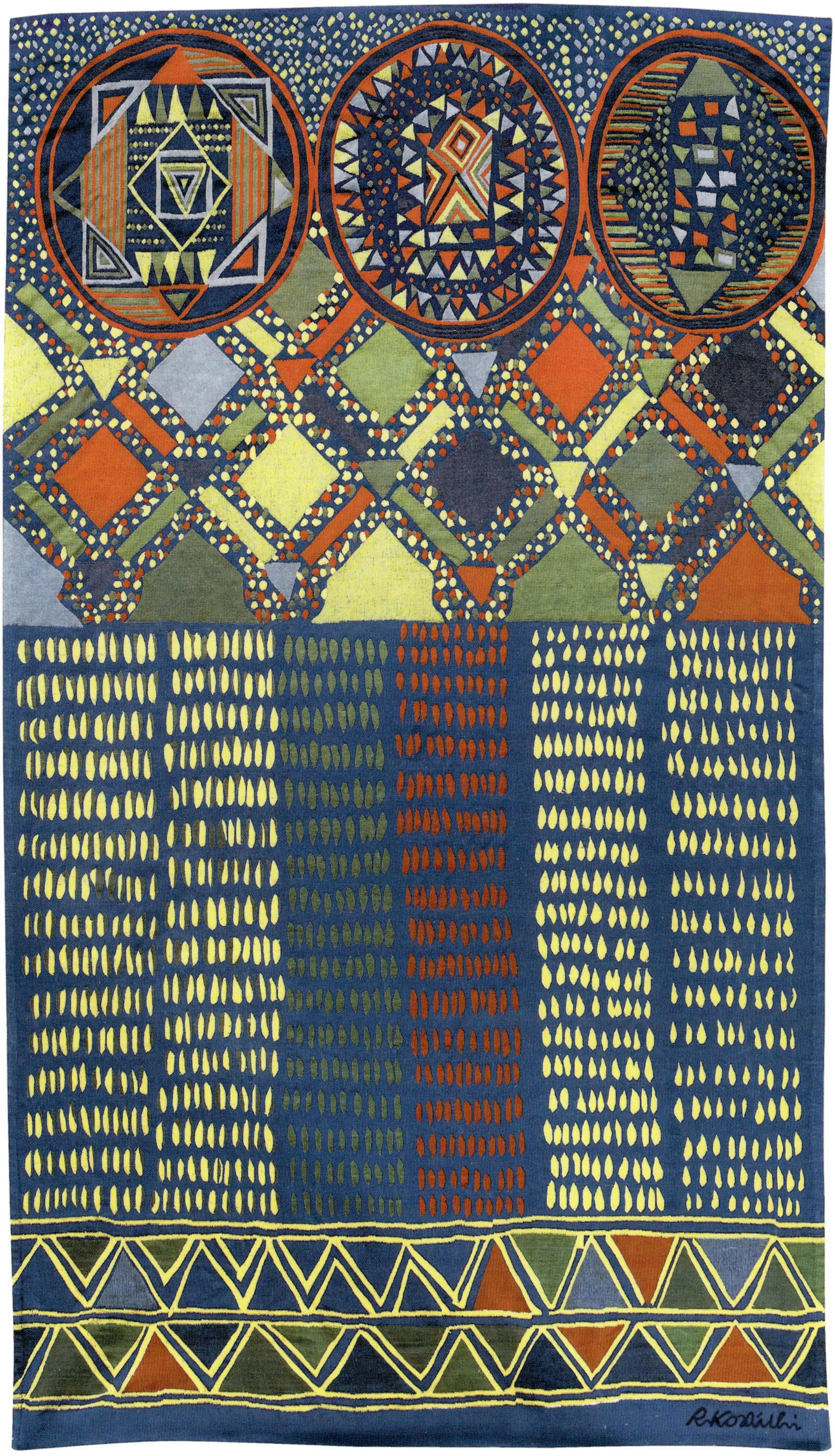

149

Arman

1928-2005

UNTITLED

signed on the top overlap
acrylic and paint tubes on canvas
81.3 BY 60.3CM.; 32 BY 23¾IN.

35,000-45,000 US$
128,000-164,000 QAR

PROVENANCE
Private Collection, Florida
Acquired directly from the above by the present owner

This work is registered as number 9498 in the archives of Madame Denyse Durand-Ruel.

Beginning in the late 1950's and early 1960's, Arman accumulated troves of everyday household goods, refuse, toys, tools and musical instruments, systematically arranging, slicing, burning and destroying them then displaying them on an artistic platform. The gathering of the objects reflected an attempt to understand society as if their accumulation granted sanctuary and control; toys and trash to regulate mass consumerism, gasmasks and swords to restrain conflict and angst. The obliteration and preservation of the objects reflected a desire to slow down the fast pace of our existence and observe, learn and adapt to the lessons we can take away from their presence. As the artist noted, "I believe that in the desire to accumulate there is a need for security and that in destruction, in cutting up, can be found the wish to stop time." (Exhibition Catalogue, Houston, Museum of Fine Arts, *Arman 1955-1991: A Retrospective*, 1991, p. 41)

One of the most frequent muses for Arman has been musical instruments. In addition to his friendships with experimental musicians such as Pierre Schaeffer, it has been noted that the artist, "whose father played the cello, whose first wife was a composer, and whose own deepest concerns are visual, was especially drawn to the violin for its intimate connection with harmony, and [...] its graceful, ageless, and physically perfect shape." (Jan van der Marck, *Arman*, New York 1984, p. 31) For the artist, the musical instrument represented the ideal object to comprehend the present via a direct continuity with the past: "Traditional subject matter for figurative artists [...] has a certain quality of permanence, and it allows the artists to develop his style trough a subject that is always recognizable; in time, it becomes the platform for his style. I discovered that musical instruments [...] express this kind of permanence [...] They are very good props for an artist, because you can do a great deal with them, and their identity will survive." (Exhibition Catalogue, Houston, Museum of Fine Arts, *Arman 1955-1991: A Retrospective*, 1991, p. 92)

The present work perfectly exemplifies Arman's desire to connect with the past while remaining relevant to the present. Predecessors to the Luth de Syrie, called an "Oud" emerged as long as 5000 years ago and to this day, remains a popular instrument throughout the world. The instrument itself, finely inlayed, represents the history of the arts and the highest achievements of man; humanity's ability to convert chaos to a finer and higher purpose. However, by dividing the Oud, Arman strips it of its potential energy. Ironically, in its new state, the work becomes infinitely more powerful. Without an ability to produce sound, we are left only with the image. Yet, dramatically sliced and displayed in bronze, the instrument becomes not only a tangible link to the past, but a hope for man's potential greatness in the future.

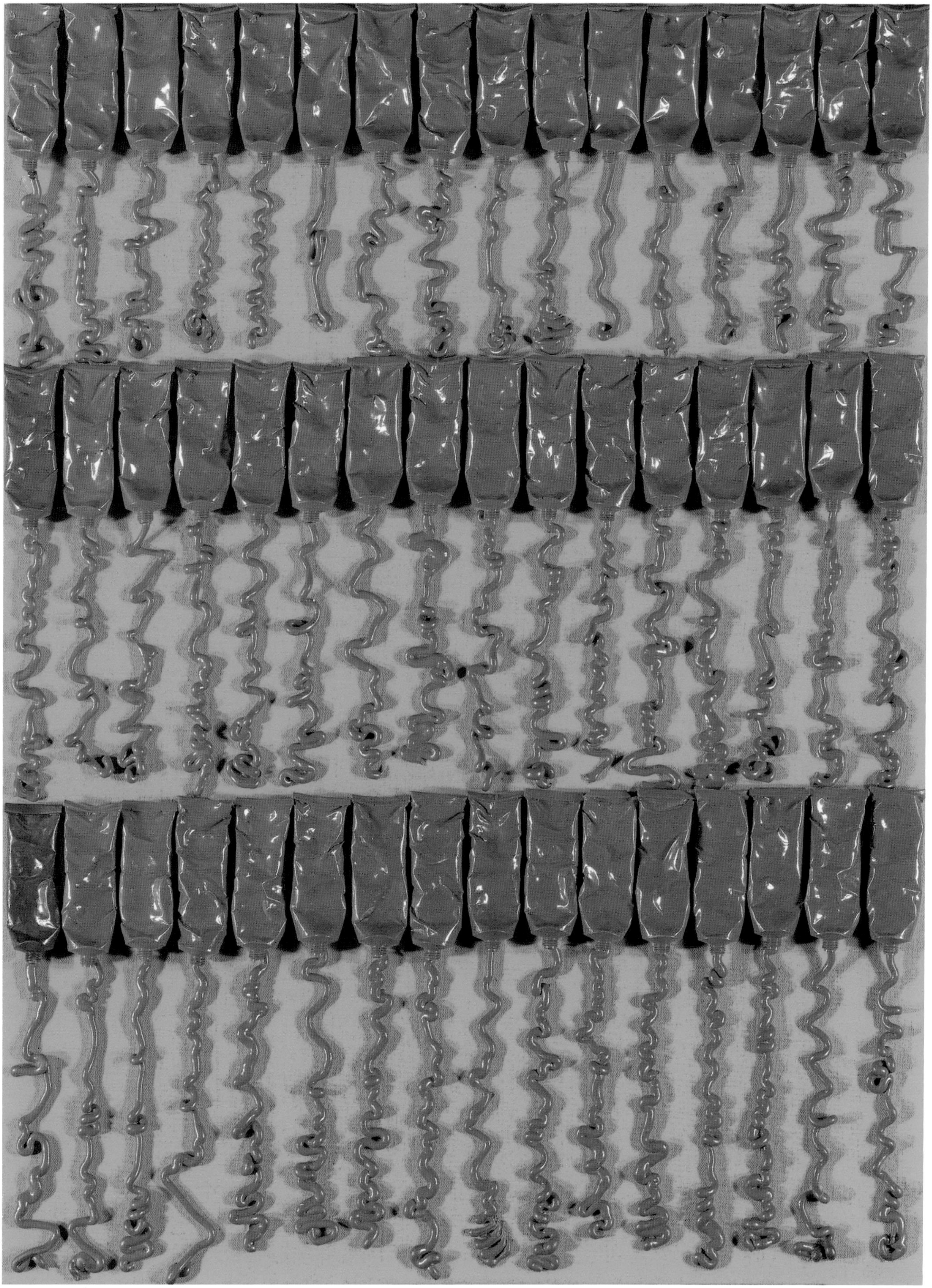

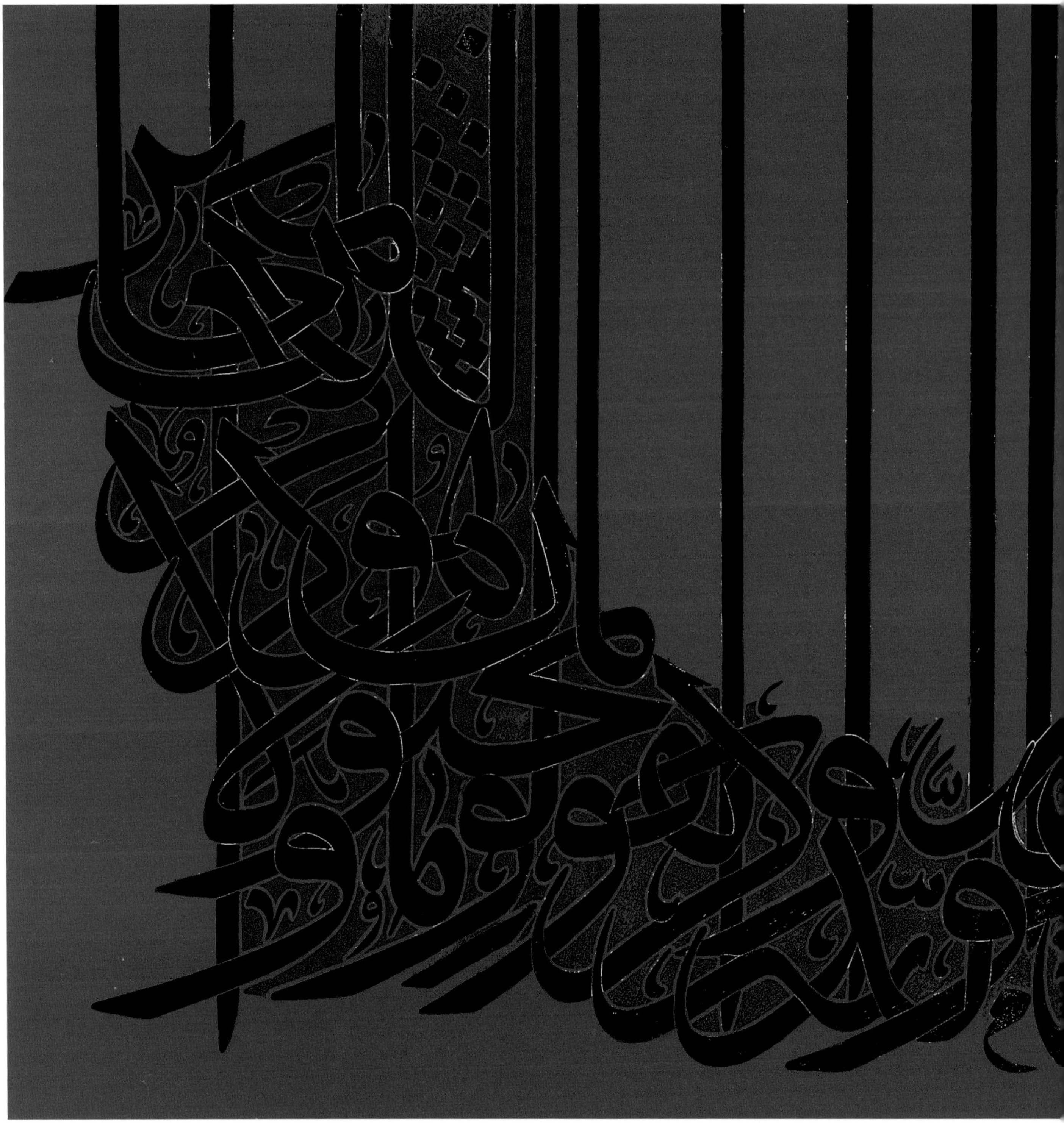

150

Nasrollah Afjei

b. 1933

VA EN YAKADOLLAZINA KAFAROO

signed and dated *2007*
oil on canvas
150 BY 300CM.; 59 BY 118IN.

100,000-150,000 US$
364,000-550,000 QAR

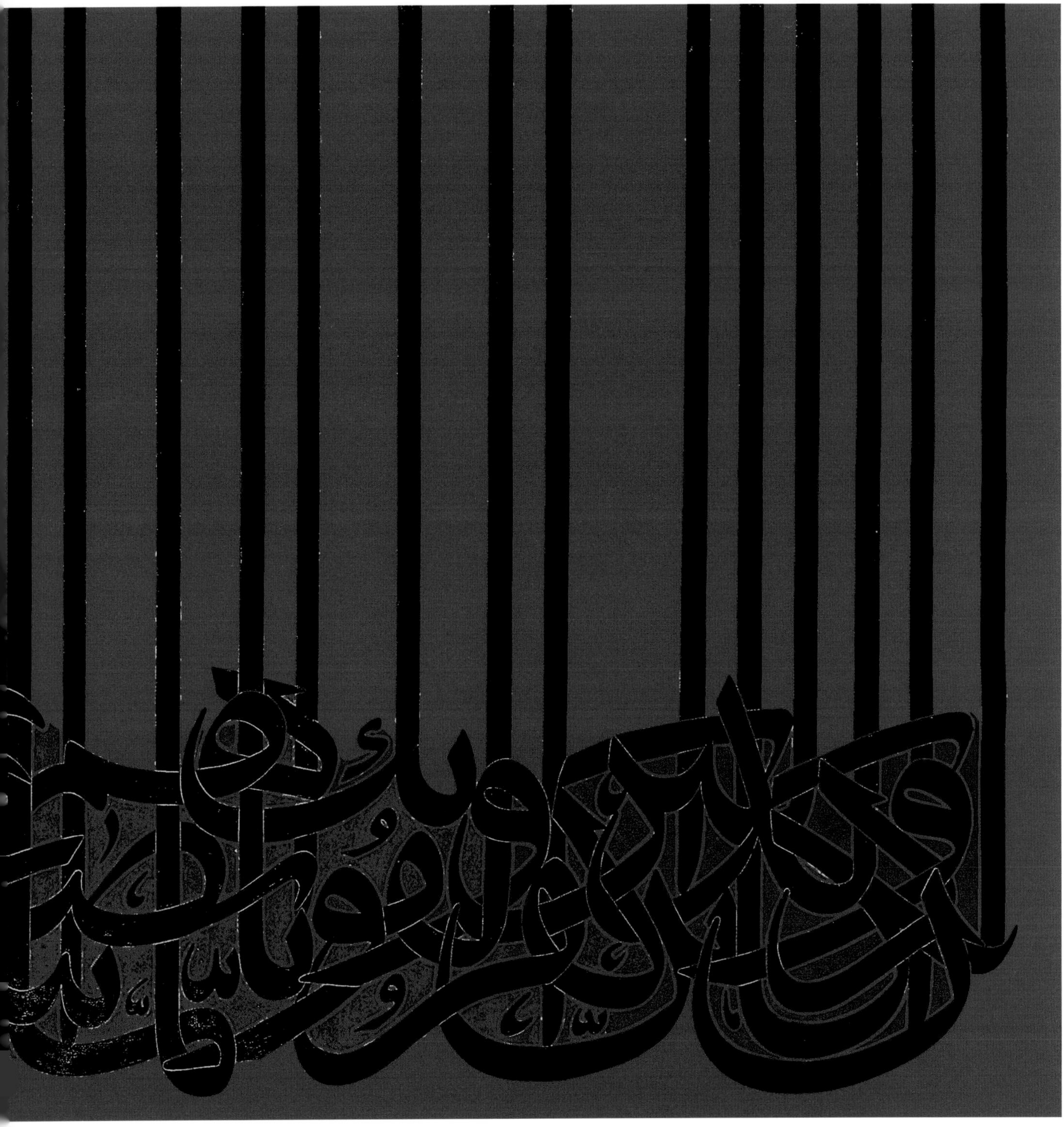

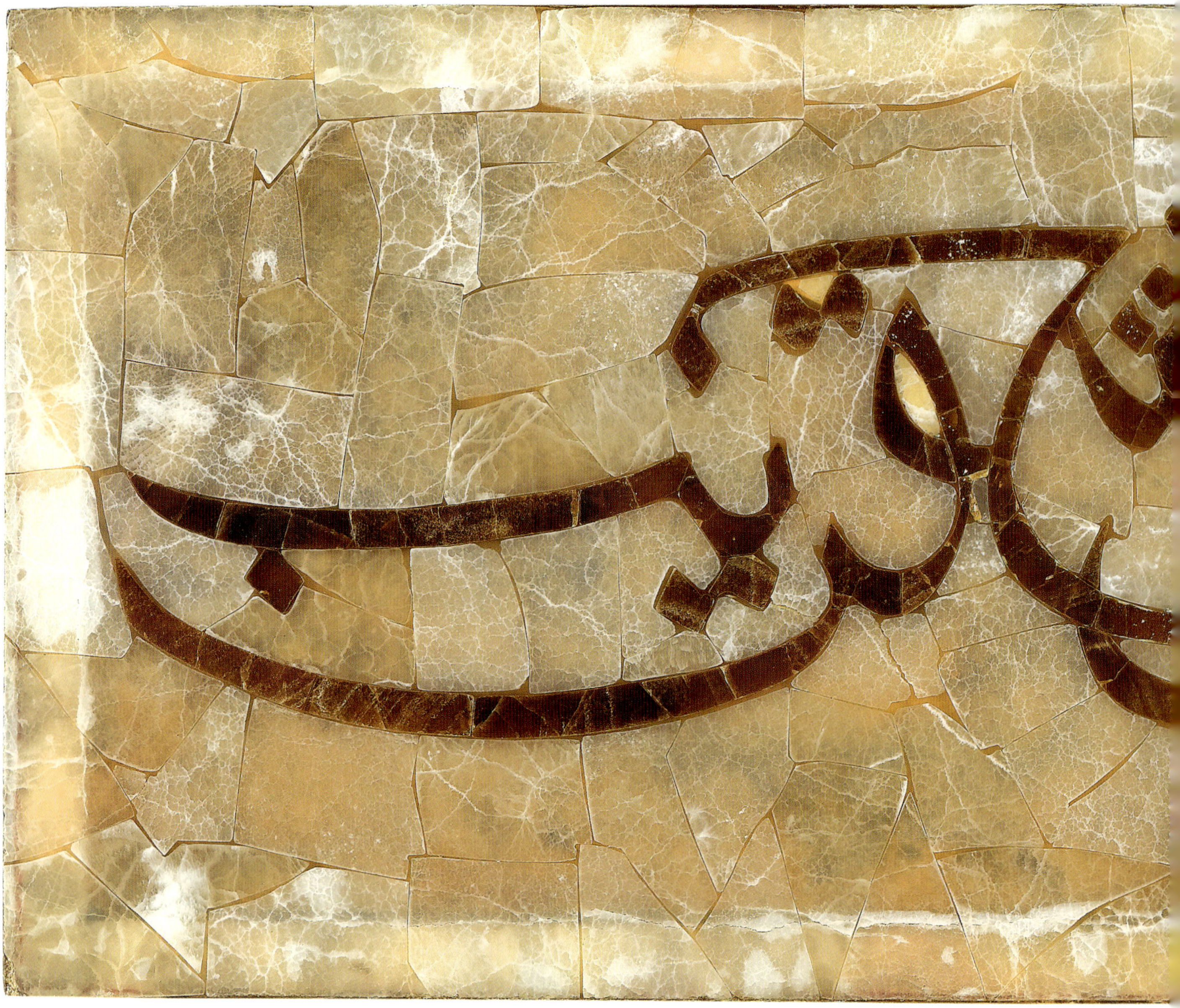

151

Ismail Gulgee

1926 - 2007

﴿ نَصْرٌ مِنَ اللَّهِ وَفَتْحٌ قَرِيبٌ ﴾

Help from Allah and Victory at hand

titled

agat mosaic set with gold leaf in a metal mount

32.5 BY 81.8CM.; 12¾ BY 32¼IN.

Executed in 1971.

80,000-120,000 US$

292,000-437,000 QAR

PROVENANCE

Acquired directly from the artist in 1972

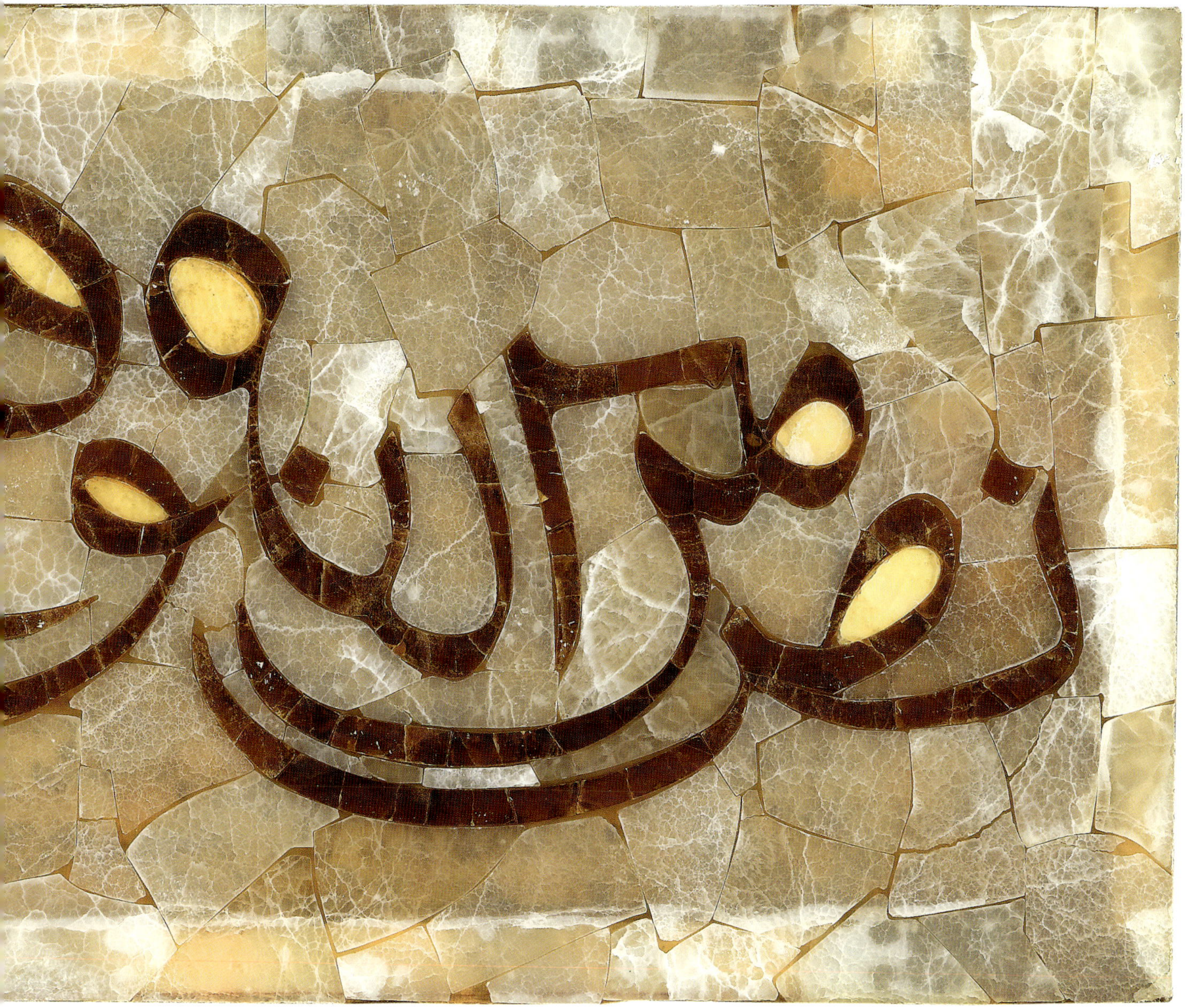

SOTHEBY'S AUTHENTICITY GUARANTEE

If Sotheby's sells an item which subsequently is shown to be a "counterfeit", subject to the terms below Sotheby's will set aside the sale and refund to the Buyer the total amount paid by the Buyer to Sotheby's for the item, in the currency of the original sale.

For these purposes, "counterfeit" means a lot that in Sotheby's reasonable opinion is an imitation created to deceive as to authorship, origin, date, age, period, culture or source, where the correct description of such matters is not reflected by the description in the catalogue (taking into account any Glossary of Terms). No lot shall be considered a counterfeit by reason only of any damage and/or restoration and/or modification work of any kind (including repainting or over-painting).

Please note that this Guarantee does not apply if either:-

(i) the catalogue description was in accordance with the generally accepted opinion (s) of scholar(s) at the date of the sale, or the catalogue indicated that there was a conflict of such opinions; or

(ii) the only method of establishing at the date of the sale that the item was a counterfeit would have been by means of processes not then generally available or accepted, unreasonably expensive or impractical to use; or likely to have caused damage to the lot or likely (in Sotheby's reasonable opinion) to have caused loss of value to the lot; or

(iii) there has been no material loss in value of the lot from its value had it been in accordance with its description.

To the fullest extent permitted by Qatar law, this Guarantee is provided for a period of five (5) years after the date of the relevant auction, is solely for the benefit of the Buyer and may not be transferred to any third party. To be able to claim under this Guarantee, the Buyer must:

(i) notify Sotheby's in writing within three (3) months of receiving any information that causes the Buyer to question the authenticity or attribution of the item, specifying the lot number date of the auction at which it was purchased and the reason why it is thought to be counterfeit; and

(ii) return the item to Sotheby's in the same condition as at the date of sale to the Buyer and be able to transfer good title in the item free from any third party claims arising after the date of the sale.

Sotheby's has discretion to waive any of the above requirements.

Sotheby's may require the Buyer to obtain at the Buyer's cost the reports of two independent and recognised experts in the field, mutually acceptable to Sotheby's and the Buyer. Sotheby's shall not be bound by any reports produced by the Buyer, and reserves the right to seek additional expert advice at its own expense. In the event Sotheby's decides to rescind the sale under this Guarantee, it may refund to the Buyer the reasonable costs of up to two mutually approved independent expert reports.

2/09 DOHA_GUARANTEE MAIN

GLOSSARY OF TERMS

The following are examples of the terminology used in this catalogue. Any statement as to authorship, attribution, origin, date, age, provenance and condition is a statement of opinion and is not to be taken as a statement of fact.

Please read carefully the terms of the Authenticity Guarantee and the Conditions of Business for Buyers set out in this catalogue, in particular Conditions 3 and 4.

1 GIOVANNI BELLINI
In our opinion **a work by the artist.** (When the artist's forename(s) is not known, a series of asterisks, followed by the surname of the artist, whether preceded by an initial or not, indicates that in our opinion the work is by the artist named.

2 The term **signed** and/or **dated** and/or **inscribed** means that in our opinion the signature and/or date and/or inscription are from the hand of the artist.

3 The term **bears** a signature and/or **date** and/or **inscription** means that in our opinion the signature and/or date and/or inscription have been added by another hand.

4 Dimensions are given height before width.

10/01 NBS_GLOS_IMPS CTP

Please note that all lots are sold subject to our Conditions of Business for Buyers and Authenticity Guarantee, which are set forth at the back of the catalogue and Conditions of Business for Sellers which are available from Sotheby's offices on request.

EMBARGO OF IMPORTATION OF PERSIAN/IRANIAN WORKS OF ART TO THE U.S.A.
Those clients considering purchasing Persian/Iranian works of art with the intention of exporting them to the U.S.A., should enquire of the relevant U.S. Government Department regarding the proper importation of such items. The Expert Department does however remain available to assist buyers with such enquiries, so far as is practicable. Buyers should be aware that Sotheby's does not represent that this approval will be granted.

COLLECTION OF LOTS
All lots will be transferred from the saleroom to Agility Warehouse after 9pm on the day of the sale. Collection can be made from the warehouse from 23 March 2009. PLEASE REFER TO THE GUIDE FOR PROSPECTIVE BUYERS IN THIS CATALOGUE.

Exceptions to this procedure will be notified by auction room notice and will be announced at the time of the sale. After 30 days, storage charges will commence.

SAFETY AT SOTHEBY'S
Sotheby's is concerned for your safety while you are on our premises and we endeavor to display items safely so far as is reasonably practicable. Nevertheless, should you handle any items on view at our premises, you accept liability for your acts which are at your own risk and without liability for Sotheby's or the seller.

Some items can be large and/or heavy and can be dangerous if mishandled. Should you wish to view or inspect any items more closely please ask for assistance from a member of the Sotheby's staff to ensure your safety and the safety of the property on view.

Some items on view may be labeled "PLEASE DO NOT TOUCH". Should you wish to view these items you must ask for assistance from a member of the Sotheby's staff, who will be pleased to assist you.

Thank you for your co-operation.

BUYERS OF LARGE PAINTINGS
Please note that all paintings specified in the catalogues as measuring 5ft x 5ft (152cm x 152cm) or more, excluding frame, will be transferred to Agility warehouse on the afternoon of the sale.

ESTIMATES IN QATARI RIYALS
As guide to potential buyers, estimates for this sale are also shown in Qatari Riyals and US Dollars. The estimates printed in the catalogues in US Dollars have been converted at the following rate, which was current at the time of printing. These estimates may have been rounded:
US$1 : QAR 3.63994

By the date of the sale this rate is likely to have changed, and buyers are recommended to check before bidding.

During the sale Sotheby's may provide a screen to show currency conversions as bidding progresses. This is intended for guidance only and all bidding will be in US Dollars. Sotheby's is not responsible for any errors or omissions in the operation of the currency converter.

Payment for purchases is due in US Dollars, however the equivalent amount in any other currency will be accepted at the rate prevailing on the day that payment is received in cleared funds.
Settlement is made to vendors in the currency in which the sale is conducted, or in any other currency on request at the rate prevailing on the day that payment is made by Sotheby's.

NOTICE REGARDING BURMESE JADITE AND RUBIES
Jadeite and Rubies of Burmese origin and articles of jewellery containing jadeite or rubies of Burmese origin all less than 100 years old may not be imported into the US. The inability of import of any such items shall not justify cancellation or rescission of the sale contract or any delay in payment. Please check with the specialist department if you are uncertain as to whether a lot is subject to these import restrictions, or any other restrictions on importation or exportation.

CLOCKS
Although condition reports may be given on request, such reports are statements of opinion only and may not specify all mechanical replacements or imperfections to the movement, case, dial, pendulum, separate base(s) or dome. All dimensions are approximate.

WRISTWATCHES
All wristwatches are sold as viewed and cannot be returned on the grounds that repairs have been carried out or parts supplied by anyone other than the named makers. There will be no viewing of watches and wristwatches on the day of sale.

Watches may not be taken apart whilst on view. Prospective buyers or their agents wishing to do so should make an appointment with the watch department for a private view the week before the sale.

Watches in water-resistant cases have been opened to examine movements but no warranties are made that the watches are currently water-resistant.

Please note that we do not guarantee the authenticity of any individual component parts, such as wheels, hands, crowns, crystals, screws, bracelets and leather bands, since subsequent repairs and restoration work may have resulted in the replacement of original parts.

Please be advised that straps made of material derived from endangered or otherwise protected species (ie. alligator and crocodile) are not sold with the watches and are for display purposes only. We reserve the right to remove these straps prior to shipping.

Furthermore, in reference to watch bands, we do not guarantee the material of manufacture. Please be advised that the purchaser will be responsible for complying with any applicable export and import matters, particularly in relation to endangered species and the United States Department of Fish and Wildlife Services.

We make no representation or warranty as to the condition of any lot sold.

R Important Notice regarding Importation into the United States of Rolex Watches
Sotheby's cannot arrange for the delivery of Rolex watches to the United States because U.S. laws restricts the import of Rolex watches. The buyer or a designated agent may collect the property in the country of sale.

2/09 DOHA_NOTICE_QAR

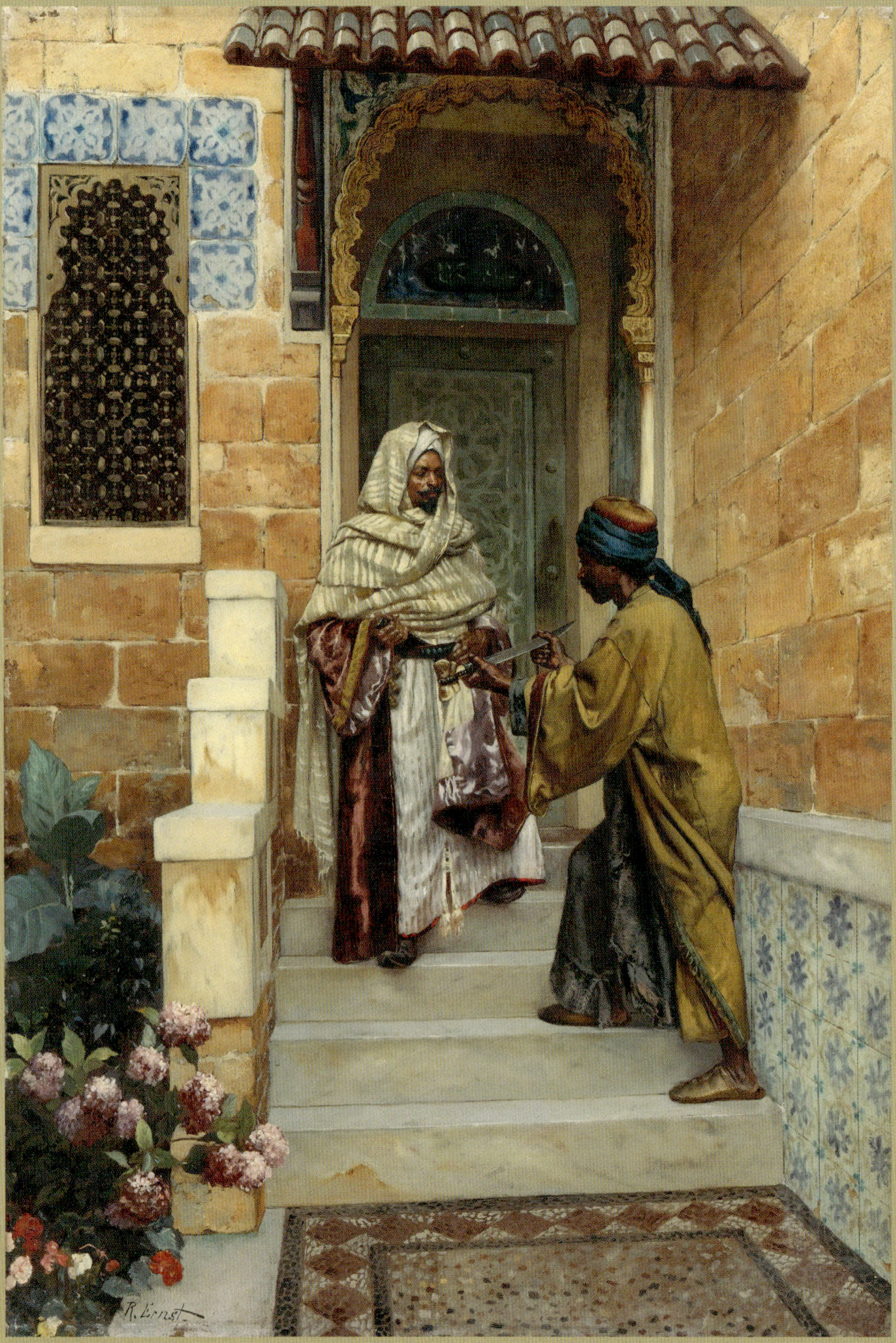
R. Ernst

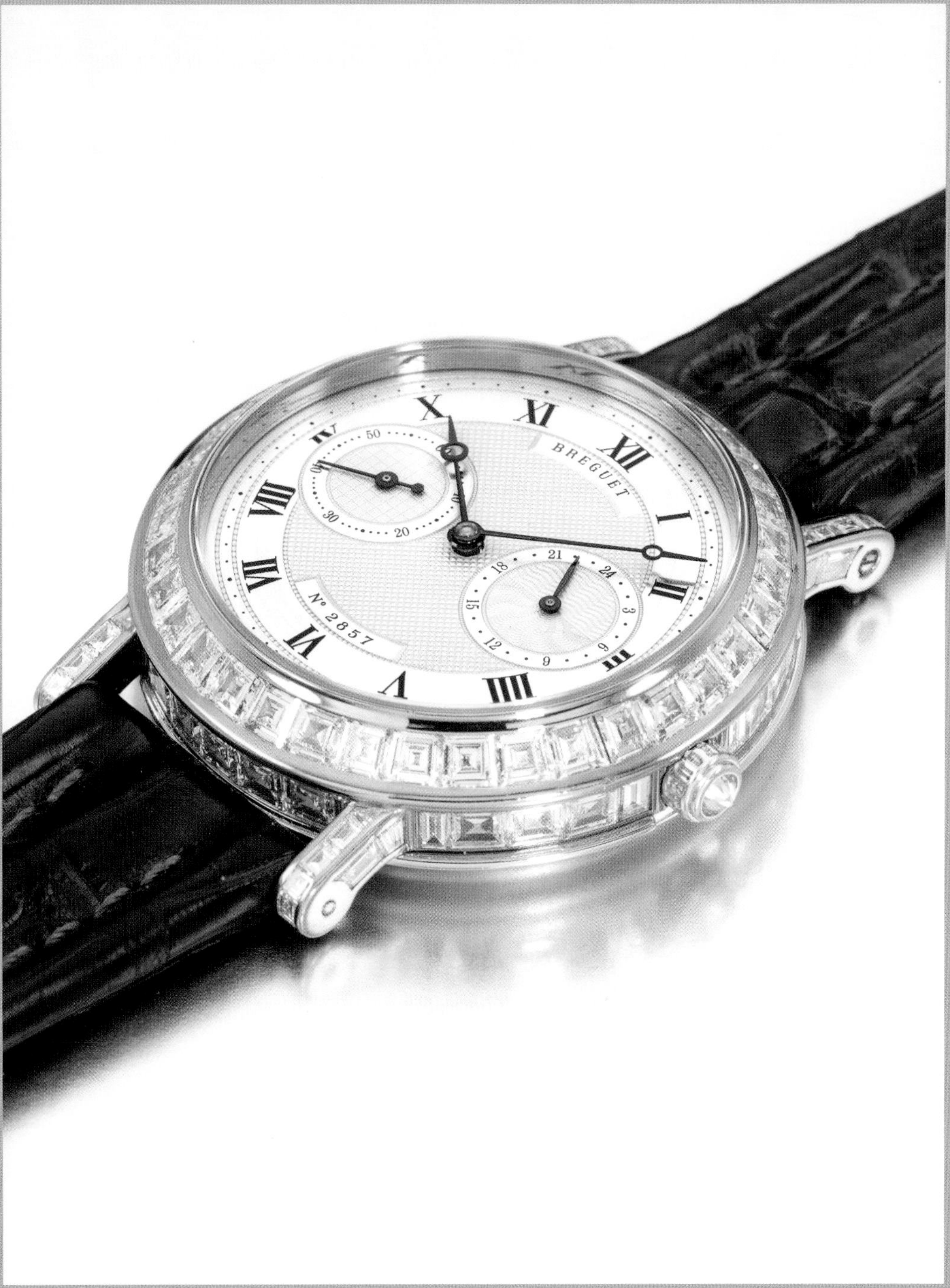
BREGUET
N° 2857

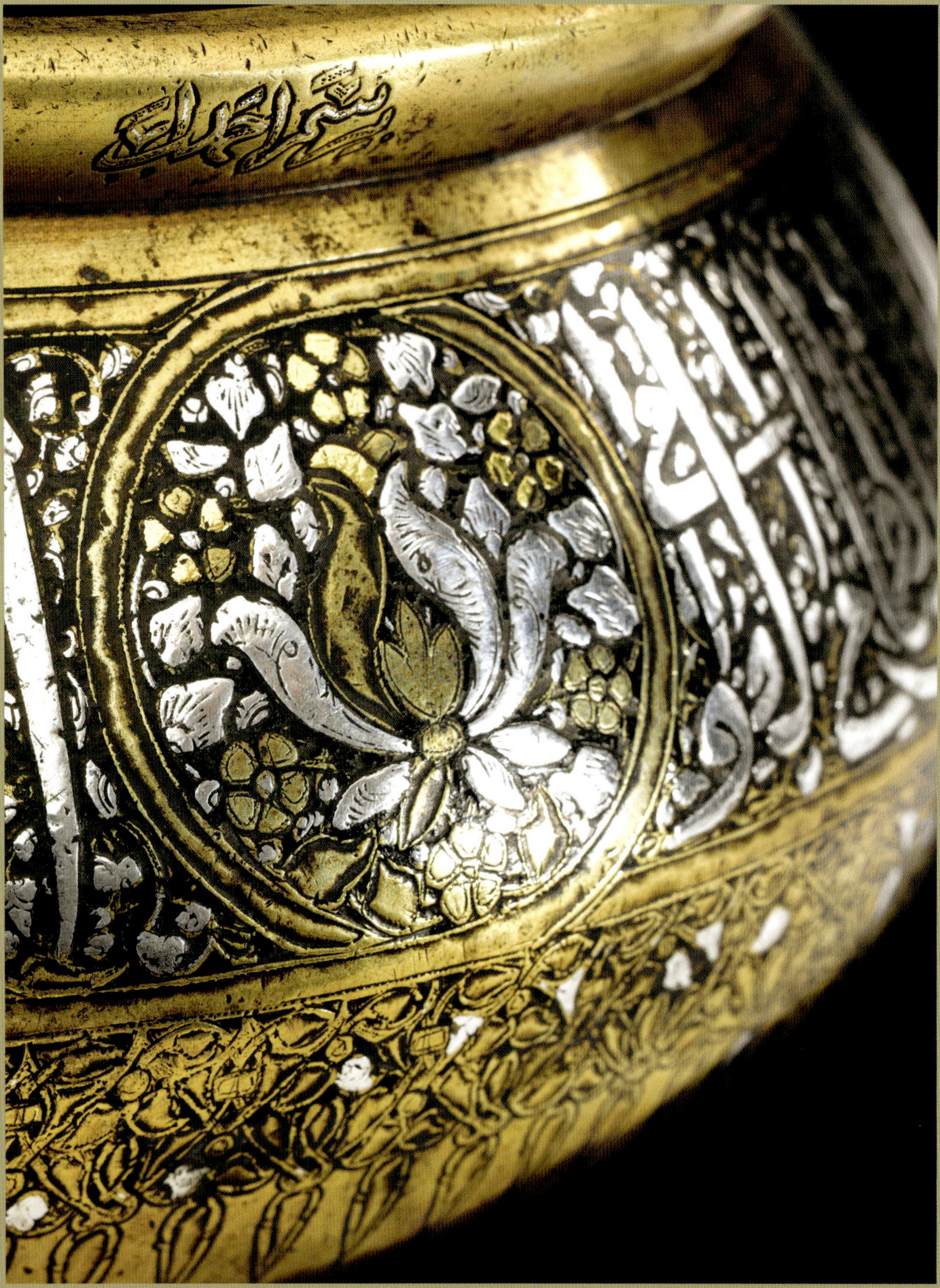

Buying at Auction The following pages are designed to give you useful information on how to buy at auction. Sotheby's staff as listed at the front of this catalogue will be happy to assist you. However, it is important that you read the following information carefully and note that Sotheby's acts for the seller: you should refer in particular to Conditions 3 and 4 of the Conditions of Business for Buyers printed in this catalogue. Prospective bidders should also consult www.sothebys.com for the most up to date cataloguing of the property in this catalogue.

Provenance In certain circumstances, Sotheby's may print in the catalogue the history of ownership of a work of art if such information contributes to scholarship or is otherwise well known and assists in distinguishing the work of art. However, the identity of the seller or previous owners may not be disclosed for a variety of reasons. For example, such information may be excluded to accommodate a seller's request for confidentiality or because the identity of prior owners is unknown given the age of the work of art.

Buyer's Premium A buyer's premium will be added to the hammer price and is payable by the buyer as part of the total purchase price. The buyer's premium is 25% of the hammer price up to and including US$50,000, 20% of any amount in excess of US$50,000 up to and including US$1,000,000, and 12% of any amount in excess of US$1,000,000.

GCC Import Tax at 5% will be payable on the hammer price of all lots. Please read carefully the "WAREHOUSE, STORAGE AND COLLECTION" section printed in this catalogue.

1. Before the Auction

Catalogue Subscriptions If you would like to take out a catalogue subscription, please ring +44 (0) 20 7293 6444.

Pre-sale Estimates Pre-sale estimates are intended as a guide for prospective buyers. Any bid between the high and low pre-sale estimates would, in our opinion, offer a chance of success. However, all lots can realise prices above or below the pre-sale estimates.

It is advisable to consult us nearer the time of sale as estimates can be subject to revision. The estimates printed in the auction catalogue do not include the buyer's premium or GCC import tax.

Pre-sale Estimates in US Dollars and Qatari Riyals Although the sale is conducted in US dollars, the pre-sale estimates in some catalogues are also printed in Qatari Riyals. The rate of exchange is the rate at the time of production of this catalogue. Therefore, you should treat the estimates in Qatari Riyals as a guide only.

Symbol Key The following key explains the symbols you may see inside this catalogue.

○ Guaranteed Property
The seller of lots with this symbol has been guaranteed a minimum price from one auction or a series of auctions. This guarantee may be provided by Sotheby's, by a third party or jointly by Sotheby's and a third party. Third parties providing all or part of a guarantee benefit financially if a guaranteed lot is sold successfully and may incur a loss if the sale is not successful. If every lot in a catalogue is guaranteed, the Important Notices in the sale catalogue will so state and this symbol will not be used for each lot.

△ Property in which Sotheby's has an Ownership Interest
Lots with this symbol indicate that Sotheby's owns the lot in whole or in part or has an economic interest in the lot equivalent to an ownership interest.

⋑ Irrevocable Bids
Lots with this symbol indicate that a party has provided Sotheby's with an irrevocable bid on the lot that will be executed during the sale at a value that ensures that the lot will sell. The irrevocable bidder, who may bid in excess of the irrevocable bid, will be compensated based on the final hammer price in the event he or she is not the successful bidder. If the irrevocable bidder is the successful bidder, he or she will be required to pay the full Buyer's Premium and will not be otherwise compensated. If the irrevocable bid is not secured until after the printing of the auction catalogue, a pre-lot announcement will be made indicating that there is an irrevocable bid on the lot.

V̲ Interested Parties
Lots with this symbol indicate that parties with a direct or indirect interest in the lot may be bidding on the lot, including (i) the beneficiary of an estate selling the lot, or (ii) the joint owner of a lot. If the interested party is the successful bidder, they will be required to pay the full Buyer's Premium. In certain instances, interested parties may have knowledge of the reserve. In the event the interested party's possible participation in the sale is not known until after the printing of the auction catalogue, a pre-lot announcement will be made indicating that interested parties may be bidding on the lot.

□ No Reserve
Unless indicated by a box (□), all lots in this catalogue are offered subject to a reserve. A reserve is the confidential hammer price established between Sotheby's and the seller and below which a lot will not be sold. The reserve is generally set at a percentage of the low estimate and will not exceed the low estimate for the lot. If any lots in the catalogue are offered without a reserve, these lots are indicated by a box (□). If all lots in the catalogue are offered without a reserve, a Special Notice will be included to this effect and the box symbol will not be used for each lot.

Condition of Lots Prospective buyers are encouraged to inspect the property at the pre-sale exhibitions. Solely as a convenience, Sotheby's may provide condition reports. The absence of reference to the condition of a lot in the catalogue description does not imply that the lot is free from faults or imperfections. Please refer to Condition 3 of the Conditions of Business for Buyers printed in this catalogue.

Electrical and Mechanical Goods All electrical and mechanical goods are sold on the basis of their artistic and decorative value only, and should not be assumed to be operative. It is essential that prior to any intended use, the electrical system is checked and approved by a qualified electrician.

2. Bidding in the Sale

Bidding at Auction Bids may be executed in person by paddle during the auction, in writing prior to the sale or by telephone.

Auction speeds vary, but average between 50 and 120 lots per hour. The bidding steps are generally in increments of approximately 10% of the previous bid.

Please refer to Conditions 5 and 6 of the Conditions of Business for Buyers printed in this catalogue.

Bidding in Person To bid in person, you will need to register for and collect a numbered paddle before the auction begins. Registration can be made during the viewing days and the day of the sale. Government issued proof of identity will be required. In addition a bank reference may be required.

Should you be the successful buyer of a lot, please ensure that your paddle can be seen by the auctioneer and that it is your number that is called out. Should there be any doubts as to price or buyer, please draw the auctioneer's attention to it immediately.

All lots sold will be invoiced to the name and address in which the paddle has been registered and cannot be transferred to other names and addresses.

Please do not mislay your paddle; in the event of loss, inform a member of Sotheby's staff immediately. At the end of the sale, please return your paddle to the registration desk.

Absentee Bids If you cannot attend the auction, we will be happy to execute written bids on your behalf. A bidding form can be found at the back of this catalogue. This service is free and confidential. Lots will always be bought as cheaply as is consistent with other bids, the reserves and Sotheby's commissions. In the event of identical bids, the earliest received will take precedence. Always indicate a "top limit" - the hammer

2/09 DOHA_BUY MAIN_A

price to which you would bid if you were attending the auction yourself. "Buy" and unlimited bids will not be accepted. Please refer to Condition 5 of the Conditions of Business for Buyers printed in this catalogue.

Telephone absentee bids must be confirmed before the sale by letter or fax. Fax number for bids only: +974 452 8334.

To ensure a satisfactory service, please ensure that we receive your bids by letter or fax at least 24 hours before the sale.

Bidding by Telephone If you cannot attend the auction, it is possible to bid on the telephone. As the number of telephone lines is limited, it is necessary to make arrangements for this service 24 hours before the sale. Where Sotheby's landlines are used, bids will be recorded.

We also suggest that you leave a maximum bid which we can execute on your behalf in the event we are unable to reach you by telephone. Where possible, multi-lingual staff are available to execute bids for you. Please refer to Condition 5 of the Conditions of Business for Buyers printed in this catalogue.

Employee Bidding Sotheby's employees may bid only if the employee does not know the reserve and fully complies with Sotheby's internal rules governing employee bidding.

Bidding by Noortman Master Paintings Noortman Master Paintings, an independently managed subsidiary of Sotheby's in the USA, may bid for and/or purchase any lot. Sotheby's accepts no responsibility to other bidders in connection with permitting Noortman to bid and/or purchase any lot.

US Economic Sanctions The United States maintains economic and trade sanctions against targeted foreign countries, groups and organisations. US buyers will please note that US persons are generally prohibited from selling, buying or otherwise dealing with property belonging to members, residents, nationals or the governments of these countries, organisations or groups.

3. The Auction

Conditions of Business The auction is governed by the Conditions of Business and Authenticity Guarantee. These apply to all aspects of the relationship between Sotheby's and actual and prospective bidders and buyers. Anyone considering bidding in the auction should read them carefully. They may be amended by way of notices posted in the saleroom or by way of announcement made by the auctioneer.

Consecutive and Responsive Bidding The auctioneer may open the bidding on any lot by placing a bid on behalf of the seller. The auctioneer may further bid on behalf of the seller, up to the amount of the reserve, by placing consecutive or responsive bids for a lot.

Please refer to Condition 6 of the Conditions of Business for Buyers printed in this catalogue.

Please note that should you be the winning bidder on a lot, on the fall of the hammer on that lot, you are contractually obligated to complete the purchase of that lot.

4. After the Auction

Payment Payment is due immediately after the sale and may be made by the following methods: US dollar cash, US dollar banker's draft, US dollar travellers cheques, US dollar cheque, wire transfer in US dollars, and credit card (Visa & Master Card) up to a limit of US$50,000, and debit cards.

- It is against Sotheby's general policy to accept single or multiple related payments in the form of cash or cash equivalents in excess of the local currency equivalent of US$10,000.
- It is Sotheby's policy to request any new clients or buyers preferring to make a cash payment to provide: proof of identity (by providing some form of government issued identification containing a photograph, such as a passport, identity card or driver's licence) and confirmation of permanent address. Thank you for your co-operation.

Cheques and drafts should be made payable to Sotheby's.

Although personal and company cheques drawn in US dollars are accepted, you are advised that property will not be released until such cheques have cleared unless you have a pre-arranged Cheque Acceptance Facility. Forms to facilitate this are available from cashiers.

Bank transfers should be made to:
HSBC Bank Middle East Limited, P.O. Box 57, Doha, Qatar.
Account Name: Sotheby's Qatar (O.P.C.)
Account No. 001-393412-050
Telephone: +974 438 2100, Facsimile: +974 441 6353
Telex: 4204 HSBC DH,
Swift Address: BBMEQAQX

Please include your name, Sotheby's account number and invoice number with your instructions to your bank. Please note that we reserve the right to decline payments received from anyone other than the buyer of record and that clearance of such payments will be required. Please contact our Client Accounts Department if you have any questions concerning clearance.

For absentee payments by credit card below US$50,000 please contact cashiers on +974 409 7130 during the sale and on +44 (0) 20 7293 5220 after the sale.

We reserve the right to seek identification of the source of funds received.

The Conditions of Business require buyers to pay immediately for their purchase. However, in limited circumstances and with the seller's agreement, Sotheby's may offer buyers it deems creditworthy the option of paying for their purchases on an extended payment term basis. Generally credit terms must be arranged prior to the sale. In advance of determining whether to grant the extended payment terms, Sotheby's may require credit references and proof of identity and residence.

Collection It is Sotheby's policy to request proof of identity on collection of a lot. Lots will be released to you or your authorised representative when full and cleared payment has been received by Sotheby's. If you are in doubt about the location of your purchases, please contact the Sale Administrator prior to arranging collection. Removal, interest, storage and handling charges will be levied on uncollected lots. Please refer to Condition 7 of the Conditions of Business for Buyers printed in this catalogue, and to the Warehouse, Storage and Collection page in this catalogue.

Storage Storage and handling charges may apply. For information concerning post sale storage and charges, please see the Warehouse, Storage and Collection Information at the back of this catalogue. Please refer to Condition 7 of the Conditions of Business for Buyers printed in this catalogue, and to the Warehouse, Storage and Collection page in this catalogue.

Loss or Damage Buyers are reminded that Sotheby's accepts liability for loss or damage to lots for a maximum period of thirty (30) days after the date of the auction. Please refer to Condition 7 of the Conditions of Business for Buyers printed in this catalogue.

Shipping Sotheby's Shipping Logistics can advise buyers on exporting and shipping property. You can contact the Shipping advisor on the number set out in the front of this catalogue.

Purchases will be despatched as soon as possible upon clearance from the Client Accounts department and receipt of your written despatch instructions and of any export licence or certificates that may be required. Despatch will be arranged at the buyer's expense. Sotheby's may receive a fee for its own account from the agent arranging the despatch. Estimates and information on methods available can be provided upon request; enquiries should be marked for the attention of the Sotheby's Shipping advisor as set out in the front of this catalogue. Additionally, a

2/09 DOHA_BUY MAIN_B

form to provide shipping instructions will be attached to the back of the buyer's invoice.

Your shipper will include a quote for transit insurance. All shipments should be unpacked and checked on delivery and any discrepancies notified to the transit insurer or shipper immediately.

Export The export of any lot from Qatar or import into any other country may be subject to one or more export or import licences being granted. It is the buyer's responsibility to obtain any relevant export or import licence. The denial of any licence required or delay in obtaining such licence cannot justify the cancellation of the sale or any delay in making payment of the total amount due.

Sotheby's, upon request and for an administrative fee, may apply for a licence to export your lot(s).

Sotheby's recommends that you retain all import and export papers including licences, as in certain countries you may be required to produce them to governmental authorities.

Endangered Species Items made of or incorporating plant or animal material, such as coral, crocodile, ivory, whalebone, tortoiseshell etc., irrespective of age or value may require a licence or certificate prior to exportation and require additional licences or certificates upon importation to any country in the EU. Please note that the ability to obtain an export licence or certificate does not ensure the ability to obtain an import licence or certificate in another country, and vice versa. For example, it is illegal to import elephant ivory under 100 years old into the United States. Sotheby's suggests that buyers check with their own government regarding wildlife import requirements prior to placing a bid. It is the buyer's responsibility to obtain any export or import licences and/or certificates as well as any other required documentation (please refer to Condition 10 of the Conditions of Business for Buyers printed in this catalogue).

5. Additional Services

Pre-sale Auction Estimates Sotheby's will be pleased to give preliminary pre-sale auction estimates for your property. This service is free of charge and is available from Sotheby's experts in New Bond Street on week days between 9:00 am and 4:30 pm. We advise you to make an appointment with the relevant expert department. Upon request, we may also travel to your home to provide preliminary pre-sale auction estimates.

Valuations The Valuation department provides written inventories and valuations throughout Europe for many purposes including insurance, probate and succession division, asset management and tax planning. Valuations can be tailored to suit most needs. Fees are highly competitive. For further information please contact the Valuation department on +44 (0)20 7293 6422, fax +44 (0)20 7293 5957.

2/09 DOHA_BUY MAIN_C

WAREHOUSE, STORAGE AND COLLECTION INFORMATION

All purchases can be collected on the day of the sale and until 20th March 2009 at The Ritz Carlton Hotel, Doha Qatar. After 20th March the lots will be relocated and stored at Agility Warehouse and will be available for collection by appointment from 23rd March 2009. The Agility office hours are: Sunday to Thursday from 8.00am till 5.00pm.

All sold lots will be available at:
Agility Warehouse, No. 41,
PO Box 22670, Doha, Qatar
Phone: +974 450 0017
Mobile: +974 580 7310
Fax: +974 460 6846
Contact: Mr. Rrajesh G. Kotean
Email: VCA@agilitylogistics.com

Sotheby's Shipping representative:
Martin de Meyer
Martin.DeMeyer@sothebys.com
From the 14th – 20th March 2009:
Tel: +974 409 7140 / F: +974 409 7103
Pre 14th March and post 20th March:
Tel: +31 20 550 22 49 / Fax: +31 20 550 23 49

Sotheby's London
Sue Swan
shipping.exports@sothebys.com
Tel: +44 20 7293 64 18
Fax: +44 20 7293 59 52

Lots will only be released to you or your authorised representative when full and cleared payment has been received by Sotheby's, appropriate identification has been provided, and a release note has been produced by our cashiers.

Purchasers wishing to collect lots from Agility Warehouse must ensure that their payment has been cleared prior to collection and that a release note has been forwarded to the warehouse by the cashiers at Sotheby's.

WHEN	METHOD	WHERE	CHARGES DUE	PACKING	WHO
18.-20.03.2009	On-site collection	Ritz Carlton Doha	5% GCC tax on hammer price. Export documentation provided on request	Bubble Wrap: Free	Please contact our shipping desk on site
18.-20.03.2009	Immediate shipping	Ritz Carlton Doha	We can take your shipping instructions and pass them to the shipper – if requested a quote will be issued in advance	As per requested instructions	Please pass the instructions to our shipping representative on site
23.03.–20.04.2009	Warehouse collection	Agility Warehouse (details above)	5% GCC tax on hammer price. If export documentation needed it can be provided on request. Handling fee depends on size – minimum US$ 50.00 per lot	Bubble Wrap: Free	Please pre-alert our shipping representative in advance (contact details above)
After 20.04.09	Late collection at Warehouse and delayed shipping	Agility Warehouse	5% GCC tax on hammer price. If export customs documentation needed it can be provided on request. Storage charges will commence. Please contact our shipping representative for the storage charges. The minimum handling fee is US$ 50.00 per lot	All packing costs will be charged to the buyer of the lot(s)	Please inform our shipping representative in advance of your plans for extended storage as charges are to be paid in advance (contact details above)

Please note:

- Storage at Agility Warehouse is free of charge until 20th April 2009. After that date all sold lots are subject to a handling and storage fee as mentioned above, payable to Sotheby's prior to collection.
- As set out in the Conditions of Business, buyers are reminded that Sotheby's accept liability for loss and damage to lots until 20th April 2009. Please refer to Condition 7 of the Conditions of Business for Buyers printed in this catalogue. Buyers are reminded that it is their responsibility to arrange adequate insurance for purchased lots.
- The export of any lots from Qatar or import into any other country may be subject to one or more export or import licences being granted. It is the buyer's responsibility to obtain any relevant export or import licences. The denial of any licence required or delay in obtaining such licence cannot justify the cancellation of the sale or any delay in making payment of the total amount due. Sotheby's upon request and for an administrative fee may apply for a licence to export your lot(s).
- Where exports are made within three months of the date of sale, the 5% GCC tax will not be charged if, before or at the point of invoicing, the buyer instructs Sotheby's to export the property from the GCC. If such an instruction is made after payment a refund will be made for the 5% GCC tax amount. Where the buyer carries purchases from Qatar personally or uses the services of another shipper, Sotheby's will charge the 5% GCC tax due as a deposit and refund it if the lot has been exported within three months of the date of sale and the appropriate documentary proof of export from the GCC has been provided. Buyers carrying their own property should obtain hand-carry papers from the shipping department to facilitate this process.
- Shipments can only be made if the purchase has been fully paid including any additional costs (handling and storage charges) and the shipping charges have been paid in advance to the shipper.

2/09 DOHA_MAIN_STORAGE

The nature of the relationship between Sotheby's, Sellers and Bidders and the terms on which Sotheby's (as auctioneer) and Sellers contract with Bidders are set out below.

Bidders' attention is specifically drawn to Conditions 3 and 4 below, which require them to investigate lots prior to bidding and which contain specific limitations and exclusions of the legal liability of Sotheby's and Sellers. The limitations and exclusions relating to Sotheby's are consistent with its role as auctioneer of large quantities of goods of a wide variety. Bidders should pay particular attention to these Conditions.

1. Introduction
(a) Sotheby's and Sellers' contractual relationship with prospective Buyers is governed by:

(i) these Conditions of Business;
(ii) the Conditions of Business for Sellers displayed in the saleroom and which are available upon request from Sotheby's UK salerooms or by telephoning +44 (0)20 7293 6152;
(iii) Sotheby's Authenticity Guarantee as printed in the sale catalogue; and
(iv) any additional notices and terms printed in the sale catalogue, including the Guide for Prospective Buyers, in each case as amended by any saleroom notice or auctioneer's announcement at the auction.

(b) As auctioneer, Sotheby's acts as representative for the Seller. A sale contract is made directly between the Seller and the Buyer. However, Sotheby's may own a lot (and in such circumstances acts in a principal capacity as Seller) and/or may have a legal, beneficial or financial interest in a lot as a secured creditor or otherwise.

2. Common Terms
In these Conditions of Business:

Bidder is any person considering, making or attempting to make a bid, by whatever means, and includes Buyers;
Buyer is the person who makes the highest bid or offer accepted by the auctioneer, and includes such person's principal when bidding as agent;
Buyer's Expenses are any costs or expenses due to Sotheby's from the Buyer and any Artist's Resale Right levy payable in respect of the sale of the Property, including an amount in respect of any applicable taxes thereon;
Buyer's Premium is the commission payable by the Buyer on the Hammer Price at the rates set out in the Guide for Prospective Buyers;
Counterfeit is as defined in Sotheby's Authenticity Guarantee;
Hammer Price is the highest bid accepted by the auctioneer by the fall of the hammer (in the case of wine, as apportioned pro-rata by reference to the number of separately identified items in that lot), or in the case of a post-auction sale, the agreed sale price;
Noortman is Noortman Master Paintings BV, an independently managed subsidiary of Sotheby's (U.S.);
Purchase Price is the Hammer Price and applicable Buyer's Premium and taxes;
Reserve is the (confidential) minimum Hammer Price at which the Seller has agreed to sell a lot;
Seller is the person offering a lot for sale (including their agent, executors or representatives (other than Sotheby's));
Sotheby's means Sotheby's Qatar (O.P.C.) with Commercial Registration No. 41076, P.O. Box 27111, Doha, Qatar;
Sotheby's Company means both Sotheby's in the USA and any of its subsidiaries and Sotheby's Diamonds SA and its subsidiaries.

3. Duties of Bidders and of Sotheby's in respect of items for sale
(a) Sotheby's knowledge in relation to each lot is partially dependent on information provided to it by the Seller, and Sotheby's is not able to and does not carry out exhaustive due diligence on each lot. Bidders acknowledge this fact and accept responsibility for carrying out inspections and investigations to satisfy themselves as to the lots in which they may be interested.

(b) Each lot offered for sale at Sotheby's is available for inspection by Bidders prior to the sale. Sotheby's accepts bids on lots solely on the basis that Bidders (and independent experts on their behalf, to the extent appropriate given the nature and value of the lot and the Bidder's own expertise) have fully inspected the lot prior to bidding and have satisfied themselves as to both the condition of the lot and the accuracy of its description.

(c) Bidders acknowledge that many lots are of an age and type which means that they are not in perfect condition and that Bidders have had the opportunity to inspect the lots. All lots are offered for sale in the condition they are in at the time of the auction (whether or not Bidders are in attendance at the auction). Condition reports may be available to assist when inspecting lots. Catalogue descriptions and condition reports may on occasions make reference to particular imperfections of a lot, but Bidders should note that lots may have other faults not expressly referred to in the catalogue or condition report. Illustrations are for identification purposes only and will not convey full information as to the actual condition of lots.

(d) Information provided to Bidders in respect of any lot, including any estimate, whether written or oral and including information in any catalogue, condition or other report, commentary or valuation, is not a representation of fact but rather is a statement of opinion genuinely held by Sotheby's. Any estimate may not be relied on as a prediction of the selling price or value of the lot and may be revised from time to time in Sotheby's absolute discretion.

(e) No representations or warranties are made by Sotheby's or the Seller as to whether any lot is subject to copyright or whether the Buyer acquires copyright in any lot.

(f) Subject to the matters referred to Conditions 3(a) to 3(e) above and to the specific exclusions contained at Condition 4 below, Sotheby's shall exercise such reasonable care when making express statements in catalogue descriptions or condition reports as is consistent with its role as auctioneer of lots in the sale to which these Conditions relate, and in the light of (i) the information provided to it by the Seller; (ii) scholarship and technical knowledge; and (iii) the generally accepted opinions of relevant experts, in each case at the time any such express statement is made.

2/09 DOHA_COB_MAIN_A

(g) Bidders agree that Noortman may bid for and/or purchase any lot.

4. Exclusions and limitations of liability to Buyers

(a) Sotheby's shall refund the Purchase Price to the Buyer in circumstances where it deems that the lot is a Counterfeit and each of the conditions of the Authenticity Guarantee has been satisfied.

(b) In the light of the matters in Condition 3 above and in light of the Bidders' ability to inspect items and the other matters set out in Conditions 4(a) and 4(e) to the fullest extent permitted by Qatar law, neither any Sotheby's Company nor the Seller:

(i) is liable for any errors or omissions in information provided to Bidders by Sotheby's (or any Sotheby's Company), whether orally or in writing, whether negligent or otherwise, except as set out in Condition 3(f) above;
(ii) gives any guarantee or warranty, to the fullest extent permitted by Qatar law, to Bidders and any implied warranties and conditions are excluded (save in so far as such obligations cannot be excluded by law) other than the express warranties given by the Seller to the Buyer in Condition 2 of the Sellers' Conditions of Business;
(iii) accepts responsibility to any Bidders in respect of acts or omissions, to the fullest extent permitted by Qatar law, (whether negligent or otherwise) by Sotheby's in connection with the conduct of auctions or for any matter relating to the sale of any lot (including the act of permitting Noortman to bid for and/or purchase any lot).

(c) Unless Sotheby's owns a lot offered for sale, it is not responsible for any breach of these conditions by the Seller.

(d) Without prejudice to Condition 4(b) and to the extent permitted by Qatar law, any claim against Sotheby's or the Seller by a Bidder is limited to the Purchase Price with regard to that lot. Neither Sotheby's nor the Seller shall under any circumstances be liable for any consequential losses.

(e) To the fullest extent permitted by Qatar law, Sotheby's and the Seller's liability is excluded in respect of death or personal injury caused by the negligent acts or omissions of Sotheby's or the Seller.

5. Bidding at Auction

(a) Sotheby's has absolute discretion to refuse admission to the auction. Bidders must complete a Paddle Registration Form and supply such information and references as required by Sotheby's. Bidders act as principal unless they have Sotheby's prior written consent to bid as agent for another party. Bidders are personally liable for their bid and are jointly and severally liable with their principal if bidding as agent.

(b) Sotheby's advises Bidders to attend the auction but will seek to carry out absentee written bids which are in US$ and, in Sotheby's opinion, clear and received sufficiently in advance of the sale of the lot, endeavouring to ensure that the first received of identical written bids has priority.

(c) Where available, written and telephone bids are offered as an additional service for no extra charge, at the Bidder's risk and shall be undertaken with reasonable care subject to Sotheby's other commitments at the time of the auction; Sotheby's therefore cannot accept liability for failure to place such bids save where such failure is unreasonable. Where Sotheby's landlines are used, telephone bids will be recorded.

6. Conduct of the Auction

(a) Unless otherwise specified, all lots are offered subject to a Reserve, which shall be no higher than the low presale estimate at the time of the auction.

(b) The auctioneer has discretion at any time to refuse any bid, withdraw any lot, re-offer a lot for sale (including after the fall of the hammer) if he believes there may be error or dispute, and take such other action as he reasonably thinks fit.

(c) The auctioneer will commence and advance the bidding at levels and in increments he considers appropriate and is entitled to place a bid or series of bids on behalf of the Seller up to the Reserve on the lot, without indicating he is doing so and whether or not other bids are placed.

(d) Subject to Condition 6(b), the contract between the Buyer and the Seller is concluded on the striking of the auctioneer's hammer, whereupon the Buyer becomes liable to pay the Purchase Price.

(e) Any post-auction sale of lots offered at auction shall incorporate these Conditions as if sold in the auction.

7. Payment and Collection

(a) Unless otherwise agreed, payment of the Purchase Price for a lot and any Buyer's Expenses are due by the Buyer in US Dollars immediately on conclusion of the auction (the "Due Date") notwithstanding any requirements for export, import or other permits for such lot.

(b) Title in a purchased lot will not pass until Sotheby's has received the Purchase Price and Buyer's Expenses for that lot in cleared funds. Sotheby's is not obliged to release a lot to the Buyer until title in the lot has passed and appropriate identification has been provided, and any earlier release does not affect the passing of title or the Buyer's unconditional obligation to pay the Purchase Price and Buyer's Expenses.

(c) The Buyer is obliged to arrange collection of purchased lots within thirty days of the auction. Purchased lots are at the Buyer's risk (and therefore their sole responsibility for insurance) from the earliest of i) collection or ii) thirty days after the auction. Until risk passes, Sotheby's will compensate the Buyer for any loss or damage to the lot up to a maximum of the Purchase Price paid. Buyers should note that Sotheby's assumption of liability for loss or damage is subject to the exclusions set out in Condition 6 of the Conditions of Business for Sellers.

(d) For all items stored by a third party and not available for collection from Sotheby's premises, the supply of authority to release the Items to the Buyer shall constitute collection by the Buyer.

(e) All packing and handling is at the Buyer's risk. Sotheby's will not be liable for any acts or omissions of third party packers or shippers.

(f) The Buyer of any firearm is solely responsible for obtaining all valid firearm or shotgun certificates or certificates of registration as a firearms dealer, as may be required by the regulations in force in Qatar relating to firearms or other weapons at the time of the sale, and for complying with all such regulations, whether or not notice of such is published in the Sale Catalogue. Sotheby's will not deliver a firearm to a Buyer unless the Buyer has first supplied evidence to Sotheby's satisfaction of compliance with this Condition.

8. Remedies for non-payment

Without prejudice to any rights the Seller may have, if the Buyer without prior agreement fails to make payment for the lot within five days of the auction, Sotheby's may in its sole discretion and to the fullest extent permitted by Qatar law (having informed the Seller) exercise one or more of the following remedies:

2/09 DOHA_COB_MAIN_B

(a) store the lot at its premises or elsewhere at the Buyer's sole risk and expense;

(b) cancel the sale of the lot;

(c) set off any amounts owed to the Buyer by a Sotheby's Company against any amounts owed to Sotheby's by the Buyer in respect of the lot;

(d) reject future bids from the Buyer or render such bids subject to payment of a deposit;

(e) charge interest at 6% per annum above HSBC Bank in Doha, Qatar Base Rate, from the Due Date to the date the Purchase Price and relevant Buyer's Expenses are received in cleared funds;

(f) exercise a lien over any of the Buyer's property which is in the possession of a Sotheby's Company. Sotheby's shall inform the Buyer of the exercise of any such lien and within 14 days of such notice may arrange the sale of such property and apply the proceeds to the amount owed to Sotheby's;

(g) resell the lot by auction or private sale, with estimates and reserves at Sotheby's discretion. In the event such resale is for less than the Purchase Price and Buyer's Expenses for that lot, the Buyer will remain liable for the shortfall together with all costs incurred in such resale;

(h) commence legal proceedings to recover the Purchase Price and Buyer's Expenses for that lot, together with interest and the costs of such proceedings on a full indemnity basis; or

(i) release the name and address of the Buyer to the Seller to enable the Seller to commence legal proceedings to recover the amounts due and legal costs. Sotheby's will take reasonable steps to notify the Buyer prior to releasing such details to the Seller.

9. Failure to collect purchases

(a) If the Buyer pays the Purchase Price and Buyer's Expenses but fails to collect a purchased lot within thirty calendar days of the auction, the lot will be stored at the Buyer's expense (and risk) at Sotheby's or with a third party.

(b) If a purchased lot is paid for but not collected within six months of the auction, the Buyer authorises Sotheby's, having given notice to the Buyer, to arrange a resale of the item by auction or private sale, with estimates and reserves at Sotheby's discretion. The proceeds of such sale, less all costs incurred by Sotheby's, will be forfeited unless collected by the Buyer within two years of the original auction.

10. Export and Permits

It is the Buyer's sole responsibility to obtain any necessary export, import, firearm, endangered species or other permit for the lot. Without prejudice to Conditions 3 and 4 above, Sotheby's and the Seller make no representations or warranties as to whether any lot is subject to export or import restrictions or any embargoes. The denial of any permit or licence shall not justify cancellation or rescission of the sale contract or any delay in payment.

11. General

(a) All images and other materials produced for the auction are the copyright of Sotheby's, for use at Sotheby's discretion.

(b) Notices to Sotheby's should be in writing and addressed to the department in charge of the sale, quoting the reference number specified at the beginning of the sale catalogue. Notices to Sotheby's clients shall be addressed to the last address formally notified by them to Sotheby's.

(c) Should any provision of these Conditions of Business be held unenforceable for any reason, the remaining provisions shall remain in full force and effect.

(d) These Conditions of Business are not assignable by any Buyer without Sotheby's prior written consent, but are binding on Buyers' successors, assigns and representatives. No act, omission or delay by Sotheby's shall be deemed a waiver or release of any of its rights.

(e) The materials listed in Condition 1(a) above set out the entire agreement and understanding between the parties with respect to the subject matter hereof. It is agreed that, save in respect of liability for fraudulent misrepresentation, no party has entered into any contract pursuant to these terms in reliance on any representation, warranty or undertaking which is not expressly referred to in such materials.

12. Data Protection

In connection with the management and operation of our business and the marketing and supply of Sotheby's Companies' services, or as required by law, we may ask clients to provide personal information about themselves or obtain information about clients from third parties (e.g. credit information). If clients provide Sotheby's with information that is defined by law as "sensitive", they agree that Sotheby's Companies may use it for the above purposes. Sotheby's Companies will not use or process sensitive information for any other purpose without the client's express consent.

If you would like further information on Sotheby's policies on personal data, or to make corrections to your information, please contact us on +44 (0)20 7293 6667.

If you would prefer not to receive details of future events please call the above number.

In order to fulfil the services clients have requested, Sotheby's may disclose information to third parties (e.g. shippers). Some countries do not offer equivalent legal protection of personal information to that offered within the EU. It is Sotheby's policy to require that any such third parties respect the privacy and confidentiality of our clients' information and provide the same level of protection for clients' information as provided within the EU, whether or not they are located in a country that offers equivalent legal protection of personal information. By agreeing to these Conditions of Business, clients agree to such disclosure.

Clients will please note that for security purposes, Sotheby's premises are subject to video recording. Telephone calls e.g. telephone bidding/voicemail messages may also be recorded.

13. Law and Jurisdiction

Governing Law These Conditions of Business and all aspects of all matters, transactions or disputes to which they relate or apply shall be governed by and interpreted in accordance with Qatar law.

Jurisdiction For the benefit of Sotheby's, all Bidders and Sellers agree that the Courts of Qatar are to have exclusive jurisdiction to settle all disputes arising in connection with all aspects of all matters or transactions to which these Conditions of Business relate or apply. All parties agree that Sotheby's shall retain the right to bring proceedings in any court other than the Courts of Qatar.

Service of Process All Bidders and Sellers irrevocably consent to service of process or any other documents in connection with proceedings in any court by facsimile transmission, personal service, delivery by mail or in any other manner permitted by Qatar law, the law of the place of service or the law of the jurisdiction where proceedings are instituted, at the last address of the Buyer or Seller known to Sotheby's or any other usual address.

2/09 DOHA_COB_MAIN_C

NOTES

Our staff are available by email using FIRSTNAME.LASTNAME@SOTHEBYS.COM

UNITED KINGDOM AND IRELAND

London

LONDON BOND STREET
Henry Wyndham
Chairman
Patrick van Maris van Dijk
Managing Director, Europe
George Bailey
Chairman, Business Development

34-35 New Bond Street
London W1A 2AA
TEL: +44 (0)20 7293 5000
FAX: +44 (0)20 7293 5989

Regional Representatives

KENT, EAST & WEST SUSSEX, SURREY & HAMPSHIRE
William Lucy
Billingshurst, Sussex
TEL: +44 (0)1403 833500
FAX: +44 (0)1403 833599

GLOUCESTERSHIRE, WARWICKSHIRE, WORCESTERSHIRE, HEREFORDSHIRE, OXFORDSHIRE, NORTHAMPTONSHIRE AND SOUTH WALES
John Harvey
Ullenwood, nr. Cheltenham
Gloucestershire
TEL: +44 (0)1242 510500
FAX: +44 (0)1242 250252
Thomas Lloyd ‡
Kilgetty, Pembrokeshire
TEL/FAX: +44 (0)1646 651493
Mary Miller ‡
Towcester, Northamptonshire
TEL: +44 (0)1327 860 020
FAX: +44 (0)1327 860 612

DEVON, CORNWALL, DORSET, SOMERSET AND WILTSHIRE
Elizabeth d'Erlanger
Tiverton, Devon
TEL: +44 (0)1884 243663
FAX: +44 (0)1884 258692
Elizabeth Fortescue ‡
Lostwithiel, Cornwall
TEL/FAX: +44 (0)1208 871133
Charles Hignett ‡
Bath, Somerset
TEL: +44 (0)1225 840101
FAX: +44 (0)1225 840696

EAST ANGLIA
The Lord Cranworth ‡
Woodbridge, Suffolk
TEL: +44 (0)1473 735581
FAX: +44 (0)1473 738278
Sara Foster ‡
Fakenham, Norfolk
TEL: +44 (0)1328 700032
FAX: +44 (0)1328 700155

THE NORTH, NORTH WALES & THE MIDLANDS
Chantal Cookson ‡
Meldon, Northumberland
TEL: +44 (0)1670 775123
Matthew Festing OBE ‡
Hexham, Northumberland
TEL: +44 (0)1434 240725
FAX: +44 (0)1434 240726
The Marchioness of Linlithgow ‡
Powys, Wales
TEL: +44 (0)1691 648646
FAX: +44 (0)1691 648664
Judith Heelis ‡
Appleby-in-Westmorland, Cumbria
TEL/FAX: +44 (0)1768 352806

CHANNEL ISLANDS
Clare d'Abo
Jersey
TEL: +44 (0)20 7293 5363
Antony Matheson
Guernsey
TEL: +44 (0)1481 233065
FAX: +44 (0)1481 233048

SCOTLAND & BORDERS
Anthony Weld Forester
Angus Milner Brown
7 Howe Street
Edinburgh EH3 6TE
TEL: +44 (0)131 558 7799
FAX: +44 (0)131 556 5568

IRELAND & NORTHERN IRELAND
Arabella Bishop
Anne Dillon
16 Molesworth Street
Dublin 2, Ireland
TEL: +353 1 671 1786
FAX: +353 1 679 7844
William Montgomery ‡
Newtownards, Co. Down
TEL: +44 (0)28 4278 8668
FAX: +44 (0)28 4278 8652

EUROPE AND MIDDLE EAST

Austria

Andrea Jungmann
Managing Director
Palais Wilczek
Herrengasse 5,
A-1010 Vienna
TEL: +43 1 512 4772
FAX: +43 1 513 4867

Belgium

BRUSSELS
Count Hubert d'Ursel
Chairman
Monique Bréhier
Deputy Chairman
Cédric Lienart
Managing Director
32 rue Jacques Jordaens
1000 Brussels
TEL: +32 2 648 0080
FAX: +32 2 648 0757
Chantal de Spot ‡
TEL: +32 475 971 534

ANTWERP
Valerie Meijer-Albada Jelgersma ‡
TEL: +32 486 506 555

Czech Republic

Filip Marco ◆
Pod Homolkou 22
150 00 Praha 5
TEL/FAX: +420 224 237 298

Denmark

Nina Wedell-Wedellsborg ◆
Vognmagergade 9
1120 Copenhagen K
TEL: +45 33 13 55 56
FAX: +45 33 93 01 19

France

PARIS
Guillaume Cerutti
Président
Princesse de Beauvau Craon
Présidente d'honneur, France
Deputy Chairman, Europe
Jeremy Durack
Secrétaire Général
76 Rue du Faubourg St. Honoré
75008 Paris
TEL: +33 1 53 05 53 05
FAX: +33 1 47 42 22 32

BORDEAUX
Alain de Baritault
TEL/FAX: +33 5 56 58 72 04

LILLE
Pascale Bomy
TEL: +33 6 07 60 79 62

LYON
Robert du Marais
TEL/FAX: +33 6 08 84 19 49

MARSEILLE
Florence Vidal
TEL/FAX: +33 4 91 48 65 59

MONTPELLIER
Béatrice Viennet
TEL: +33 4 67 24 95 72
FAX: +33 4 67 24 93 52

NANTES
François d'Hautpoul
TEL/FAX: +33 2 40 69 14 89

STRASBOURG
Marie-France Ludmann
TEL/FAX: +33 3 88 60 00 61

Germany

FRANKFURT
Dr. Philipp Herzog von Württemberg
Managing Director-Germany
Vice Chairman, Europe
Nina Buhne
Mendelssohnstrasse 66
D-60325 Frankfurt-am-Main
TEL: +49 69 74 07 87
FAX: +49 69 74 69 01

MUNICH
Heinrich Graf von Spreti
President-Germany
Odeonsplatz 16
D-80539 München
TEL: +49 89 291 31 51
FAX: +49 89 299 271

COLOGNE
Ursula Niggemann
Vice President-Germany
St. Apern - Strasse 17-21
D-50667 Köln
TEL: +49 221 20 7170
FAX: +49 221 257 4359

HAMBURG
Dr. Katharina Prinzessin zu Sayn-Wittgenstein
Tesdorpfstrasse 22
D-20148 Hamburg
TEL: +49 40 44 40 80
FAX: +49 40 410 70 82

HANNOVER
Susanne von Lüneburg ‡
TEL: +49 53 01 13 66
FAX: +49 53 01 12 27

Greece

Constantine Frangos
TEL: +44 (0)20 7293 5704
FAX: +44 (0)20 7293 5923
MOBILE: +30 69 4059 2317

* Associate of Sotheby's
‡ Consultant
◆ Representative

KEY
Sale Rooms

12/08 NBS_INTL OFF_A

Our staff are available by email using FIRSTNAME.LASTNAME@SOTHEBYS.COM

Hungary
Countess Dr. Soraya Stubenberg ‡
TEL: +43 676 566 90 92

Israel
Rivka Saker
Chairman
Sigal Mordechai
Co-Managing Director
Michelle Pollak
Co-Managing Director
11 Yehuda Halevi Street
Tel Aviv 65135, Israel
TEL: +972 3 560 1666
FAX: +972 3 560 8111

Italy
Claudia Dwek
Co-Chairman
Mario Tavella
Co-Chairman
MILAN
Filippo Lotti
Managing Director
Palazzo Broggi
Via Broggi 19,
20129 Milan
TEL: +39 02 295001
FAX: +39 02 29518595
BOLOGNA
Daniela Amati Jovi ‡
TEL: +39 0 51 331 382
FLORENCE
Clementina Bartolini Salimbeni
TEL: +39 0 55 247 9021
FAX: +39 0 55 247 9563
ROME
Luisa Lepri
Director
Palazzo Colonna
Piazza SS, Apostoli, 61
00187 Rome
TEL: +39 0 6 699 41791
FAX: +39 0 6 679 6167
TURIN
Laura Russo
Director
Corso Galileo Ferraris 18B
10121 Turin
TEL: +39 0 11 544898
FAX: +39 0 11 547675

Luxembourg
Please refer all enquiries to
Count Hubert d'Ursel
in the Brussels Office
TEL: +32 2 648 0080
FAX: +32 2 648 0757

Middle East & Gulf Region
Roxane Zand
Director, Middle East Department
TEL: +44 (0) 207 293 6200
TEL: +44 (0) 7809 58 7388
FAX: +44 (0) 207 293 6903

Qatar
Nigel Harrison
General Manager
PO Box 27111,
Level 15, Commercial Bank Plaza,
Al Markhiya Street #60, Doha
TEL: +974 452 8333
FAX: +974 452 8334

Monaco
Mark Armstrong
Director
Est-Ouest, 24, Boulevard
Princesse Charlotte, B.P. 45,
MC 98001 Monaco Cedex
TEL: +377 93 30 88 80
FAX: +377 93 25 24 98

Netherlands
AMSTERDAM
Mark Grol
Managing Director
Eveline van Oirschot
Chairman
De Boelelaan 30
1083 HJ Amsterdam
TEL: +31 20 550 22 00
FAX: +31 20 550 22 22

Norway
Ingeborg Astrup ◆
Bjørnveien 42, 0774 Oslo
TEL: +47 22 1472 82
FAX: +47 22 49 38 36

Portugal
Maria do Rosario
Horta e Costa ◆
Rua das Amoreiras, 103
1250-022 Lisbon
TEL: +35 1 213 713 310
FAX: +35 1 213 713 319

Russia
Mikhail Kamensky
General Director
4, Bldg 2, Romanov Pereulok,
125009, Moscow
TEL: +7 495 772 96 88
FAX: +7 495 772 96 89

Spain
MADRID
Pablo Melendo
Managing Director
Flavia Hohenlohe
Chairman
Alexandra Schader ‡
Contemporary Art Consultant
Alfonso XI, 7 bajo dcha
28014 Madrid
TEL: +34 91 576 5714
FAX: +34 91 781 2490

BARCELONA
Aurora Zubillaga
Aribau 175, Entlo. 2B
08036 Barcelona
TEL: +34 93 414 0866
FAX: +34 93 200 8361

Sweden
STOCKHOLM
Peder Isacson
Managing Director
Arsenalsgatan 2,
111 47 Stockholm
TEL: +46 8 679 5478
FAX: +46 8 611 4826

Switzerland
Maria Kelly
General Manager
GENEVA
Caroline Lang
Managing Director
13 Quai du Mont Blanc
CH - 1201 Geneva
TEL: +41 22 908 4800
FAX: +41 22 908 4801
ZURICH
Dr. Claudia Steinfels
Managing Director
Dr. Brigit Bernegger
Director
Talstrasse 83
CH - 8021 Zurich
TEL: +41 44 226 2200
FAX: +41 44 226 2201
LUGANO
Iris Fabbri ◆
Riva Caccia 4a
CH - 6900 Lugano
TEL: +41 91 993 3060
FAX: +41 91 993 3061

Turkey
Oya Delahaye
Ayazaga Mahallesi Meydan Sokak
Beybi Giz Plaza Kat: 27
34396 Maslak, Istanbul
TEL: +90 212 335 6442
FAX: +90 212 335 2500

Africa
South Africa
JOHANNESBURG
Stephan Welz & Co (Pty) Ltd*
Mark A. Kretschmer
Chairman
Jack Rosewitz
Vice Chairman
13 Biermann Avenue
Rosebank, Johannesburg 2196
TEL: +27 11 880 3125/9
FAX: +27 11 880 2656

CAPE TOWN
Stephan Welz & Co (Pty) Ltd*
Alphen Hotel, Alphen Drive
Constantia 7806, Cape Town
TEL: +27 21 794 6461
FAX: +27 21 794 6621

ASIA
China
BEIJING
Jackie Lien
Chief Representative
Zhang Rui
Resident Representative
Room 110, Building 1
21 Jian Guo Men Wai Da Jie
Beijing 100020, China
TEL: +86 10 8532 2323
FAX: +86 10 8532 2366
SHANGHAI
Jackie Lien
Chief Representative
Room 2803, Plaza 66
1266 Nanjing Road (W)
Shanghai 200040, PRC
TEL: +86 21 6288 7500
FAX: +86 21 6288 7200

Hong Kong
HONG KONG
Patti Wong
Chairman, Asia
Kevin Ching
Chief Executive Officer, Asia
Suites 3101-3106
One Pacific Place
88 Queensway
Hong Kong
TEL: +852 2524 8121
FAX: +852 2810 6238

Indonesia
The Capital Residence
Ground Floor
Sudirman Central Business
District, Lot 24
Jl. Jend. Sudirman Kav. 52-53
Jakarta 12190, Indonesia
TEL: +62 21 5797 3603
FAX: +62 21 5797 3604

Japan
Yasuaki Ishizaka
Managing Director
Fuerte Kojimachi Bldg. 3F
1-7 Kojimachi
Chiyoda-ku, Tokyo 102
TEL: +81 3 3230 2755
FAX: +81 3 3230 2754

Korea
c/o Hong Kong Office
TEL: +852 2524 8121
FAX: +852 2810 6238

2/09 NBS_INTL OFF_B

Our staff are available by email using FIRSTNAME.LASTNAME@SOTHEBYS.COM

Malaysia
Walter Cheah ‡
TEL: +60 3 2070 0319
FAX: +60 3 2070 6833

Philippines
c/o Hong Kong Office
TEL: +852 2524 8121
FAX: +852 2810 6238

Singapore
SINGAPORE
Esther Seet
Managing Director
1 Cuscaden Road
01- 01 The Regent Singapore
Singapore 249715
TEL: +65 6732 8239
FAX: +65 6737 0295

Taiwan, R.O.C.
Winnie Chang
Managing Director
Suite 3203, 32F No.333, Sec. 1,
Keelung Road, Taipei,
Taiwan 110, R.O.C.
TEL: +886 02 2757 6689
FAX: +886 02 2757 6679

Thailand
Wannida Saetieo
Country Manager
2nd Floor, Sukhothai Hotel
13/3 South Sathorn Rd
Bangkok 10120, Thailand
TEL: +662 286 0788
TEL: +662 286 0789
FAX: +662 286 0787

Australia
Justin Miller
Chairman
Lesley Alway
Managing Director
MELBOURNE
926 High Street, Armadale
Melbourne, Victoria 3143
TEL: +61 3 9509 2900
FAX: +61 3 9563 5067
SYDNEY
Queen's Court, Level 1
118-122 Queen Street
Woollahra
New South Wales 2025
TEL: +61 2 9362 1000
FAX: +61 2 9362 1100

LATIN AMERICA

Argentina
BUENOS AIRES
Adela Mackinlay de Casal
Edificio Kavanagh
San Martin 1068 PB
C1004AAV - Capital Federal
Argentina
TEL: +54 11 5032 8600
FAX: +54 11 5032 3330

Brazil
RIO DE JANEIRO
Katia Mindlin Leite Barbosa*
Caixa Postal 62619
Rio de Janeiro
RJ CEP 22250-970, Brazil
TEL: +55 21 2553 1946
FAX: +55 21 2553 4594
Heloise Guinle*
Estrada da Gavea 611
Bloco 1, Apt 2503
São Conrado
22610-000 Gavea
Rio de Janeiro, Brazil
TEL: +55 21 3322 4500
FAX: +55 21 3322 6397
SÃO PAULO
Pedro Corrêa do Lago*
Rua Dinamarca 92
São Paulo, SP 01449-040, Brazil
TEL: +55 11 3063 5455
FAX: +55 11 3082 6987

Chile
Cecilia Miquel*
Av. Presidente Riesco, 3641
Dpto. 401, Las Condes
Santiago, Chile
TEL: +562 231 8936
FAX: +562 335 6459

Mexico
MEXICO CITY
Carolina Morales
Campos Eliseos 325-5
Polanco, Mexico 11560 D.F.
TEL: +5255 5281 2100
TEL: +5255 5281 2200
FAX: +5255 5280 7136
MONTERREY
Barbara Perusquia de Lobeira*
Via Triumphalis 127 PTE.
Fuentes Del Valle
Monterrey 66220, Nuevo Leon
TEL: +52 81 8675 7573
TEL: +52 91 8675 7574
FAX: +52 81 129 5081

Venezuela
Diana Boccardo*
dboccardo@cantv.net
TEL/FAX: +58 212 285 5794

U.S.A.

Offices and Associates
HEADQUARTERS
NEW YORK
William F. Ruprecht
President & Chief Executive Officer
1334 York Avenue
New York, New York 10021
TEL: +1 212 606 7000
FAX: +1 212 606 7107

BALTIMORE
Aurelia Bolton*
Elizabeth Schroeder*
660 Kenilworth Drive, Suite 204,
Towson, Maryland 21204
TEL: +1 410 296 1100
FAX: +1 410 296 4433

CHICAGO
Helyn D. Goldenberg
Chairman, Midwest
Cathy Busch
Director
Cassie Spencer
Trusts & Estates
Gary F. Metzner
Fine Arts
Marjorie S. Susman*
188 East Walton Place
Chicago, Illinois 60611
TEL: +1 312 475 7900
FAX: +1 312 664 5295

DALLAS
Eve Reid*
TEL: +1 646 387 6765

HOUSTON
Aliyya Stude*
TEL: +1 713 594 8874

LOS ANGELES
Lisa Hubbard
International Jewelry
9665 Wilshire Blvd.
Beverly Hills, California 90212
TEL: +1 310 274 0340
FAX: +1 310 274 0899

MIAMI
Axel Stein
Director
Douglas Entrance
800 Douglas Road
Suite 125
Coral Gables, Florida 33134
TEL: +1 305 448 7882
FAX: +1 305 448 7168

MINNEAPOLIS/ST. PAUL
Laura MacLennan*
5108 Newton Avenue South
Minneapolis, Minnesota 55419
TEL: +1 612 308 2550

MONTANA
Kathryn Wilmerding Heminway
Bar 20 Ranch
West Boulder Reserve
McLeod, Montana 59052
TEL: +1 406 222 9399
FAX: +1 406 222 0051

NEW ENGLAND
William S. Cottingham
Director
Patricia Ward
Business Representative
67½ Chestnut St.
Boston, Massachusetts 02108
TEL: +1 617 367 6323
FAX: +1 617 367 4888

NEW YORK CITY
Barbara Cates*
Lee Copley Thaw
International Representative
TEL: +1 212 606 7000

PALM BEACH
David G. Ober
Chairman, Southeast
Hope P. Kent*
Louis J. Gartner*
Virginia Guest Valentine
International Representative
317 Peruvian Avenue
Palm Beach, Florida 33480
TEL: +1 561 833 2582
FAX: +1 561 655 4583

PHILADELPHIA
Angela Hudson
Director
Wendy Foulke*
18 Haverford Station Road
Haverford, Pennsylvania 19041
TEL: +1 610 649 2600
FAX: +1 610 649 7995

SAN FRANCISCO
Jennifer Foley Biederbeck
Mrs. Prentis Cobb Hale*
Mrs. John N. Rosekrans
International Representative
214 Grant Avenue, Suite 350
San Francisco, California 94108
TEL: +1 415 772 9028
FAX: +1 415 772 9031

SANTA BARBARA
Carolyn Amory*
PO Box 5736
Montecito, California 93159
TEL: +1 805 695 8344
FAX: +1 805 969 6811

Canada
David P. Silcox
President
9 Hazelton Avenue
Toronto, Ontario M5R 2E1
TEL: +1 416 926 1774
FAX: +1 416 926 9179
Ira R. Hopmeyer
Chairman & CEO
Canadian Art Sales in Association
with Ritchie's Auctioneers
380 King Street East
Toronto, Ontario M5A 1K9
TEL: +1 416 364 1864
FAX: +1 416 364 0704

KEY
Sale Rooms

1/09 NBS_INTL OFF._C

Sotheby's
EST. 1744

BIDDING FORM

SALE NUMBER
D09001

SALE TITLE
CONTEMPORARY ART

SALE DATE
18 MARCH 2009

IMPORTANT

Please note that the execution of written and telephone bids is offered as an additional service for no extra charge, and at the bidder's risk. It is undertaken subject to Sotheby's other commitments at the time of the auction. To the fullest extent permitted by Qatar law, Sotheby's therefore cannot accept liability for failure to place such bids, whether through negligence or otherwise.

Please note that we may contact new clients to request a bank reference.

Sotheby's will require sight of government issued ID and proof of address prior to collection of purchases (do not send originals).

FOR WRITTEN/FIXED BIDS

- Bids will be executed for the lowest price as is permitted by other bids or reserves.
- "Buy" or unlimited bids will not be accepted and we do not accept "plus one" bids. Please place bids in the same order as in the catalogue.
- Alternative bids can be placed by using the word "or" between lot numbers.
- Where appropriate your written bids will be rounded down to the nearest amount consistent with the auctioneer's bidding increments.

FOR TELEPHONE BIDS

- Please clearly specify the telephone number on which you may be reached at the time of the sale, including the country code. We will call you from the saleroom shortly before your lot is offered.

TITLE (EG. MR, MRS, DR) OR COMPANY NAME IF APPLICABLE ______

FIRST NAME ______ LAST NAME ______

SOTHEBY'S CLIENT ACCOUNT NO. (IF KNOWN) ______

ADDRESS ______

POSTCODE ______

TELEPHONE (HOME) ______ (BUSINESS) ______

EMAIL ______ FAX ______

WE WOULD LIKE TO SEND YOU MARKETING MATERIALS AND NEWS CONCERNING SOTHEBY'S, OR ON OCCASION THIRD PARTIES. IF YOU PROVIDE YOUR E-MAIL ADDRESS WE WILL CONTACT YOU FOR THIS PURPOSE.

MOBILE NO ______ VAT NO. (IF APPLICABLE) ______

☐ PLEASE TICK IF THIS IS A NEW ADDRESS & GIVE PREVIOUS FULL POSTCODE ______

PLEASE WRITE CLEARLY AND PLACE YOUR BIDS AS EARLY AS POSSIBLE, AS IN THE EVENT OF IDENTICAL BIDS, THE EARLIEST BID RECEIVED WILL TAKE PRECEDENCE.
BIDS SHOULD BE SUBMITTED IN US$ DOLLARS AT LEAST 24 HOURS BEFORE THE AUCTION.

LOT NUMBER	LOT DESCRIPTION	MAXIMUM US DOLLAR PRICE (EXCLUDING PREMIUM AND TAXES) OR TICK FOR PHONE BID
		US$
		US$
		US$
		US$
		US$
		US$
		US$
		US$
		US$
		US$

TELEPHONE NUMBER DURING THE SALE (TEL. BIDS ONLY) ______

PLEASE SEE OVERLEAF FOR DETAILS OF WHERE TO SEND THIS FORM.

I hereby agree that if I am the highest bidder at the fall of the auctioneer's hammer for that lot, I will be contractually bound to complete the purchase of that lot on the terms of the Conditions of Business for that sale.

I consent to the use of this information and any other information obtained by Sotheby's in accordance with the Guide for Absentee Bidders and Conditions of Business. If you would like further information on Sotheby's policies on personal data, or to make corrections to your information, please contact us on +44 (0)20 7293 6667. I am aware that all telephone bid lines will be recorded.

Signed ______ **Dated** ______

Witness Name ______ **Witness Signature** ______ **Dated** ______

PAYMENT IS DUE IMMEDIATELY AFTER THE SALE IN US$ DOLLARS. FULL DETAILS ON HOW TO PAY ARE INCLUDED IN THE GUIDE FOR BUYERS. **OR:** PLEASE CHARGE MY CREDIT / DEBIT CARD FOR MY PURCHASES IN THIS SALE. WE ACCEPT VISA, MASTERCARD, DEBIT CARDS, BUT NOT AMERICAN EXPRESS OR DINERS CLUB. NB. ONLY PAYMENTS UP TO A MAXIMUM OF US$50,000 MAY BE PAID BY CREDIT CARD. **PAYMENT MUST BE MADE BY THE INVOICED PARTY.**

NAME ON CARD ______ TYPE OF CARD ______

CARD NUMBER ☐☐☐☐☐☐☐☐☐☐☐☐☐☐☐☐

START DATE (IF APPLICABLE) ☐☐ ☐☐ EXPIRY DATE ☐☐ ☐☐ ISSUE NUMBER ☐ SWITCH ONLY

☐☐☐ 3 LAST DIGITS OF SECURITY CODE ON SIGNATURE STRIP

INVOICE IF YOU ARE SUCCESSFUL AND WOULD LIKE YOUR INVOICE SENT TO THE ABOVE EMAIL OR FAX, PLEASE TICK BOX ☐. A COPY WILL FOLLOW BY POST.
SHIPPING IF YOU ARE SUCCESSFUL AND WOULD LIKE US TO CONTACT YOU REGARDING SHIPPING, PLEASE TICK HERE ☐.

2/09 DOHA_BIDSLIP

If you are unable to attend an auction in person, you may give Sotheby's Bid Department instructions to bid on your behalf by completing the form overleaf.

This service is free and confidential.

Please record accurately the lot numbers, descriptions and the top hammer price you are willing to pay for each lot.

We will try to purchase the lot(s) of your choice for the lowest price possible and never for more than the top amount you indicate.

"Buy" or unlimited bids will not be accepted.

Alternative bids can be placed by using the word "OR" between lot numbers.

Bids must be placed in the same order as in the catalogue.

This form should be used for one sale only – please indicate the sale number, title and date on the form.

Please place your bids as early as possible, as in the event of identical bids the earliest received will take precedence. Wherever possible bids should be submitted at least twenty-four hours before the auction.

Where appropriate, your bid will be rounded down to the nearest amount consistent with the auctioneer's bidding increments.

Absentee bids, when placed by telephone, are accepted only at the caller's risk and must be confirmed by letter or fax to the Bid Department on +974 452 8334.

Please note that the execution of written bids is offered as an additional service for no extra charge at the bidder's risk and is undertaken subject to Sotheby's other commitments at the time of the auction; to the fullest extent permitted by Qatar law Sotheby's cannot accept liability for failure to place such bids, whether through negligence or otherwise.

Successful bidders will receive an invoice detailing their purchases and giving instructions for payment and clearance of goods.

Successful buyers are earnestly requested to arrange early collection of their goods as they will incur storage charges after 20th April 2009.

Bidders on large objects are recommended to check on the day of the auction whether they have been successful.

All bids are subject to the conditions of business applicable to the sale, a copy of which is available from Sotheby's offices or by telephoning +974 452 8333. Conditions of Business particularly relevant to buyers are also set out in the sale catalogue.

It is against Sotheby's general policy to accept single or multiple related payments in the form of cash or cash equivalents in excess of the local currency equivalent of US$10,000.

It is Sotheby's policy to request any new clients or purchasers preferring to make a cash payment to provide: proof of identity (by providing some form of government issued identification containing a photograph, such as a passport, identity card or driver's licence) and confirmation of permanent address.

We reserve the right to seek identification of the source of funds received.

In connection with the management and operation of our business and the marketing and supply of Sotheby's Companies' services, or as required by law, we may ask clients to provide personal information about themselves or obtain information about clients from third parties (e.g. credit information). If clients provide Sotheby's with information that is defined by law as "sensitive", they agree that Sotheby's Companies may use it for the above purposes. Sotheby's Companies will not use or process sensitive information for any other purpose without the client's express consent. If you would like further information on Sotheby's policies on personal data, or to make corrections to your information, please contact us on +44 (0)207 293 6667.

In order to fulfil the services clients have requested, Sotheby's may disclose information to third parties (e.g. shippers). Some countries do not offer equivalent legal protection of personal information to that offered within the EU. It is Sotheby's policy to require that any such third parties respect the privacy and confidentiality of our clients' information and provide the same level of protection for clients' information as provided within the EU, whether or not they are located in a country that offers equivalent legal protection of personal information. By signing this Absentee Bid Form you agree to such disclosure. Clients will please note that for security purposes, Sotheby's premises are subject to video recording. Telephone calls e.g. telephone bidding/voicemail messages may also be recorded.

Please mail or fax your bidding form to:

Sotheby's Qatar (O.P.C.),
P.O. Box 27111,
Level 15, Commercial Bank Plaza
Al Markhiya Street #60
Doha, Qatar

Up to and including March 13th.
Tel: +974 452 8333
Fax: +974 452 8334

From March 14th to March 20th.
Tel: +974 409 7120
Fax: +974 409 7102

Mixed Sources
Product group from well-managed forests and other controlled sources
www.fsc.org Cert no. SGS-COC-004826
© 1996 Forest Stewardship Council
FSC

The paper used in this catalogue was manufactured at a mill that has been awarded the ISO 14001 and the Eco Management Audit Scheme certificates for environmental management.

2/09 DOHA_AB BID MAIN

PHOTOGRAPHY DONALD THOMPSON JAMIE GOVIER | CATALOGUE DESIGNER MICHAEL MOLLOY JONATHAN WILLS | COLOUR EDITOR TOM BROWN
PRODUCTION CONTROLLER ROBYN ERBE | REPRO/PRINT SOT/MID

For further information and full listing of all Specialist departments and Services, go to: sothebys.com

12/08 NBS_BOD

(أ) أن تقوم بتخزين القطعة في المنشآت التابعة لها أو في أي مكان آخر، وذلك على نفقة **المشتري** فقط وعلى مسؤوليته الحصرية لجهة المخاطر؛
(ب) أن تقوم بإلغاء عملية بيع القطعة؛
(ج) أن تقوم بخصم أي مبالغ مستحقة على **شركة سوذبيز إلى المشتري** من أي مبالغ مستحقة على **المشتري** إلى **سوذبيز** فيما يتصل بالقطعة المذكورة؛
(د) أن تقوم برفض أي مزايدات مستقبلية من هذا **المشتري** أو أن تشترط عليه دفع عربوناً أو مبلغاً ما كوديعة؛
(هـ) أن تقوم بإضافة فائدة تزيد بنسبة ٦% على معدل الفائدة الأساسي لبنك إتش إس بي سي في الدوحة HSBC Bank في السنة اعتباراً من **موعد الاستحقاق** وحتى تاريخ استلام **ثمن الشراء ونفقات المشتري** ذات الصلة من **المشتري**، وبأموال خالصة؛
(و) أن تقوم بالحجز على أي ممتلكات **للمشتري** تكون موجودة في حيازة **شركة سوذبيز**. ويجب أن تقوم **سوذبيز** بإخطار **المشتري** بأنها قامت بإجراء هذا الحجز، ويحق لها أن تقوم خلال ١٤ يوماً من تاريخ هذا الإخطار بإجراء الترتيبات اللازمة لبيع الممتلكات المحتجزة واستخدام عائدات البيع لسداد المبلغ المستحق لها؛
(ز) أن تقوم بإعادة بيع القطعة في المزاد أو في عملية بيع خاصة، وفقاً للأسعار التقديرية **والأسعار الاحتياطية** التي تحددها **سوذبيز** حسب تقديرها الخاص. وإذا كان سعر إعادة البيع أقل من **ثمن الشراء ونفقات المشتري** عن تلك القطعة، يظل **المشتري** مسؤولاً عن دفع فرق السعر بالإضافة إلى كافة التكاليف الأخرى التي يتم تكبدها في عملية إعادة البيع؛
(ح) أن ترفع دعوى قانونية لاستعادة **ثمن الشراء ونفقات المشتري** عن تلك القطعة، بالإضافة إلى الفوائد والمصاريف المرتبطة بهذه الدعوى وعلى أساس التعويض الكامل عنها؛
(ط) أن تقوم بالكشف عن اسم وعنوان **المشتري إلى البائع** لكي يتسنى له رفع دعوى قانونية لاسترداد المبالغ المستحقة وأتعاب المحاماة، على أن تقوم **سوذبيز** باتخاذ الخطوات المعقولة لإخطار المشتري قبل أن تقوم بالكشف عن هذه المعلومات **للبائع**.

٩. عدم استلام القطع المشتراة

(أ) إذا قام **المشتري** بدفع **ثمن الشراء ونفقات المشتري** دون أن يقوم باستلام القطعة المشتراة خلال ثلاثين يوم شمسياً من تاريخ المزاد، يتم تخزين القطعة المشتراة بالمزاد على نفقة **المشتري** (ومسؤوليته لجهة المخاطر) في منشآت **سوذبيز** أو منشآت أي طرف ثالث.
(ب) في حال سداد المدفوعات مع عدم استلام القطعة المشتراة بالمزاد خلال ستة أشهر من تاريخ المزاد، يقوم **المشتري** بتفويض **سوذبيز** (بعد إخطار **المشتري**) بإجراء الترتيبات لإعادة بيع القطعة في المزاد أو في عملية بيع خاصة وفقاً للأسعار التقديرية **والأسعار الاحتياطية** التي تحددها **سوذبيز** حسب تقديرها الخاص، بعد إخطار **المشتري** بذلك. وتقوم **سوذبيز** بمصادرة عائدات هذا البيع بعد خصم التكاليف التي تحملتها **سوذبيز**، ما لم يقم **المشتري** بتحصيلها خلال مدة سنتين من تاريخ المزاد الأصلي.

١٠. التصدير والتصاريح

إن استحصال أي تصاريح لازمة للتصدير أو الاستيراد أو الأسلحة النارية أو المخلوقات المهددة بالانقراض أو غيرها من التصاريح الأخرى الخاصة بالقطعة المشتراة، يقع على عاتق **المشتري** دون غيره. وبدون الإخلال بالشرطين ٣ و ٤ أعلاه، لا تقدم **سوذبيز** أو **البائع** أي بيانات توضيحية أو ضمانات عما إذا كانت أي قطعة من القطع المباعة بالمزاد تخضع لقيد أو حظر بخصوص الاستيراد أو التصدير. كما أن عدم الحصول على أي تصاريح أو تراخيص لا تعد أساساً أو مبرراً لإلغاء أو إبطال عقد البيع أو لتأخير أي مدفوعات مستحقة.

١١. عموميات

(أ) جميع الصور والمواد الأخرى التي يتم إنتاجها من أجل المزاد تعتبر ضمن حقوق التأليف والنسخ والنشر المحفوظة **لسوذبيز** على أن تكون لها حرية التصرف فيها.

(ب) جميع الإخطارات إلى **سوذبيز** يجب أن تكون كتابية وموجهة إلى الإدارة المسؤولة عن عملية البيع، مع ذكر رقم المرجع المحدد في بداية كتالوج البيع. أما الإخطارات الموجهة لزبائن **سوذبيز** فيتم إرسالها إلى آخر عنوان قاموا بإبلاغ **سوذبيز** رسمياً به.

(ج) في حال اعتبار أي من هذه الشروط التجارية غير قابل للتنفيذ لأي سبب من الأسباب، تبقى جميع الشروط المتبقية سارية ونافذة بشكل كامل؛

(د) إن جميع حقوق المشتري الواردة هذه **الشروط التجارية** غير قابلة للتنازل عنها إلا بعد الحصول على موافقة كتابية مسبقة من **سوذبيز**، وإنما تعتبر هذه الشروط ملزمة لوَرَثة **المشترين** وممثليهم والأشخاص المتنازل لهم من قبلهم. ولا يعتبر أي تصرف أو إغفال أو تأخير من جانب **سوذبيز** تنازلاً أو تخلياً عن أي من الحقوق الخاصة بها.

(هـ) تمثل المواد المبينة في الشرط ١(أ) أعلاه الاتفاق والتفاهم الكامل بين الأطراف بشأن مضمون هذه المواد والأحكام. ومن المتفق عليه، باستثناء المسؤولية في حالات التمثيل الإحتيالي، بأن أي طرف لم يقم بإبرام أي عقد بموجب هذه الشروط والأحكام بالاستناد إلى أي بيانات توضيحية أو ضمانات أو تعهدات لم يتم الإشارة إليها بشكل صريح ضمن هذه المواد.

١٢. حماية البيانات الحاسوبية

من الممكن أن نطلب من زبائننا تقديم بعض البيانات الشخصية عنهم، أو أن نحصل على هذه البيانات عنهم من أطراف ثالثة (مثل معلومات الائتمان)، وذلك فيما يتصل بإدارة وتشغيل أعمالنا التجارية وأعمال التسويق وتوفير الخدمات من جانب **شركات سوذبيز**، أو وفقاً لما يقتضيه القانون. وفي حال حصول **سوذبيز** من الزبائن على بيانات يصنفها القانون بأنها بيانات "حساسة"، يوافق الزبائن على السماح **لشركات سوذبيز** باستخدام هذه البيانات في الأغراض الآنفة الذكر. ولا تقوم **شركات سوذبيز** باستخدام أو معالجة هذه البيانات في أي أغراض أخرى بدون موافقة صريحة من الزبون.

إذا أردت الحصول على مزيد من المعلومات حول سياسات **سوذبيز** الخاصة بالبيانات الشخصية، أو أردت تصحيح أي من البيانات الخاصة بك، يُرجى الاتصال برقم الهاتف: 6667 7293 20(0) 44+.

وإذا كنت تفضل عدم استلام أي تفاصيل عن أحداث أخرى في المستقبل، يُرجى الاتصال بالرقم المذكور أعلاه.

لكي تتمكن **سوذبيز** من تقديم الخدمات التي يطلبها الزبائن، يمكن لسوذبيز الكشف عن المعلومات لأطراف ثالثة (مثل شركات الشحن). إن بعض الدول لا تقدم نفس المستوى من الحماية القانونية للبيانات الشخصية الذي تقدمه دول الاتحاد الأوروبي ، إلا أن سياسة **سوذبيز** تقضي بأن تفرض قيام تلك الأطراف الثالثة باحترام خصوصية وسرية المعلومات والبيانات الخاصة بزبائنها وتوفير نفس المستوى من الحماية لبيانات الزبائن كالذي توفره دول الاتحاد الأوربي، سواء أكانت هذه الأطراف متواجدة أم لا في إحدى الدول التي توفر نفس المستوى من الحماية القانونية للبيانات الشخصية. وبموافقتهم على هذه الشروط، يوافق الزبائن أيضاً على هذا الكشف عن تلك البيانات.

نوجه عناية زبائننا إلى أن منشآت **سوذبيز** تخضع للتسجيلات المرئية (الفيديو) لأغراض أمنية. كما أن المكالمات الهاتفية، مثل المزايدة عن طريق الهاتف أو رسائل البريد الصوتي، قد يتم تسجيلها أيضاً.

١٣. القانون والنظام القضائي

القانون النافذ: هذه **الشروط التجارية** وكافة الجوانب المتصلة بأي أمر من الأمور، بالإضافة إلى كافة المعاملات أو النزاعات المرتبطة بها أو المطبقة عليها، يجب أن تخضع لأحكام القانون القطري، ويتم تفسيرها وفقا لتلك الأحكام.

النظام القضائي: لتحقيق مصلحة **سوذبيز**، يوافق كافة **المزايدين والبائعين** على أن تكون المحاكم القطرية هي السلطة القضائية الوحيدة التي لها الحق تسوية كافة النزاعات التي تنشأ فيما يتصل بكافة الجوانب الخاصة بكافة الأمور أو المعاملات المرتبطة بهذه **الشروط التجارية** أو التي تنطبق عليها هذه الشروط. ويوافق جميع الأطراف على أن تحتفظ **سوذبيز** بحقها في رفع الدعاوى أمام أي محكمة أخرى غير المحاكم القطرية.

التبليغ بالإجراءات القضائية: يوافق جميع **المزايدين والبائعين** موافقة نهائية لا رجوع عنها على أن يتم التبليغ بالإجراءات القضائية، أو غيرها من الوثائق الأخرى التي لها علاقة بالدعاوى لدى أي محكمة، عن طريق الفاكس أو التسليم باليد أو الإرسال بالبريد، أو من خلال أي وسيلة أخرى يسمح بها القانون القطري أو قانون البلد الذي يتم فيه التبليغ أو القانون

(و) مع مراعاة الأحكام المذكورة في الشروط ٣(أ) إلى ٣(هـ) أعلاه، ومراعاة الاستثناءات المحددة المتضمنة في الشرط ٤ أدناه، تقوم **سوذبيز** ببذل العناية المعقولة عند التعبير عن رأيها الصريح سواء في الوصف المذكور في الكتالوج أو في التقارير عن حالة القطع بما ينسجم مع دورها كدلال للقطع المعروضة للبيع والتي تتعلق بها هذه الشروط، وفي ضوء (١) المعلومات المقدمة من **البائع**، (٢) والمعارف والخبرات والمعلومات الفنية، (٣) والآراء المتعارف عليها بشكل عام من الخبراء المعنيين، في كل حالة في الوقت الذي تعبر فيه عن رأيها الصريح.

(ز) يوافق **المزايدون** على أن من حق **شركة نورتمان** المزايدة و/ أو الشراء لأي من القطع المعروضة للبيع.

٤. الاستثناءات والمحدوديات المتعلقة بمسؤوليات المشترين

(أ) تلتزم **سوذبيز** بإعادة **ثمن الشراء** إلى **المشتري** في الحالات التي تعتبر فيها أن القطعة المباعة مزيفة، وأن كافة الشروط الواردة في **ضمان الأصالة** تمت مراعاتها.

(ب) في ضوء الأمور المشار إليها في الشرط ٣ أعلاه، وفي ضوء قدرة المشتري في تفحص القطع المعروضة و الأمور الأخرى الواردة في الشرطين ٤(أ) و ٤(هـ) و إلى الحد الأقصى المسموح به في القانون القطري ، فإن كلا من **شركة سوذبيز والبائع**:

(١) غير مسؤول عن أي خطأ أو إهمال في أي من المعلومات التي تقدمها **سوذبيز** (أو أي **من شركات سوذبيز**) إلى **المزايدين**، سواء أكانت هذه المعلومات شفهية أو كتابية، وبصرف النظر عما إذا كان ذلك يعود إلى الإهمال أو غير ذلك، باستثناء ما هو محدد في الشرط ٣(و) أعلاه؛

(٢) لا يقدم أي ضمان أو كفالة، إلى الحد الأقصى المسموح به في القانون القطري، **للمزايدين** ولا أي ضمانات أو شروط ضمنية (باستثناء الالتزامات التي لا يمكن استبعادها بموجب القانون) غير الضمانات والكفالات الصريحة التي يقدمها **البائع** إلى **المشتري** في الشرط ٢ من **الشروط التجارية للبائعين؛**

(٣) لا يتحمل أي مسؤولية تجاه **المزايدين** عما قامت به **سوذبيز** أو عما لم تقم به، إلى الحد الأقصى المسموح به في القانون القطري، (سواء بسبب الإهمال أو غير ذلك) فيما يتصل بطريقة إجراء المزادات أو بأي من الأمور الأخرى التي لها علاقة ببيع أي من القطع (بما في ذلك السماح لشركة **نورتمان** بالمزايدة و/ أو الشراء لأي من القطع المعروضة).

(ج) لا تتحمل **سوذبيز** أية مسؤولية عن قيام **البائع** بانتهاك أي من هذه الشروط، ما لم تكن **سوذبيز** هي المالكة للقطعة المعروضة للبيع بالمزاد.

(د) بدون الإخلال بالشرط ٤(ب) وإلى الحد المسموح به في القانون القطري، أي ادعاء يرفعه **المزايد** ضد **سوذبيز أو البائع**، يجب أن يقتصر فقط على **ثمن الشراء** للقطعة المباعة بالمزاد. ولا تتحمل **سوذبيز** ولا **البائع** أية مسؤولية بأي حال من الأحول عن أية خسائر تبعية.

(هـ) وإلى الحد الأقصى المسموح به في القانون القطري **سوذبيز** أو **البائع** ولا يحدّ من مسؤولياتهما بخصوص أي مزاعم كاذبة بغرض الاحتيال، أو بخصوص وفاة أي من الأشخاص أو إصابته بالأذى نتيجة الإهمال أو التقصير من جانب **سوذبيز** أو **البائع**.

٥. المزايدة في المزاد

(أ) يكون **لسوذبيز** الحرية المطلقة في عدم السماح لشخص ما بالدخول في المزاد. ويجب على **المزايدين** ملء **استمارة تسجيل اللافتة الرقمية**، وتقديم المعلومات والبيانات التي تطلبها **سوذبيز**. ويجب أن يعمل **المزايد** كشخص أصيل ما لم يحصل على موافقة خطية مسبقة من **سوذبيز** بأن يقوم بالمزايدة كوكيل عن طرف آخر. ويعتبر **المزايد** مسؤولاً شخصياً عن المزايدات التي يقوم بها، بالإضافة إلى أنه مسؤول بالتكافل والتضامن مع الشخص الأصيل الذي قام بتوكيله إذا قام بالمزايدة كوكيل.

(ب) تنصح **سوذبيز المزايدين** بحضور جلسات البيع بالمزاد، ولكنها تسعى أيضاً لإجراء المزايدات الكتابية الغيابية التي تتم بالدولار الأمريكي، وتكون واضحة، حسب تقدير **سوذبيز**، ويتم تسليمها مسبقاً قبل بيع القطعة بفترة كافية من الوقت، وهي تحاول أن تضمن الأولوية **للمزايدة** الخطية المسلمة قبل غيرها في حال تعادل المزايدات المقدمة.

(ج) يتم تقديم خدمة المزايدة الهاتفية أو المزايدة الكتابية، في حال توافرها، كخدمة إضافية بدون مقابل، وعلى مسؤولية **المزايد** الشخصية، على أن يتم تنفيذها بعناية معقولة وبما يتماشى مع الالتزامات الأخرى **لسوذبيز** في موعد المزاد، ولذلك لا تتحمل **سوذبيز** أية مسؤولية عن الإخفاق في تقديم المزايدات إلا إذا كان هذا الإخفاق بدون مبرر معقول. سيتم تسجيل المزايدات في حالة استخدام خطوط الهاتف للمزايدة..

٦. طريقة إجراء المزاد

(أ) ما لم يرد نصّ بغير ذلك، يتم تحديد **سعر احتياطي** لكافة القطع المعروضة للبيع، وهذا **السعر الاحتياطي** يجب ألا يزيد في موعد المزاد عن الحدّ الأدنى للسعر التقديري للقطعة قبل المزاد.

(ب) يكون لدار المزاد حق التقدير في أي وقت من الأوقات بأن يرفض أي مزايدة أو أن يقوم بسحب أي قطعة من القطع المعروضة للبيع، أو يقوم بإعادة عرض أي من القطع التي تم عرضها سابقاً (بما فيها الحالة التي يكون فيها قد ضرب المطرقة مسبقاً)، إذا كان يعتقد أن هناك خطأً أو خلافاً محتملاً، ويحق له اتخاذ الإجراء الذي يراه مناسباً بشكل معقول.

(ج) يقوم دار المزايدة بتحديد المستوى الذي تبدأ منه المزايدة، ومستوى الزيادة التي يرى أنها ملائمة، ومن حقه أيضاً أن يزايد أو يقدم سلسلة من المزايدات بالنيابة عن **البائع** إلى أن يصل إلى **السعر الاحتياطي** للقطعة، بدون أن يشير إلى قيامه بذلك أو إلى ما إذا كانت هناك مزايدات أخرى أم لا.

(د) مع مراعاة الشرط ٦(ب)، يتم إبرام العقد بين **المشتري والبائع** من اللحظة التي يقوم ممثل دار المزايدة بضرب المطرقة، ومنذ هذه اللحظة يصبح **المشتري** ملزماً بسداد **ثمن الشراء**.

(هـ) أي بيع يتم بعد المزاد للقطع التي كانت معروضة في المزاد يجب أن تنطبق عليه هذه الشروط وكأن عملية البيع تمت أثناء المزاد.

٧. الدفع والاستلام

(أ) ما لم يتم الاتفاق على غير ذلك، يستحق **ثمن الشراء** للقطعة على **المشتري** بالإضافة إلى **نفقات المشتري** بالدولار الامريكي، وذلك فور انتهاء المزاد (ويُشار إليه بـ **"موعد الاستحقاق"**) بصرف النظر عما إذا كانت هناك أي متطلبات أخرى تتعلق بتصدير أو استيراد تلك القطعة.

(ب) لا يتم نقل ملكية القطعة المشتراة إلا بعد أن تحصل **سوذبيز** على **ثمن الشراء** وعلى **نفقات المشتري** عن تلك القطعة، وذلك بأموال خالصة. وتعتبر **سوذبيز** غير ملزمة بتسليم أي قطعة إلى **المشتري** إلا بعد أن تنتقل ملكية هذه القطعة إليه ويتم إبراز دليل ملائم حول هويته، وأي تسليم مبكر للقطعة لا يؤثر على نقل حق الملكية، ولا على الالتزام غير المشروط من جانب **المشتري** بدفع **ثمن الشراء ونفقات المشتري**.

(ج) يلتزم **المشتري** بإجراء الترتيبات اللازمة لاستلام القطع المشتراة من المزاد خلال ثلاثين يوم من انتهاء المزاد. كما تعتبر القطع المشتراة على مسؤولية **المشتري** لناحية المخاطر (وهو يتحمل أيضاً وبصورة حصرية مسؤولية التأمين عليها)، وذلك منذ (١) موعد استلامه لها، أو (٢) بعد مرور ثلاثين يوم على انتهاء المزاد، على أن ينطبق الموعد الأسبق زمنياً بين هذين الموعدين. وإلى أن تزول المخاطر المحتملة، تقوم **سوذبيز** بتعويض **المشتري** عن الخسائر أو الأضرار التي يمكن أن تلحق بالقطعة المشتراة وبحدّ أقصى لا يتجاوز **ثمن الشراء** المدفوع. ويجب أن ينتبه **المشترون** إلى أن **سوذبيز** تتحمل هذه المسؤولية عن الخسائر أو الأضرار مع مراعاة الاستثناءات الواردة في الشرط ٦ من **الشروط التجارية للبائعين**.

(د) بالنسبة للقطع التي يتم تخزينها لدى طرف ثالث ولا تكون متوفرة للاستلام من المنشآت التابعة **لسوذبيز**، يعتبر إصدار التفويض بالتسليم **للمشتري** وكأنه استلام للقطعة من قبل **المشتري**.

(هـ) تتم كافة أعمال التعليب والتغليف والمناولة على مسؤولية **المشتري** لجهة المخاطر، حيث أن **سوذبيز** لا تكون مسؤولة عن أي عمل أو إهمال من جانب أي طرف ثالث يقوم بالتعليب أو التغليف أو الشحن.

(و) عند شراء أي أسلحة نارية، يعتبر **المشتري** وحده هو المسؤول عن الحصول على كافة الشهادات أو التسجيلات التي تثبت أنه تاجر للأسلحة النارية وفقاً لما قد تقتضيه القواعد التنظيمية المعمول بها في إنجلترا وويلز أو في اسكتلندا (حسبما ينطبق) بشأن الأسلحة النارية أو أي أسلحة أخرى في موعد البيع، ويكون مسؤولاً عن التقيد بجميع تلك القواعد، بصرف النظر عما إذا كان قد ورد إخطار بذلك في كتالوج البيع أم لا. ولا تقوم **سوذبيز** بتسليم أي أسلحة نارية إلى **المشتري** إلا بعد أن يقدم الدليل الذي تطمئن إليه **سوذبيز** بشأن التقيد بهذا الشرط.

٨. الإجراءات العلاجية في حالة عدم الدفع

بدون الإخلال بأي من الحقوق التي يتمتع بها **البائع**، إذا أخفق **المشتري**، وبدون اتفاق مسبق، في تسديد ثمن القطعة المشتراة خلال خمسة أيام من تاريخ المزاد، يحق **لسوذبيز** أن تقوم حسب تقديرها الحصري و إلى الحد

الشروط التجارية للمشترين

فيما يلي توضيح لطبيعة العلاقة بين **سوذبيز والبائعين والمزايدين**، بالإضافة إلى الشروط والأحكام التي تقوم بموجبها **سوذبيز** (بصفتها الدلال) **والبائعون** بالتعاقد مع **المزايدين**.

إننا نلفت نظر المزايدين على وجه التحديد إلى الشرطين ٣ و ٤ ، اللذان يحتمان عليهم الاستقصاء عن القطع المعروضة بالمزاد قبل المزايدة عليها، بالإضافة إلى ما يتضمنه هذان الشرطان من محدوديات واستثناءات للمسؤولية القانونية التي تقع على **سوذبيز والبائعين**. وتتماشى هذه المحدوديات والاستثناءات للمسؤوليات القانونية التي تتحملها **سوذبيز** مع دورها كدار مزايدة يقوم ببيع كميات كبيرة من البضائع ذات التشكيلة المتنوعة والواسعة في المزاد. ويجب على **المزايدين** الانتباه على وجه الخصوص إلى هذين الشرطين.

١. مقدمة

(أ) تخضع العلاقة التعاقدية **لسوذبيز والبائعين** مع **المشترين** المحتملين لما يلي:-

(١) **الشروط التجارية** هذه ؛

(٢) **الشروط التجارية للبائعين** التي يتم عرضها في قاعة المزاد، والتي يمكن الحصول عليها عند الطلب من قاعات المزاد التابعة **لسوذبيز** في المملكة المتحدة، أو من خلال الاتصال برقم الهاتف: 44+(0)20 7293 6152؛

(٣) **ضمان الأصالة** من **سوذبيز** حسبما هو مطبوع في كتالوج البيع بالمزاد؛

(٤) الإخطارات والشروط الإضافية المطبوعة في كتالوج البيع بالمزاد، بما فيها **دليل المشترين**، مع التعديلات التي تجري على كل منها بأي من الإخطارات التي يتم الإعلان عنها في قاعة المزاد أو يعلن عنها الدلال نفسه داخل قاعة المزاد.

(ب) إن **سوذبيز**، بصفتها دار مزايدة، تعمل كوكيل عن **البائع**. ويتم إبرام عقد بيع بين **البائع والمشتري** مباشرة، ولكن من الممكن في بعض الأحيان أن تكون **سوذبيز** هي المالك الأصلي للقطعة المباعة (وفي هذه الحالة تتصرف **سوذبيز** بصفتها **البائع**)، و/ أو تكون لها أي مصلحة قانونية أو منفعة مالية في القطعة المباعة، بصفتها الدائن المضمون أو غير ذلك.

٢. المصطلحات العامة

فيما يلي تفسير الكلمات الواردة في إطار **الشروط التجارية**:

المُزايد: هو أي شخص ينوي أو يقوم، أو يحاول القيام، بالمزايدة بأي وسيلة من الوسائل، ويشمل ذلك **المشترين**؛

المشتري: هو الشخص الذي يقدم أعلى سعر مزايدة أو سعر شراء معروض يقبله دار المزايدة، ويشمل ذلك الشخص الأصيل في حال المزايدة عن طريق الوكيل؛

نفقات المشتري: هي التكاليف أو المصاريف المستحقة **لسوذبيز** على المشتري، أو أي رسوم خاصة بحق الفنان في إعادة البيع للآخرين والتي يستحق دفعها بخصوص بيع القطعة، ويشمل ذلك أية ضرائب مستحقة. ؛

الرسم الإضافي على المشتري: هو العمولة المستحقة على **المشتري** كنسبة من سعر إرساء المزاد، حسب المعدلات المذكورة في **دليل المشترين المحتملين**؛

المزيف: هو ما تم تعريفه في **ضمان الأصالة** من **سوذبيز**؛

سعر إرساء المزاد: هو أعلى سعر شراء معروض يقبله دار المزايدة بضرب المطرقة (في حالة النبيذ، يكون هذا السعر متناسباً مع كل حصة من الحصص مع الإشارة إلى عدد البنود المعرّفة بشكل منفصل في القطعة المباعة)؛ وفي حالة البيع بعد المزاد، يكون **سعر إرساء المزاد** هو سعر البيع المتفق عليه؛

شركة نورتمان: هي شركة "نورتمان ماستر بينتنغز المحدودة Noortman Master Paintings BV"، إحدى الشركات التابعة **لسوذبيز**، والتي تخضع لإدارة مستقلة؛

ثمن الشراء: هو سعر إرساء المزاد بالإضافة إلى الرسم الإضافي على المشتري مع الضرائب المترتبة؛

السعر الاحتياطي: هو الحدّ الأدنى (السرّي) لسعر إرساء المزاد الذي وافق **البائع** على بيع القطعة به؛

البائع: هو الشخص الذي يعرض إحدى القطع للبيع في المزاد، ويشمل ذلك الوكيل ، أو منفذ وصيته أو ممثله الشخصي (غير **سوذبيز**)؛

سوذبيز: تعني سوذبيز (ش.ش.و.) رقم السجل التجاري ٤١٠٧٦ و صندوق بريد ٢٧١١١، الدوحة ، قطر.

شركة سوذبيز: تعني شركة **سوذبيز** الموجودة في الولايات المتحدة الأمريكية وأية شركة من الشركات التابعة لها، بالإضافة إلى شركة **سوذبيز دياموندس إس إيه** Sotheby's Diamonds S.A. والشركات التابعة لها.

٣. واجبات كل من المزايدين وسوذبيز فيما يتعلق بالقطع المعروضة للبيع بالمزاد:

(أ) تعتمد المعلومات المتوافرة لدى **سوذبيز** عن كل قطعة من القطع بشكل جزئي على ما يقدمه **البائع** من معلومات، إذ لا يتسنى **لسوذبيز** القيام بالتقصي الدقيق اللازم عن كل قطعة من القطع المعروضة للبيع بالمزاد. ويقر **المزايدون** بهذه الحقيقة، ويقبلون أن يتحملوا مسؤولية القيام بالمعاينات والاستقصاءات اللازمة حول القطع التي قد يرغبون في شرائها، وللدرجة التي يقتنعون بها.

(ب) الفرصة متاحة أمام **المزايدين** لأن يقوموا قبل عملية البيع بتفحص أي من القطع المعروضة للبيع بالمزاد لدى **سوذبيز**. إن **سوذبيز** لا تقبل المزايدة على القطع إلا على أساس أن **المزايدين** (والخبراء المستقلين الموكلين نيابة عنهم إلى المدى الذي يتناسب مع طبيعة وقيمة القطع المعروضة للبيع بالإضافة إلى الخبرة المتوافرة لدى **المزايدين**) قد قاموا بالمعاينة الكاملة للقطع المعروضة للبيع قبل المزايدة عليها، واطمأنوا لحالتها ومدى مطابقتها للوصف المذكور لها.

(ج) يقر **المزايدون** أن العديد من القطع المعروضة للبيع في المزاد هي من حيث العمر و النوع في حالة غير مثالية و بأن الفرصة سنحت للمزايدين لتفحص القطع المعروضة. كما أن كافة القطع المعروضة للبيع يتم عرضها في الحالة الراهنة لها في موعد المزاد (سواء أكان **المزايد** حاضراً في المزاد أم لا). كما يمكن أن تتوافر تقارير عن حالة هذه القطع للمساعدة في تفحصها. وقد يشير الوصف المذكور في الكتالوج، أو التقارير حول حالة القطع، في بعض الأحيان إلى عيوب خاصة موجودة في إحدى القطع، ولكن يحب أن ينتبه **المزايدون** إلى أن القطع المعروضة للبيع يمكن أن تحتوي أيضاً على عيوب أخرى لم تتم الإشارة إليها بشكل صريح في الكتالوج أو في التقارير الخاصة بحالة هذه القطع. والغرض من الإيضاحات الواردة هو تحديد هوية القطعة فقط، وهي لا تمثل المعلومات الكاملة عن الحالة الفعلية للقطعة.

(د) إن المعلومات التي يتم توفيرها **للمزايدين** بخصوص أي من القطع، سواء أكانت كتابية أو شفهية، بما في ذلك أي سعر تقديري أو المعلومات الواردة في الكتالوج أو التقرير عن حالة القطعة أو غيره من التقارير الأخرى أو التعليقات أو التقييمات، لا تمثل حقيقة مسلمة، وإنما تعبر عن وجهة النظر الحقيقية **لسوذبيز**. كما لا يجوز الاعتماد على الأسعار التقديرية للتنبؤ بسعر البيع أو بقيمة القطعة المعروضة، ويجوز أيضاً تغيير تلك الأسعار من وقت لآخر حسب التقدير المطلق **لسوذبيز**.

(هـ) لا تقدم **سوذبيز** أو **البائع** أي بيانات توضيحية أو ضمانات حول ما إذا كانت أي من القطع المعروضة تخضع لأي من حقوق التأليف أو النسخ أو النشر أم لا، أو ما إذا كان **المشتري** سوف يكتسب أياً من حقوق التأليف أو النسخ أو النشر لأي منها.

في حالة قيام **سوذبيز** ببيع إحد القطع وتبين بعد ذلك أنها مزيفة، تقوم **سوذبيز** بإلغاء عملية البيع وإعادة المبلغ الكامل الذي دفعه **المشتري** مقابل هذه القطعة بنفس العملة التي تمت بها عملية البيع الأصلية.

ولهذه الأغراض، تعني كلمة **"مزيف"** الكثير من الأشياء التي ترى **سوذبيز** أن الغرض منها هو التقليد أو الغش لشخصية المؤلف أو الفنان أو الكاتب الذي قام بالعمل أو لمنشأ هذا العمل أو تاريخه أو عمره أو عصره أو ثقافته أو مصدره، عندما لا يظهر الوصف السليم لمثل هذه الأمور في الكتالوج الخاص (مع الأخذ في الاعتبار مسرد المصطلحات). ولا يتم النظر إلى أي قطعة باعتبارها مزيفة بسبب وجود أي تلف و/ أو إصلاح و/ أو تعديل من أي نوع (بما في ذلك إعادة الرسم أو الطلاء فوق الرسم الموجود). يُرجى الانتباه إلى أن هذا **الضمان** لا ينطبق في الحالات التالية:

(١) إذا كان الوصف الموجود في الكتالوج يتوافق مع الآراء المتفق عليها بشكل عام بين الخبراء والمتخصصين في تاريخ عملية البيع، أو إذا كان الكتالوج قد أشار إلى وجود آراء متضاربة حول هذا الأمر؛
(٢) إذا كانت الطريقة الوحيدة المتاحة في تاريخ البيع لإثبات زيف القطعة المباعة تتم من خلال عمليات لم تكن بصورة عامة متوفرة أو مقبولة في حينه، أو إذا كانت الطريقة غير عملية أو باهظة بشكل غير معقول، أو إذا كان من المرجح أن تؤدي إلى تلف القطعة المباعة أو من المرجح أن تؤدي إلى فقدان قيمتها (حسب الرأي المعقول **لسوذبيز**)؛
(٣) إذا لم يحدث فقدان في قيمة القطعة المباعة عن قيمتها لو كانت متماشية مع الوصف الذي ورد لها في الكتالوج.

يتوفر هذا **الضمان** لمدة خمس (٥) سنوات بعد تاريخ المزاد الذي تمت فيه عملية البيع، والمنتفع الوحيد من هذا **الضمان** هو **المشتري**، ولا يجوز تحويل هذا **الضمان** إلى أي طرف ثالث. ولكي يتمكن **المشتري** من الانتفاع بهذا **الضمان** يجب عليه القيام بما يلي:

(١) إخطار **سوذبيز** كتابياً خلال ثلاثة (٣) أشهر من تاريخ حصوله على أية معلومات جعلته يشك في أصالة القطعة التي اشتراها أو في صحة نسبتها للمؤلف أو الفنان إلخ، مع تحديد رقم القطعة التي اشتراها، والتاريخ الذي تم فيه المزاد، والأسباب الذي تجعله يعتقد أنها مزيفة؛
(٢) أن يقوم بإعادة القطعة التي اشتراها من **سوذبيز** في نفس الحالة التي اشتراها عليها، وأن يكون قادراً على تحويل ملكية القطعة دون أن تنشأ أي مطالبات لأي طرف ثالث بعد تاريخ البيع.

ويحق **لسوذبيز** أن تتنازل، حسب تقديرها، عن أي من الشروط والمتطلبات المذكورة أعلاه. كما يمكن أن تطلب **سوذبيز** من **المشتري** أن يقوم، وعلى نفقته، باستحصال تقريرين من خبيرين مستقلين ومعترف بهما في هذا المجال، على أن يقبل بهما كل من **المشتري** و**سوذبيز**. ولا تكون **سوذبيز** ملزمة بأي من التقارير التي يقدمها **المشتري**، وهي تحتفظ بحقها في الحصول على رأي الخبراء الإضافيين، وذلك على نفقتها الخاصة. وفي حال اتخاذ سوذبيز قراراً بإلغاء عملية البيع بموجب هذا **الضمان**، فإنها قد تقوم عندئذ بتسديد التكاليف المعقولة التي دفعها **المشتري** عن تقارير خبير مستقل أو خبيرين مستقلين فقط (لا أكثر) كانا قد تم الاتفاق المتبادل عليهما.

CATALOGUE PRICE
US$60 AT THE GALLERY | US$68 BY MAIL | US$78 OVERSEAS
FOR SUBSCRIPTIONS CALL 44 (0)20 7293 6444